BRITAIN
AND THE BRITISH

THE BRITISH COMMON PEOPLE
[1746–1938]
by G. D. H. Cole & Raymond Postgate

". . . a more thorough survey of the whole history of the British working classes than anyone else has hitherto attempted."
— *The Nation*

THE BRITISH EMPIRE
BEFORE THE AMERICAN REVOLUTION
by Lawrence H. Gipson

". . . the most significant historical work currently being written in the United States, to be compared favorably in every way with the histories of Francis Parkman."
— *New York Herald Tribune Books*

THE ANATOMY OF BRITISH SEA POWER
by Arthur J. Marder

The rise of British naval strength during the formative years 1880–1905. "Complete and reliable."
— Capt. Dudley W. Knox, U. S. Navy Department

THESE ARE BORZOI BOOKS, PUBLISHED BY
Alfred A. Knopf

The English People

Et *penitus toto divisos orbe Britannos."*

—VIRGIL

"Non Angli sed angeli."

—POPE GREGORY THE GREAT

"A nation of shopkeepers."

—ADAM SMITH

". . . the English people are sweet,
And we might as well get used to them because when
they slip and fall
They always land on their own or somebody else's feet."

— OGDEN NASH

THE

English People

IMPRESSIONS
AND OBSERVATIONS
BY

D. W. Brogan

NEW YORK · ALFRED A. KNOPF · 1943

13367

TO

CECILIA REEVES

"The lot is fallen unto thee in a fair ground;
yea, thou hast a goodly heritage."

Preface

THAT THERE has been a good deal of criticism of Britain and the British Empire in the United States is natural and not, in itself, unfortunate. But in war, nerves are frayed and tempers on edge. Waves of feeling which are in themselves natural, spontaneous, and defensible may, in fact, help the Axis by stressing national incompatibilities and ignoring what the nations have in common. That American criticism of the English people and the British Empire had reached the point of being a danger was the view held by a good many intelligent Americans when I was in America this spring. It was a danger, they thought, to American unity and to American efficiency. It weakened faith in the desirability as well as in the possibility of the victory of the United Nations. I did not see the situation so tragically as did many of my American friends. But that there were and that there will be waves of distrust, irritation, and dislike of the English we may take for granted. That these waves of anger or annoyance may be a danger may also be taken for granted. I can well believe that anything that can be done, not to reduce anti-English feeling as such, but to bring its premises to the light, is worth doing. That the anti-English feeling would persist or be even more intense if the Americans knew the English better is possible, but I do not believe it. So when Mrs. Knopf suggested that I should write a book on the English for the

American public, I could not simply say no. My disqualifications are many and will appear, or some of them will, to readers of this book. But as it was my old teacher, Arthur Schlesinger, and the most acute of American commentators on the English scene, Mr. Edward R. Murrow, of the Columbia Broadcasting System, who suggested my name to Mrs. Knopf, my diffidence was a little diminished. (None of them has seen what they rashly bargained for.)

I have tried to write a book that is candid, relevant, and serious. I have not tried to paint a picture of a mythical England that is all Old World charm or all character and uprightness. I have not tried to conceal the fact that a great deal of the most English sides of English life are the oddest and least defensible. Nor have I tried to conceal my belief that in fields where comparison with the United States is reasonable, the result is not always favourable to the United States.

One personal explanation seems called for. Although I live in England, I have as far as is known to me no English blood at all. And by a series of accidents I had lived for periods running from weeks to months in Paris, Rome, New York, and Washington before I had spent more than one night in London. In England I am still a foreigner of a kind, cut off by my Irish and Scottish background and ancestry from many of the spontaneously English reactions of true-born Englishmen. And, without striving for any pedantic uniformity, when I write "English" or "England," I usually mean the English people and England, not the British people and Britain. After all, the English people, not the British people or the British Empire, are the basic problem to the American people and to Hitler.

It is possible that a certain apparent indifference to high moral verbal principles made manifest in this book may shock people. I don't think that I am indifferent to principles in politics. I believe in the Rights of Man and in government by the people. But as a student of politics I think that harm is done to the securing of the Rights of Man and of government by the people if it is forgotten that in democratic government "democratic" is the adjective, and that problems of government are not problems in private morality. The pursuit in politics of moral and intellectual perfection to the disregard of the possible is one of the greatest moral and intellectual sins of high-minded or, at any rate, righteously-minded "Anglo-Saxons." As M. Roussy de Sales has pointed out, we have escaped from the juvenile illusion that we can live happily ever after in our private lives, that we can organize that small sphere perfectly, live with our wives (or husbands) in perfect amity, raise our children without any serious difficulties, keep our friends and improve our enemies without compromise or failures. But whereas the man who will be content with nothing less than a perfect solution to his private problems, who insists on the infallibility of his own judgment and the right to expect impeccability from his friends and colleagues, is rightly regarded as pathological and lucky if he is only kept under observation, the same type, when this attitude is transferred to public affairs, claims the respect due to superior wisdom and is entitled to lecture, not to say hector, the more sensible and less credulous members of the community. It used to be thought easier to arrange the affairs of a small circle that one knew intimately than to decide what ought to be done when the problem was made more complex by a great increase in scale. But the new quack doctors of political medicine have changed all that. Tackle all the problems at once; insist not merely that nothing but the best is good enough for you, but that nothing but the perfect solution is good enough for you. Abolish war and poverty and intolerance and racial discrimination and religious bias and pride and sadism—all at one go. Do this by manifestoes and meetings. If the sins and follies of the human race are not abolished overnight by a petition to Congress from five hundred perfectionists in a New York hotel, so much the worse for the human race. They have had their chance. To run for Congress, successfully, in California on a program of unlimited Oriental immigration would take a lot of time, energy, and political tact. The manifesto method, petitioning away many thousand years of sinful history, is easier and, morally, more uplifting. It is easier to ask for the moon than to guide fallen men by candlelight. And many of those who do ask for the moon would be extremely puzzled to know what to do with it if they got it. Many of them are like the type of man or woman who always finds good reasons for not marrying, reasons which boil down to a demand for the perfect partner, which conceals a fear that maybe marriage, with its imperfections thick upon it, would be too much for the perfectionist. This type of all-or-nothing reformer may, of course, simply be dressing up despair of "the so-called human race," wishing that

> *All that the brigand apple brought*
> *And this foul world were dead at last.*

But with others it is a simple, honest, and cheery conviction that even if they cannot and do not apply these rigorous standards to their friends or to private problems, they can handle an aggregate of problems provided the resultant general problem is *big* enough. So they cannot be bothered with any but complete solutions; time is no object, and unless a political cure lasts forever, it is not worth having. A Chinese emperor, when greeted with the traditional "ten thousand years," knew that his courtiers did not expect him to live to be a hundred and was not shocked at this pessimism or hypocrisy. But both England and America are full of people who would not settle for ten thousand years; they want an eternity and a perfection that their ancestors wisely expected only in the next world.[1]

In war-time the perfectionist is on top of his world. War is so absurd, it involves so many unpleasant, almost intolerable, morally dangerous, and economically and physically repulsive courses of

---

[1] There is a true sense in which the United States Constitution is the oldest planned political solution in the world. Yet it is only 153 years since it began to work. There are people alive still whose parents could have talked with its chief maker, James Madison. There are people alive who fought in the great Civil War, caused by its inadequacies. All the same, by human standards the American Constitution has been a success.

action that normally sensible people do (and should) think harder about their duty and the true policy to be followed. How much happier is the role of the panacea-monger! He has, first of all, the easy job of pointing out that war is a bad thing. Here he has all sensible people with him, but like any moral absolutist, he refuses to admit that a bad thing can yet be less bad than an alternative course of action, or that the highly probable consequences of a course of action must be borne in mind in making a choice about it. The man who now says that nothing can be worse than war should examine carefully *why* he thinks war is bad and decide whether what he objects to in war is absent from the kind of world a surrender to Hitler would produce. He can, of course, assert that Hitler would be touched or the German people awakened to the acceptance of views that they have shown even less signs of being willing to adopt than have the English or Americans. But that kind of assertion is less plausibly made (since it involves a view of the power of moral example that the ordinary sensual man finds it hard to accept) if it is merely asserted in New York or London instead of being tried out in a German concentration camp or in the conquered countries.

But the perfectionists are not so numerous and not so dangerous as the believers in what I call "political plastics." These technicians are devout believers in new and immediate solutions. The past history and present complexity of most political problems do not shake their confidence in their doctrine that, with the use of this formula or that, the twisted, gnarled, tough roots of the Upas tree of human folly and wickedness can be dug up with practically no difficulty at all, and the tree itself made over into new nice, shiny gadgets that will be welcome to all peoples and used by all peoples. To believe that nothing but a profound and improbable change in most or all human institutions is alone worth striving for is a very different attitude from the belief of the plastics school that a new model government, or banking system, or filing system, is all that is needed. But the immediate results in a war, especially in a war where a country has allies, are often the same.

If nothing but heaven will do, it is obvious that in helping your allies (or your own country) you are taking something a lot short of heaven or even of purgatory as worth your faith and works. If all is fairly simple, a matter of the right blueprints and hiring the most effective social engineers, you can equally easily be distressed at the obscurantism, bad faith, and downright selfish wickedness of the people concerned. They *may*, of course, be your own countrymen, but if, as sometimes happens, the advocate of a simple political cure-all is also a candidate for the job of applying the remedy or exploiting the plastics formula, they are more likely to turn out to be the allies whom historical necessity, that unidealistic and unplastic force, has provided. Naturally this is too much for the purists and for the technicians. Are they to be involved with publicans and sinners? Or with relics of horse and buggy days? No, a thousand times, no!

It is true that a common victory means that one ally is contributing to the survival of the other and may be contributing to the survival of the least, as well as the most attractive features of the other's social system. And if one ally has no domestic weaknesses or wrongs, or shadows on the national landscape, it does share, to some degree, in the sin of the partner. Whether any nation is without sin, or, not being quite so immaculate as that, need have no fear that victory in war may postpone the reorganization that defeat would make necessary, is perhaps an open question. (The spectacle of Vichy does not suggest that defeat in the contemporary world is, in fact, a very good way of getting ready to carry out domestic or imperial reform.) If it can be taken as generally accepted that each member of the United Nations wants victory and would not be improved by defeat, and that each is dependent, at any rate for the speed and comparative cheapness of victory, on its associates, it is worth considering whether it is wise, or even justifiable, to insist on an absolutely clean bill of moral health from the associates concerned. If the victory of the United Nations is a good thing for all of them, for the world, and for each of them, a member of this alliance may be well advised to put up with the fact that the other members' records are not snowy-white, but at best tattle-tale grey. That necessity being accepted, there is, for example, no overwhelming case for anxiety about being able to look American soldiers in the eye when you think of India. The American soldier is first of all fighting for America, then for the temporary inadequate but desirable solution of the current world political problem of which the freeing of India is an important but not absolutely primary condition.

To move on. The United States and England and the British Empire are all deeply involved in a great war where, if it is not certain that none can avoid catastrophic defeat if one of the major partners gives way, it is certain that neither the British Empire nor England nor the United States can achieve victory without the others. The English people realize this. So, in all probability, do the American people, whatever some of the most vociferous politicians and publicists may say. Relations between allies or associates are always difficult. The common cause does not necessarily or often make for a common viewpoint. There are great differences in habits of life, in what may be called the system of internal priorities. These different habits of life and thought may be changed, rapidly, in war-time and very often are so changed. But there is no guarantee that they will change in the same direction. Yet the association for the common cause must go on.

The English and American peoples are thrown together at a great and decisive moment in their history. They have many things in common; they have many things in which they differ, more or less profoundly. I have stressed the things in which they differ. Sometimes one country differs for the worse, sometimes for the better; sometimes the result is merely a difference with no moral implications. I have tried to hold the balance fair. My basic object, however, has not been the pretentious one of giving out good and bad marks, but of explaining some odd features of English life to Americans. No nation keeps exactly the same character all the time or is equally conservative in all things. But no change, however rapid, will make England entirely like America during the period during which they will be compulsorily associated by the threat of German and Japanese power to their free existence. An American might wish for a better, more powerful, more amiable, and more understandable ally. But what he has got is England, and these shallow, disconnected, but not quite random chapters are an attempt to make some of the problems of Anglo-American understanding and co-operation better understood. This book is designed to be useful to and in America. If it has utility or interest in England as well, that is a piece of luck for the author which he has not deserved. But luck, good and bad, deserved and undeserved, is a great historic force. And kicking against good luck is one of the most morbid personal or national foibles.

The four quotations that face the title page represent very varying views, none of them English, of the English. Two Italians, a Scot, and an American have illustrated various aspects of the English character. I am aware (thanks to the *Oxford Dictionary of Quotations*) that Virgil thought of geographical more than spiritual isolationism; that Pope Gregory did not confuse English and angels in the epigrammatic form that tradition has sanctified, and that Adam Smith had more complicated ideas about the character of a nation of shopkeepers. Only Mr. Nash has said what he wanted to say in a perfectly quotable form. It will be evident, too, that parts of this book owe what merits they may have to Dr. G. J. Renier's book: *The English: Are They Human?* But I am sure he will forgive this pillaging by an old friend.

D. W. Brogan

London, November 22, 1942

Contents

The English People

1

The English and Themselves

SIXTEEN HUNDRED YEARS AGO Pope Gregory the Great declared that some English boys were angels, not English. Few foreigners have made any correspondingly laughable mistake since. But although the English have been called everything but angels since they began to attract notice from abroad, the kind of notice has varied from age to age. Froissart noticed that they took their pleasures sadly; Erasmus commented on the charming habit of English girls who kissed all visitors with an engaging amiability. As the English state grew more powerful, foreigners tended to concentrate on the less agreeable but more impressive sides of the English character. Native critics abounded and native patriots pointed with pride to every virtue as being characteristic of the race, including the logically inconsistent one of modesty.

The Reformation not only established as the official religion a local English variant of Christianity that had no real equivalent elsewhere in Christendom, but made parts of the national tradition such oddities as an unintelligible form of Latin. When all the other great European states turned their mediæval monarchies into absolute monarchies, the English cut the head off one king, expelled another, hired a foreign family to carry on the job under rigorous terms of employment, and in general broke all the rules of political decorum. Worse than that, they got away with it to the extent of making themselves the centre of opposition to the most powerful European state. In a series of wars they exploited victory and avoided the worst consequences of temporary setbacks. They imposed respect if not affection in Europe and began to be studied with interest by their neighbours, who, contemplating the combination of irregular conduct and world success, began to think that the English must have some method in their now notorious madness. All Europe went to school to England (and, odder still, to Scotland) in the eighteenth century.

Revolutionary ideas and even more revolutionary machines were perfected in the University of Glasgow, in the rising town of Birmingham, and in the colonies across the Atlantic which had been secured for the English tongue, the Protestant religion, and representative government by the series of victorious wars formally caused by the absence of male heirs in the two branches of the House of Habsburg. Incidental to the great result of winning North America, the same victories made it certain that English, not Dutch or French adventurers would, in the course of trade, find it necessary (and profitable) to impose peace on the anarchical politics of the great peninsula called India. More than ever, English ways of doing things were thought worth studying. The islanders had many faults; they were boorish, drunken, violent in public and private life; when they travelled abroad, they spoiled the local hotel-keepers by their lavishness, as did the Earl of Bristol, whose name was taken over in grateful remembrance by so many *hôteliers,* or they bullied and quarrelled and argued over the bill like Tobias Smollett. England was a fantastic country where anything could happen, where fantastic extremes of wealth and poverty existed side by side, where all the ordinary rules of decent behaviour were defied with apparent immunity. Even the great disaster of the loss of the rebel colonies of North America did not have the dampening effect that was confidently, not to say gladly, anticipated.

The day of England's doom, noted with satisfaction by European observers and with gloomy relish by native critics, did not last long. When the great wars of the French Revolution and then of Napoleon came, the island power proved to be unconquerable and unshakable. She hung on until the greatest of conquerors was captive. And not merely did she beat Napoleon, add vast territories to her dominions, prudently seize such useful centres of power in peace and war as Singapore, Malta, the Cape of Good Hope, and Ceylon, but she invented and put on the market a new way of life. The modern world is a world of machines. Young Englishmen went abroad not to make the grand tour, but to give Berlin her first gasworks and France her first railways. English steamships made pioneer voyages across the Atlantic, and English locomotives were shipped off to the United States to make possible the first American railroads. English fleets and armies forced the ambiguous benefits of modern civilization on the reluctant Chinese and waged as vigilant war as the United States Senate would permit on the African slave trade. Missionaries and traders introduced Christianity, commerce, and deadly disease into the South Seas. And English liberal ideas, parliamentary government, free trade, vaguely progressive religion, and Darwinian evolution were exports as universally in demand as Manchester or Glasgow cotton goods or Birmingham hardware.

Whether such power, such prestige, such wealth was ever deserved by any people is doubtful. There was a pretty unanimous vote that the English were not liked. Nasty Germans might complain of the hand-to-mouth character of English thought. Nasty Frenchmen might talk of London's dirt and disorder. Nasty Americans might sneer at English slowness and political hypocrisy. The English did not care. Virtue was its own reward and who, looking at the reward, could doubt the virtue? It was at this time that the traditional picture of England was painted by Englishmen and others. Unlike that Carthage with which Frenchmen and Germans were fond of comparing her, England was the home of one great art, literature. There were great novelists as well as great inventors, exploiters, and politicians. Thackeray and Dickens, Trollope and George Eliot were the countrymen of George Stephenson, Arkwright, James Watt, Alexander Baring, and Palmerston. Every aspect of English life was studied and criticized by natives as well as foreigners. If there was abundant complacency, there was abundant critical study, too. The Benthamites, Matthew Arnold, Carlyle, could be offset against Macaulay, Roebuck, *The Times*. Mr. Podsnap was no more a typical Englishman —and no less—than Mr. Dickens. But the picture was, in the main, painted by the complacent.

In the great Victorian heyday—that is, in the second half of Victoria's reign—the English were probably as insufferable a nation as the modern world had seen up to then. Up to then, for the complacent English traveller, paying his way and snubbing the foreigners who inhabited Rome and Dresden and Bruges and Lucerne and all the other beauty spots provided for his holiday relaxation, was a model of decorum in comparison with the German tourist whom Bismarckian prosperity permitted to take a culture cure abroad. But even the comparative amiability of the English tourist was offensive, too, for, unlike the German, he was unaffected by any doubts of his own civilization, any uneasiness at the ironical reception he got from the benighted foreigner. He was at ease in Zion, and the natives of Zion did not altogether like it.

But despite the appearances England was changing, and changing, in this respect, for the better. Her new rich bourgeois were less conscious of their climb upwards to opulence and security; her aristocracy was less purely barbarous than Matthew Arnold had painted it; her intellectual culture was less insular; the rise to wealth and power of such different but un-English societies as the United States and Germany gave rise to reflections on the possibly accidental character of English economic pre-eminence. Stanley Jevons and John Stuart Mill hinted that it was due as much to coal as to character, and the prosperity of the Ruhr and Pennsylvania suggested that there was something in the theory. The

English working classes, never as grateful for their good fortune in being English as they should have been, were becoming more and more restive. To the old radical tradition a new Marxian flavour was given. The apostle of Marxism was H. M. Hyndman, no working man, it is true, but a product of that conservative seminary, Eton College. To the old conservative tradition a new exotic flavour was given by the imperialists whose chief spokesman, Kipling, was the product of a school about as far removed from Eton as was compatible with being nice. The great ducal houses, though still rich, were no longer the richest class in the world. The collapse of agricultural prices in the late seventies began that impoverishment of the landed aristocracy which has gone on to this day, and it marked the determination of the English people of the middle and working classes not to pay the high cost of keeping the landed interest prosperous. All was no longer obviously for the best in the best of all possible countries. Englishmen began to think they might have something to learn, a point of view that John Stuart Mill, with his knowledge of France, and John Austin, with his knowledge of Germany, had totally failed to make a generation before. As far as English complacency was the cause of English unpopularity, the complacency was shaken by the time of the Diamond Jubilee of the Good Queen. Kipling, with the intuition of genius, noted the change in temper in *Recessional*. The new technically educated classes had found their spokesman in a genius with even more intuition, Mr. Wells. And after centuries in which the Irish had existed to provide comic relief for the English, the time had come when the English provided raw material for the Irish sense of fun. Mr. Shaw, Mr. Wells, German-trained politicians like Haldane and Milner, half-American businessmen like Joseph Chamberlain, these were signs of the times.

Materially speaking, the golden age of English complacency ended with the great war of 1914. But in a spiritual sense it ended with the little war with the Boer republics. Exhausting and faith-shaking as was the experience of 1914–19, it was not demoralizing. Not merely was victory finally won, but great resources of wealth, ingenuity, and courage were drawn on; easy pessimism was shown to have been as false as easy optimism had been earlier. The South African War was worse. For the defeats were humiliating and the victories unexhilarating. All the efforts of propagandists, bad poets, and baffled politicians could not make the war anything but shabby in its origin and ludicrous in its conduct. The generation that came to maturity in the years after the South African War was allergic to slogans and ideas that had evoked genuine enthusiasm a few years before. The Conservative working man who really worried about problems of Imperial strategy in Africa died out. 1914 was to show that English patriotism was as strong as ever, but it was a "Little Englander" patriotism. What did they know of England who only England knew? asked the Indian-born poet of Empire. And the answer was "Quite enough." [1]

One of the most valuable and irritating English qualities is indifference to outside criticism. Even the most acute foreign exposure of native vices or native weaknesses is normally met with complacent indifference, or with an even more eager acquiescence, an emphatic assertion of the view that the foreign critic doesn't know half of it. And it is worth noting that this national com-

[1] This view of the impact of the South African War is not susceptible of proof. It is, perhaps, in part accounted for by knowledge that an Imperially-minded uncle suggested, ironically, to a pro-Boer father that I should be christened Paul Kruger. But I think it is true, nevertheless. The ease with which the Liberal government of 1906 turned over the rule of South Africa to the Boer leaders is significant not merely of the generosity and political sagacity of Campbell-Bannerman, but of the decision of the English people that they had taken the wrong turning. The Philippines, the American equivalent of the South African conquests, are only now attaining the effective independence the Boer Republics got within ten years of their conquest. The South African equivalent of Aguinaldo was commanding British armies twelve years after his surrender. Such political wisdom would have been impossible if the English people had not become highly self-critical. And the comic character of English humiliations in South Africa, the Boer habit of taking away the trousers of prisoners and then letting them loose, helped the Englishman in the street to see through the imperial ballyhoo that had brought the countrymen of Marlborough and Wellington to such a pass.

placency broke down in 1899 and 1900. The whole world laughed at the spectacle of the greatest empire in history being held up by a few thousand farmers in top hats. And for once the English didn't laugh too. Critics of the war were mobbed, as if Kruger and Botha were more deadly enemies than Napoleon had been. Mr. Lloyd George and the pro-Boers were assailed with a vehemence that had not been needed when Hazlitt was defending Napoleon or John Bright denouncing the Crimean War. Conscience made cowards of the English people and they did not soon, perhaps ever, forgive the rulers who had put them into this absurd position.

It was perhaps this memory that accounted for the unprecedented collapse of the political sense of the English governing class between 1903 and 1914. The great secret of that governing class has always been its knowledge, its prophetic knowledge, of when it was necessary to retreat. It has more highly developed than any governing class since the great days of the Roman Republic that "sense of the possible" which Cavour, most Anglophile of great modern statesmen, regarded as the most important gift of the statesman. This gift was not conspicuous in the years before the war of 1914. The English Tory party (with which had been incorporated most of the old Whig oligarchy) abandoned all prudence. It developed an ideology and began to think of following principles to their logical conclusion. Few less English remarks can be thought of than the "damn the consequences" of Lord Milner. It was not an un-Milnerian remark, for that very able, perhaps great man was more than half German by training and temper, but what were the Tories of England doing taking the advice of a Milner against the advice of a Hicks-Beach? What were they doing following the lead of an Oriental potentate like Curzon? Or of a Scots-Canadian businessman like Bonar Law? Even their English leader, Joseph Chamberlain, was more the international entrepreneur than the English really liked. It was not only that he confused Birmingham Town Hall with the Palace of Westminster, as his son was to do after him, but, in an unfortunate sense of the term, Joseph Chamberlain was too widely travelled to be a Little Englander. He was at home in the America of Mark Hanna, but if Birmingham was in some ways like Cleveland, Birmingham was not England—and Cleveland had, after all, Tom Johnson as well as Mark Hanna, and the English public mind was becoming more sympathetic to Tom Johnsons than to Hannas.

So in the ten years before 1914, great political and social changes came about against the hysterical opposition of the so-called natural leaders of the people. They insisted on having the nature of the English Constitution inspected. The result was the enactment of the Parliament Act of 1911, which gave England a written Constitution and one which, from an American point of view, was dangerously democratic, at least in form. They offered tariffs as a cure for unemployment, and the result was the creation of a system of what is now called in the United States "social security," paid for by the rich. Faced with the genuine if belated repentance of the Englishman at the sight of the Irish refusal to accept being English as a promotion, the ruling classes lost their tempers and heads and encouraged revolutionary habits that might have plagued them had not the war of 1914 given them a chance for silent repentance. Walter Long preaching revolution, F. E. Smith weeping for threatened Christianity, distinguished soldiers encouraging mutiny, distinguished lawyers promoting rebellion, there was an apparent danger of the English political compromise collapsing, thanks to the folly of its chief beneficiaries. No wonder Chesterton wondered!

> If over private fields and wastes as wide
> As a Greek city for which heroes died,
> I owned the houses and the men inside—
> If all this hung on one thin thread of habit
> I would not revolutionize a rabbit.

And (one guess is as good as another) the bad temper and bad judgment, the verbal violence and the folly of the English Conservatives at this time may well have been induced by memories of the nonsense talked in the autumn of 1899 when it was decided to give these backward Boers a lesson—and the roles of teacher and taught were suddenly reversed, to the delight of a world that saw the English at last get their come-uppance. Fortunately for the world, that salutary lesson was not fatal.

For, despite the sabotage of order and good sense by the best people, a great and desirable transformation of English society was being carried out. One great change, perhaps the greatest of all, was the work of the Conservative government. The Education Acts of 1902 and 1903 were far more important than the noisier projects of Chamberlain and Milner. And Balfour, so ill equipped to be a political leader, was all the better equipped to sponsor this great reform while public attention was largely, though not wholly, directed elsewhere. The Liberal government that ruled from 1905 to 1914 was in its personnel probably the ablest that England has ever known. To list the membership of the government that entered the war of 1914 and compare it with that which entered the war of 1939—not to carry the comparison further—is to suffer doubts as to the inevitability of political progress.[2] The Milner-esque hankering after a unified empire with a formal constitution was ignored and the modern free alliance of the dominions, which has twice stood the most rigorous test, that of war, was in fact born. England was not well prepared for the ordeal that was to come, but she was better prepared than any of the other belligerents. There was no discomfiture so complete as that which ruined the French plan of campaign in 1914; no miscalculation so disastrous as the German ignoring of the possibility of a long war. Despite defeats like Coronel and undramatic successes like Jutland, the British Navy did what it had been planned to do: it

[2] Asquith, Haldane, Lloyd George, Winston Churchill, John Simon, Reginald McKenna, Edward Grey; these names alone, as far as ability matters, are painfully suggestive of something wrong with the present English political personnel. Even the dissenters from the war policy of the Asquith government, Morley and Burns, are critics of another calibre from our present moralistic protesters against the nature of the modern world.

imposed its will on Germany. The generally victorious German armies never had the time or the means to exploit their successes. Sea-power by itself could not have defeated Germany, but sea-power forced on Germany more and more extravagant gambles, including the last, which was the decision to defy the United States and win the war before American power could be made actual and effective. That race against time was lost and the most dramatic indication of that fact was the mutiny of the German fleet when it was decided, as a last gambler's throw, to send it out on a death-ride that might just conceivably have succeeded. It was a fine Wagnerian conception, but the rank and file of the German Navy was not so Wagnerian as its officers, and the High Seas Fleet peacefully surrendered.[3]

In the twenty years between the two wars the condition of England was getting steadily better, but the people of England and the outside world refused to notice it. Relatively, of course, England was not so powerful as she had been in 1914. The system of international trade which had worked to her and the world's advantage for the previous century received a blow from which it has never recovered. Some fears expressed immediately after the

[3] The German naval high command expected that the British Navy would try to force a battle in the North Sea and it was prepared to fight and win such a battle in the waters round the great fortress of Heligoland. In a realist, unsporting spirit, worthy of a nation of shopkeepers and of a navy prepared for action by that very ungentlemanly genius Lord Fisher, the Grand Fleet stayed away in Scapa Flow and let the High Seas Fleet sail around in its own wet triangle as much as it liked. The naval war would have been won just the same had neither fleet fired a shot. The old established Royal Navy didn't need to worry about honour, glory, the martial spirit, or anything but the real problem of how to win the war. It had the immunity from snobbery of an aristocrat who has no doubts about his social position. And this was a permanent characteristic. When the British Navy had *its* mutiny, it was not over strategy or politics or any great and emotional issue. It was over pay. The foreign observers who saw in the mutiny of 1931 the end of the British Empire were romantics. Violent discontent with the conditions of service and bad feeling rising to mutiny were quite in the tradition of the mariners of England. What was not in the least in their tradition was a refusal to fight because the chance of victory was slight.

end of the war proved to be groundless. There was no transfer of the central machinery of international banking from London to New York. It takes more than a lot of money to be a great banker. But international banking, as such, was declining. Indeed, from the English point of view a successful assumption of the old role of London by New York would have been a blessing for England, and London would have gained more by a restoration of the old economic system than it would have lost (except in *amour propre*, and English bankers are not touchy) by the primacy passing from London to New York as it had passed, around 1800, from Amsterdam to London. Nor was the panic fear of Bolshevism found to be justified. Within two or three years of the Bolshevik Revolution the Left parties all over Europe were on the defensive, increasingly afraid of losing what they had won and far enough from seeking new worlds to conquer. The old order seemed to have lots of life in it, and it had. There was great technical progress; the means of creating wealth were immensely increased in all countries but France up to the American collapse of 1929, and again in most countries, notably Britain, once the upward movement was resumed, as it was quite soon in Britain.

But English complacency, English confidence, English immunity to criticism were dying rapidly, almost too rapidly. The reading public was avid for books explaining how much better things were done in Russia or Germany or (for a time) in the United States. The countrymen of James Watt and Kelvin sometimes talked as if modern technology had been invented in Russia or America. There was some justification for the Russian *engouement*. Russian industry was just getting on its feet in 1914, so reports of what was going on there had the charm of novelty. But the American menace was no novelty. Sir John Foster Fraser was making the blood of English manufacturers run cold long before such premature prophets as Mr. Ludwell Denny found English readers for books like *America Conquers Britain*. Even the American collapse of 1929 did not restore English complacency, for attention was first of all directed to England's own troubles and,

when the worst of the crisis was over, the aspect of American life
that attracted most attention was the belated effort to construct
social services of a type with which England and Germany had
been familiar for a generation. And this imitation of English practice by the United States bred no renewal of self-confidence, as it
was at least a generation since anybody in England had regarded
the United States as being anything but a very backward country
on all questions of social legislation and administration.

No complete victory has ever bred less enthusiasm in the victors
than the Allied triumph of 1918. It is difficult to say whether
American disillusionment was more profound than English or
French. But disillusionment there was, and out of that disillusionment grew a most dangerous illusion that victory or defeat didn't
matter, that war settled nothing, that the day of old-fashioned
national pride was past, and that a sceptical, hard-boiled attitude—
"What is there in it (materially speaking) for me?"—was the beginning and end of practical wisdom. The Germans, who had
been defeated, knew better; the French know better now. The
English and Americans may still, it is to be feared, have preserved
some of that short-sighted realism whose cost is now being charged
up to them. Be that as it may, the England of the post-war years
was remarkably free from nationalist exultation. It was not only
that the fairly new imperialism proved to have shallow roots; that
was not surprising.[4] What was surprising or, at any rate, new was

[4] It is difficult to imagine any audience listening patiently to this kind of
thing, which was yet so popular in the high Kipling era: "This question
is deeper than any question of party politics; deeper than any question of
the isolated policy of our country even; deeper even than any question of
constitutional power. It is elemental. It is racial. God has not been preparing
the English-speaking and Teutonic peoples for a thousand years for nothing
but vain and idle self-contemplation and self-admiration. No! He has made
us the master organizers of the world to establish system where chaos reigns.
He has given us the spirit of progress to overwhelm the forces of reaction
throughout the earth. He has made us adepts in government that we may
administer government among savage and senile peoples. Were it not for
such a force as this the world would relapse into barbarism and night."
This kind of thing would have been laughed at in England and America

the decline in simple national pride. There was an apparent abdication of the presumption of the goodness of things English that, on the surface at least, was complete. Never had there been such a general rush of the educated classes after strange gods. All literary and artistic movements had now to be *à la mode de* Paris or Moscow or New York. The solutions for all problems were to be sought abroad. An English solution or innovation was as unheard of as an English couple in the tennis finals of Wimbledon. Proust and Lenglen, Henry Ford and Lenin, Freud and Gandhi, all had their warmest admirers in England. Even the defenders of the old traditions showed their uneasiness by ill-timed admiration for punctual trains in Italy, for mass production in Detroit. The few unshaken Englishmen talked a language that was, in great part, meaningless to the mass of their countrymen. They talked of the Empire when the word and the thing had lost concrete meaning and emotional appeal. They talked of fighting for King and Country when the whole notion of national independence and power was questioned. What they said was not untrue; it was merely unsuited to the times, and what they had to say would, to be effective, have had to be said differently. But those who saw that Mr. Churchill was using the wrong kind of language to make his point, did not like the point either.

The temper of the times was illustrated by the success of the column "This England" in the *New Statesman*. Here were pilloried, every week, foolish remarks from other organs of English opinion, remarks that often enough would not have seemed notably silly twenty years before and sometimes would not appear silly now. An even greater success was the creation of Colonel Blimp. That pugnacious officer often said things that were, are,

---

alike at almost any time after 1918, and no less laughed at in England than in America. Yet the orator, Senator Beveridge of Indiana, was no fool; he was simply expressing the intoxication of the age of Kipling and Richard Harding Davis, of Theodore Roosevelt and Cecil Rhodes. The citation is from Albert K. Weinberg: *Manifest Destiny, A Study of Nationalist Expansionism in American History,* p. 308.

[15]

and always will be silly. But sometimes they were not silly at all, and more often than is realized Blimp was replying to anti-Blimp-isms no less silly and no less dangerous than his own Blimpism. The decline in English smugness was, of course, an æsthetic gain. Never were the islanders more ready to learn, more free from arrogance, more eager to meet their critics half-way than between 1920 and 1939. They were, indeed, too eager, too humble. A little more of the old English complacency might have stiffened their rulers' backs. In the old days when to describe a thing as "un-English" was to damn it, Ribbentrops and Grandis would have had a harder time· The old English Tory and the old English Radical were sometimes stupid, but they had the courage of their convictions or prejudices. They did not think they should ignore eccentric conduct on the ground that foreigners knew best what was good for them—and their immediate neighbours. Victorian complacency would not, in itself, have prevented Munich, but it would have made it harder to represent Munich as a moral, intellectual, and prudential triumph. And Victorian complacency, while it would have annoyed the world more, would have misled it less than the new national habit of self-criticism and self-depreci-ation. Ribbentrop and Mussolini both had reason to complain of this new trick of perfidious Albion. They thought that England was to be taken over at fire-sale terms (hadn't they listened to the barkers?). But they discovered they were wrong, even when they provided the fire.

The explanation of this trick played on the Germans and the Italians, to name only the enemies and not the allies of England, is not hard to find. However internationally-minded, however adept in the sport of national fault-finding, the Englishman's Englishness is ineradicable. History, climate, general good luck, but not too good luck, have given him institutions, habits of life, a world view that can only be explained in English terms. England has played a great part in the world; the English know it; she will continue to play a great part and the English know that. And, if it comes to mere guess-work and projections of opinion into the

future, the average Englishman finds it much more easy to contemplate an England without any terrestrial neighbours than a
world without England. For a world without England would have
no adequate standards of rightness; no English marks to surpass
or to fail to attain. So it has been ever since:

Britain first at heaven's command arose from out the azure main.

Whether the rest of the world was created before or after this
decisive proof of divine power does not really matter. Fixed in this
conviction, the Englishman can afford to rise above nearly all
forms of nationalist weakness, to be his own most severe critic,
the most enthusiastic admirer of foreign, even of hostile peoples.
But at bottom he knows that being English is something that
matters more than anything else. For that reason he was not nearly
so frightened in the summer of 1940 as he ought to have been. It
was, it is true, very difficult to see how the war was to be carried on.
German efficiency, as well as German power, was greatly admired.
The guesses at the military weakness of England, though not grim
enough, were yet grim. But, after all, what did defeat, what did
surrender mean? That Germany laid down the law to England?
That sort of thing, no matter what experts said, simply wasn't
done. And it wasn't.

English Education: The Rift in the Lute

THE ENGLISH are both the most united and the most divided of great peoples. In moments of great crisis they discover hidden though not unexpected sources of national strength in their mutual trust. They do not expect to let each other down or to be let down. No nation is less subject to the panic fear of internal treason that leads to the cry *"Sauve qui peut."* When disaster comes, the Englishman does not at once look for a scapegoat; he looks for a leader or leaders. He does not think he has been betrayed—merely that his affairs have been mismanaged. He does not shout "Each for himself" but "Stick together." He may be ironical at the expense of his leaders, at moments almost bitter, but he does not demand a clean sweep and insist that the country be put under entirely new management. Despite economic stresses and acute class differences based mainly on economic differences, the English are a united people to a degree that is a source of perpetual astonishment to foreigners—French, Irish, Scotch, American. So much has been asserted by many observers, and truthfully asserted.

But within this national unity how many kinds of difference are not only allowed to exist but positively encouraged! The classes that in a crisis trust each other cannot in fact speak to each other. Even if their language is mutually intelligible (as it is not always), they have little or nothing to say to each other. At moments their sole apparent bond of union appears to be the fact that they are "English," and being English seems to have hardly any definable content at all. The resident foreigner takes many years to learn the truth that you never come to the end of the English class structure, that new castes and sub-castes are forever being discovered, new gossamer threads of social distinction being bumped into— and found to be capable of bearing pressures that would in other lands burst the most formidable social dikes. In despair, the observer may come to the conclusion that the English class structure consists of forty-odd million classes, each composed of one man or woman who is neither identical with nor equal to any other class of one man or one woman, and that the one thing these forty-odd million classes have in common is this Englishness, which may be nothing more (or less) than an unconscious acceptance of this odd state of affairs as right and natural for Englishmen.

To enter an English public house for the first time; to choose between the public, the private, the saloon bar, the lounge; to note and classify the types that frequent each of these segments of the "public house"; to begin to notice the types that, in each segment, are mutually intelligible, at ease, and unselfconscious; to note all this and to realize that this is only the elements, the arithmetic of the system—this is the beginning of wisdom.

In no Western country is class-consciousness (in the social, not the Marxian sense) so widely spread, so much taken for granted. In no Western country are national controversies, openly or covertly, so affected by the knowledge that there is an immense and most potent force of snobbery that must be allowed for by the politician, the preacher, the publicist, the artist.

This snobbery has innumerable aspects. It has been one of the great English exports, with railways, governesses, organized games;

the rich of the whole world have gone to school to modern England to find how best to enjoy the superiorities of wealth.

But the clue to the English attitude to class and social distinction is to be found in the school system. In no other country does the character of the formal education received have the permanent importance that it has in England. In all modern countries educational systems have been the subject of controversy and even of rational discussion. Should education be secular or religious? Should it be controlled locally or centrally? Should private schools, not run by the state, be allowed? Should education aim at creating a unified national character? Should it be purely literary, or scientific, or technical? Should boys be taught by women? These are only some of the controversies that have distracted educational politics in America, France, Scotland, Germany. And all of them have distracted England, too. But over and above all these controversies there has loomed in England the so-called "public school" question (or, if you like, system). Even if all the other questions had been settled quickly and amicably, this might still have remained. The other questions have not all been settled quickly or amicably, and even when they have been, the solutions adopted have been irrelevant to the problem of the public schools.

The very name of the "public schools" illustrates the complexity of the problem, for the public schools of England are, in the ordinary sense of the term, not public at all. They are not controlled by what are usually called public bodies and they are far from wishing to serve all the public. They got their name when the English state took no interest in or responsibility for education. Their title contrasted them with private schools run by individuals or unincorporated committees. The public schools were governed by self-perpetuating committees, which had control over endowments which they were supposed to administer for educational purposes as defined in the wills or deeds of gift of the founders, who varied in social rank from kings and bishops to retired sea-captains or shopkeepers. Over against these more or less ancient and more or less richly endowed schools were the private schools, set up by individuals or religious denominations, with no responsibilities to the law and with no permanent place in the educational system. Some of these private schools were good, some were bad; they can both be illustrated from the works of Dickens. Some of the public schools were good and some were bad, but, being perpetual institutions, they had a chance in their long lives to be both at different times. All schools, even the most famous, took at least one chance of being bad.

So far there is nothing extraordinary in the English situation. It could be paralleled in most European countries and in the United States. What is extraordinary is the sudden rise, in the nineteenth century, of the idea that only a "public school" could give an education fitting a boy for command in business, in politics, in the army, the civil service, even in the arts. Only in England—and there in modern times—did the idea grow up that the effects of education between the ages of thirteen and fourteen and seventeen and eighteen were decisive. All the most important lessons, intellectual, moral, and social, had to be learned then or not at all. The old saying attributed to the Jesuits: "Give us a boy from seven to twelve and we can let anybody have him after that," was transformed into an English version of a more negative kind: "If you don't give us a boy between fourteen and eighteen, nobody will ever make anything of him," or, if not anything, at least enough to justify his being a leader of the nation. Nor was this all. It became an accepted dogma of English life that the male population was divided into two classes: those with a public-school education and others. The products of the public schools were assumed to have certain valuable moral and social qualities which, if not quite unattainable by the products of other schools, were, at any rate, rarely attained by them. The public-school boy started with a bias in his favour, the outsider with a bias against him. There was nothing like this in any other European country or in the United States. There were good schools and bad schools, and some of the "goodness" of schools in all countries was social rather than intellectual; but nobody who had other serious social or financial or intellectual assets in France or Germany or the United States lived his life under the shadow of having gone to the wrong kind of school.[1] Like many sacred, traditional, and indisputably national institutions, the great English class-barrier, the exclusive character of the public schools and of the two ancient universities, is quite modern.

It was not the aristocratic eighteenth century that created the modern English class structure, but the middle period of the Victorian age. Oxford and Cambridge were far less "exclusive" in Mr. Gladstone's youth than in his old age. They were far more aristocratic, snobbish, if you like, scandalous. But they were also far more representative of all classes of society. And in this change the universities reflected the schools, reflected the creation of that most important English class-distinction, that between the upper and lower middle classes, a difference which is not purely educational and not purely economic. And it is fairly new. There is no doubt on what side of the barrier Soames Forsyte fell, but where can we place Mr. Pickwick? Into this class, talent, energy and luck could force a way, but the real conquest took two generations; the intruder was really naturalized not in his own person but in his son's.

But not only is this "traditional" class-barrier new, not old; it lasted only two generations or so in its pristine purity. Around 1900 the system was as near perfection as an economically fluid society permitted. But its day of uncontested supremacy was over. The generation of which Mr. Wells was so brilliant a representa-

[1] Henry Adams disliked the Boston Latin School because it was, he thought, a bad school, giving a sterile education; he thought the same of Harvard College. He did not lament the fact that Groton or St. Paul's did not exist in time to add (if it were possible) to the importance of being an Adams. The modern American preparatory school is often an imitation of the English public school. Even the older American boarding schools have been influenced by the social prestige borrowed from England by such comparatively new foundations as Groton. But it should be remembered that there are famous and "good" American boarding schools, like the Phillips Academies at Exeter and Andover, that are a good deal older than some very good English public schools. Even Groton is older than some quite good English schools.

tive was knocking at the door. The next generation of the poor was provided with far more effective educational weapons than Mr. Wells got in his school-days. Oxford and Cambridge abandoned their brief experiment in exclusiveness, and the public schools began to suffer from the competition of the new secondary schools—suffer not socially but scholastically—and scholastic success, thanks to the reforms of 1850–70, paid rewards in cash and prestige. The public schools preserved their social and literary prestige, and so did Oxford and Cambridge, but their heyday was over. It took a long time for this to be noticed; it is not widely noticed yet, but like so much in English life, an apparently immemorial, unchanging, unshakable institutional set-up appeared, existed in its pure form for only a short time, and either adapted itself to the new conditions or disappeared. The English educational system is now in the stage of adapting itself or of being profoundly changed.

But the England that is fighting this war and that got into this war is an England in which the old educational system of "exclusive" schools and two "ancient" universities providing nearly all the leaders in nearly all branches of life is still vigorous although already in obvious decline. It is this system that most novelists, journalists, dramatists, film-producers take for granted whether they like it or not. It is as much part of the standard picture of English life as the village ruled by the squire and the parson. And like so many things in this tradition-ridden community, the tradition is not old; its day of uncontested acceptance was short and its decline was well under way while its enemies were attacking its dominance and its friends were defending outworks of a citadel whose key positions were already open to capture.

The industrial revolution created a social problem for which England found a solution. It was an important social problem. In each generation, there emerged from the ranks new millionaires, new men who without being millionaires were yet very rich, new men who were simply prosperous. The millionaires were not the problem. Even the most caste-ridden society, in the Western world at any rate, easily finds a place for the *really* rich man. They became peers; they became baronets; they founded great landed dynasties; they soon provided aristocratic rakes, backers of slow horses and fast women, as the joke was. They also produced Peel and Gladstone, men who combined in a synthesis unknown in other countries the business habits, the financial competence of the new magnates, with the education, the tastes, the sense of public duty of the more respectable elements of the old landed aristocracy.

It was below this level that the job of assimilation was more difficult. Was England to have a large opulent class with purely business standards, cut off by habit and prejudices from the classes that provided officers for the army and navy, rulers for India, members of the professions (especially the law and the church), the "educated classes"? Was this new bourgeoisie to be a rival of the minor gentry as in France, or a docile hanger-on as it became in Germany? It was very important for England that the solution was a compromise, the fusion of the two classes.

The fusion was made possible, of course, by the absence in England of the rigid hereditary class-lines of the continent of Europe. There was no real equivalent of the rigid class-barriers of France, not to speak of such feudal anachronisms as Germany. There were no real hereditary castes. But the job of mating one set of standards to another had to be done in a hurry. It was not a matter of taking a few hundred new men in each generation into the upper classes. That had always been done. The new men were now numbered in thousands, not hundreds, and they did not come provided merely with money; they had their own ideas, their own order of values. Solid middle-class virtues and prejudices had to be adapted, not merely thrown away by the social climbers.

The job of marrying the old English social order to the new was mainly the work of the public schools. Let all the sons of the more prosperous classes, whether their prosperity was new or comparatively old, receive the same education. And not merely the same book-education—that mattered little, as Continental experience was to show—but the same social education. Let them learn to speak alike, play alike, have the same artificially uniform manners, tastes, prejudices, religious and ethical ideas. Then it would matter little whether they went into the family business, or inherited the family estate, or became successful lawyers, doctors, bishops, generals. They would be members of a class, marked off from the mass of the people by economic status, but not by that alone. And it would be a unified class, whose education would give a common background more important than the bias given by professional education or experience, so that the soldier or parson or squire would have in common links of habit and of memory that would hold them together, make it possible for them to understand one another, keep their quarrels within a common family tradition.

There existed in the public schools an instrument for the making of the uniform "upper class" that no other country could equal. The reverence for vested interests that had saved from confiscation so many apparently indefensible institutions now paid dividends. There were scattered all over England, but especially in the south, old schools, more or less well endowed, which had from their age and wealth a prestige that had little or no relation to their educational efficiency. It was necessary to take the sons of the new men away from their families if they were to be given the accent, the habits, the tastes that their parents wanted them to have but could not teach by example. So the boarding school was a necessary solution of the problem. That most of the old boarding schools were in the south and most of the new wealth in the north was all to the good from this point of view. The boy was moved from the new industrial, rapidly changing modern world into an artificially preserved sample of eighteenth-century England, rural, unchanging. The revival of religious belief in the upper classes that was the fruit of Wesleyanism, the Evangelical movement, and the fears provoked by the French Revolution made it easier to find a common religious program that reassured middle-class parents who had no desire to see their sons catch aristocratic infidelity as well as aristocratic manners.

In Rugby school and in Dr. Arnold the working model was found. The squire's son, Tom Brown, learned to be a Christian,

English gentleman and he also learned to mix with sons of lawyers, doctors, manufacturers, all of them cut off by their school status from the inhabitants of the town of Rugby. A high moral tone was insisted on; boys were made each other's keepers. The older boys were given authority over the younger as a reward for their proficiency in study. The prestige of Greek fought a losing battle against the prestige of sport, but it had more prestige than it had in smart European schools where success in school work had no extra prestige at all. A religion that was based on undisputed moral principles rather than on theological dogma reinforced the idea of the "Christian gentleman" who learned at school to control himself and others and so learned the habit and acquired the right of ruling.[2]

The transformation of the old public schools was not the work of one man at one moment. It began before Arnold at Rugby. They had their rivals, disciples, imitators. Old schools were transformed, new schools founded. The transformation of the old schools presented some difficulties. Often these schools had been founded for a particular town by a leading citizen. If they were to continue to serve only that town, they would be small or very mixed in social character. And they would not be boarding schools, or not be boarding schools for the majority. It was necessary to free the endowments of the old schools from the narrow views of the founders, to throw open the scholarships to competition with no attention paid to the place of origin or economic status of the competitors. Thus clever boys from all over England might compete for the prize of free education "on the foundation" of old and famous schools. Such a scholarship might be the only way whereby such a boy could enter a good school; it might, on the other hand, be simply an honour, of no serious economic importance to the family of the

[2] Not everybody approved the assimilation of the new and old "upper classes." "He said Rugby School is also upon a bad footing. In it are many of the Sons of Gentlemen, but more of those who are the sons of Manufacturers at Birmingham, Wolverhampton, etc. who having little sentiment of the disgrace of anything dishonorable act as their inclinations lead them. . . ." Quoted in Charles Smythe: *Simeon and Chur h Order*, p. 46.

candidate. The advantages were manifest. A school was not forced to spend its resources on the best the local small town could provide in the way of raw materials. The stigma of charity was removed from the scholarship-holder and so from academic industry. There was a lowering of the barrier, which in other countries was so high, between the boys who had to "do well" at school and those who did well without the same severe economic pressure. Both in the old schools and in the old universities the danger of creating a class of able, embittered poor intellectuals was diminished. Frenchmen coming to Oxford were surprised to learn that the industrious were not necessarily drab, nor the idle smart. Of course, games had far more prestige than studies, but then games were not an extra but a part—in some schools, at some times, the main part—of formal education. The talented boy who could get his foot on the bottom of the ladder by entering one of the good schools as a scholar had no great ground of complaint. He was given a chance to compete on fair terms, a chance which parents were glad to give him a chance to take.[3] But it was the first step that counted.

[3] For an account of the transformation of a local school see E. M. Forster's *The Longest Journey*: "For the intentions of the founder had been altered, or, at all events, amplified, and instead of educating the 'poore of my home,' he now educated the upper middle classes of England. The change had taken place not so very far back. Till the nineteenth century the grammar-school was still composed of day scholars from the neighbourhood. Then two things happened. Firstly, the school's property rose in value, and it became rich. Secondly, for no obvious reason, it suddenly emitted a quantity of bishops. The bishops, like the stars from a Roman candle, were of all colours, and flew in all directions, some high, some low, some to distant colonies, one into the Church of Rome. But many a father traced their course in the papers; many a mother wondered whether her son, if properly ignited, might not burn as bright; many a family moved to the place where living and education were so cheap, where day-boys were not looked down upon, and where the orthodox and the up-to-date were said to be combined. The school doubled its numbers. It built new class-rooms, laboratories, and a gymnasium. It dropped the prefix 'Grammar.' It coaxed the sons of the local tradesmen into a new foundation, the 'Commercial School,' built a couple of miles away. And it started boarding-houses. It had not the gracious antiquity of Eton or Winchester, nor, on the other hand, had it

The apparent democracy of the competitive system was much criticized at the time of its institution. It was not universally agreed, for instance, that the sons of the poorer residents of Rugby were wholly compensated for the transformation of their local school into a school catering for the richer classes of the whole nation by the provision of a local "commercial" school and open scholarships which the poor boys of Rugby could compete for on even terms with rich boys who were prepared for the examination in preparatory schools to which the poor boys could not afford to go. The then headmaster of Rugby, Dr. Temple,[4] admitted that the criticism might have had a great deal of truth in it "twenty years ago. There is very much less truth in it now; and I believe, as the foundations are opened, there will be less and less truth in it as time goes on, and in a very little while I think there will be no truth in it at all."[5] This was stated in good faith in 1865, but Dr. Temple's optimistic belief that boys from poor homes and local schools could compete on even terms with boys from rich homes and expensive schools, especially designed for winning scholarships at the great public schools, was unrealistic. Indeed, the preparatory schools—that is, the schools which prepare for the great public schools—are more of a class barrier than are the public schools themselves. They are privately owned, representing a vested interest which need not have any regard for public policy; their curriculum is quite different from that of the state schools, so that preparatory-school Latin is a very important class difference; and they give up their boys to the public schools at thirteen instead of eleven. The public schools still accept new boys at an age that

---

a conscious policy like Lancing, Wellington, and other purely modern foundations. Where traditions served, it clung to them. Where new departures seemed desirable, they were made. It aimed at producing the average Englishman, and, to a very large extent, it succeeded."

[4] Later Archbishop of Canterbury and father of the present Archbishop of Canterbury.

[5] *Memoirs of Archbishop Temple*, edited by E. G. Sandford, Vol. I, p. 194.

does not suit the state school system, and by insisting on a knowledge of Latin they usually bar the way to the ablest elementary-school boys.

At the university stage the same principle was applied. Help given to poor boys to aid them to pass through the universities had taken the form of scholarships and exhibitions restricted to candidates who had no other resources and, in many cases, to boys from local schools which served a limited area. Another form of help was a system of "working your way through college" as a sizar. In return for part-time work poor boys could get the mental though not the social benefits of college life. Badly fed, badly lodged, looked down on by the richer students, this university proletariat was an obstacle to the creation of a unified class of "university men." They were the oddities whom the hero of *The Way of All Flesh* was induced to meet, led out of his class by ill-timed religious zeal. From them had come not only great ornaments of English life like Samuel Johnson but men who had made their academic careers preliminaries to worldly success. Thus men like Dean Ireland made Greek pay.[6] The new system penalized the boy who had no good, cheap school close at hand and who had not the money to pay his way through one of the old or new public schools. The decline of the old grammar schools, or their rise into the rank of public schools, and the failure of central or local authorities to provide efficient secondary education weakened the competitive position of the poor boy. Even if he got to the university, he had to face the competition of equally able boys who had got a head start on him at Rugby or Clifton or St. Paul's. Canon Liddon was going a little too far, but not much, when he described this reform

[6] Leslie Stephen calculated that "a man who can secure a high place in either of our two great Triposes wins at least £5,000 in money, besides an amount of glory of which it is difficult to make an accurate valuation" (*Sketches from Cambridge*, 1936 edition, p. 26). This was written just as the new system was coming into effect. It was becoming harder for a boy starting from scratch to vault into a different economic and social class by three or four years' successful industry at Oxford or Cambridge.

as "making a present of the endowments of Oxford to the upper middle class."[7]

The importance of the reform did not stop there. For at the same time the introduction of competitive civil-service examinations made profitable, honourable, and interesting official careers, first in India and then at home, a monopoly of the boys who had competed successfully in the obstacle race of English education. And the chief obstacles were economic. A dull boy of a prosperous family could start but not finish; a bright boy of a really poor family could not start. A *really* poor boy, that is; for a day boy at Percival's Clifton or Walker's Manchester Grammar School or St. Paul's could get a first-class competitive training without having to draw too heavily on the resources of his family—by middle-class standards—but he was not really poor. But to the great majority of the English people, being a day boy at a good school was as fantastic a dream as being an Etonian. And the boy who was debarred from entering one of the public schools, even as a day boy or as a scholar, was very often debarred from receiving any decent secondary education at all. For the richer, more energetic, more successful members of the middle class had, in educational matters, an interest different from that of the poorer, less successful members of the same class. Had the old public schools remained unreformed, the strong Puritan bias of the new middle class would have kept its sons away from contagion. Had the doctrinal bias of the public schools been more definite, there would have been more Nonconformist public schools than the two or three which were, in fact, found adequate.[8] Had it been more difficult to transform local grammar schools into national "public schools," or to found new public schools whose status was not questioned by the older schools; had, in fact, the English genius for carrying out profound changes under the disguise of immovable

---

[7] *Life of Pusey*, Vol. III, p. 396.

[8] The great headmasters were nearly all Broad Churchmen like Tait, Temple, Arnold, Percival. Even Benson was theologically "broad," though ritualistically mildly "high."

conservatism failed in this field, there might have been created a united system of middle-class education. But that was not to be. The lower middle class was left to its own resources and its own standards. Both were inadequate.[9]

In all departments of life the English lower-class boy was conditioned to an acceptance of the second-best or the third-best. He was neither forced nor encouraged to be intellectually ambitious. He learned, in a dozen ways, to know his place, and the only way out of his place was normally through financial success. Matthew Arnold might lament; the Scotch might sneer; the Germans wonder. The English middle and upper class were proud of the education they received and, at the edge of the middle class, those who did not receive a public-school education paid it the sometimes bitter but always sincere compliment of envy and flattery, of more or less competent imitation.

While this unique system was being built up, England was creating a rival system of education that has far more claim to be called "public" in the normal sense of the word. Compared with Scotland, which was socially, if not politically, democratic, popular education in England was very backward; it was also backward compared with popular education in autocratic Prussia. And Puritan zeal for a reading and understanding laity to provide the audience

---

[9] "This was the line of weakness along which Victorian culture was fractured. The Middle Classes, 'the wealth and intelligence of the nation, the pride and glory of the British name' were stratified along the seam where the public schools met the grammar schools. With the social and political consequences I am not concerned. For our culture it was a major disaster. A culture is an area of inter-communication, living and alert in all directions at once, and in the late Victorian age the educated classes, already splitting into specialized interests, were dragging behind them a growing mass with no interests at all. It had thrown up the sponge, and was becoming to all intents and purposes a proletariat, and it was Northcliffe, I think, who first apprehended its existence and diagnosed its quality" (G. M. Young: *Daylight and Champaign*, p. 155). Northcliffe went, in fact, to a rather exceptionally good private school, run by the father of Mr. A. A. Milne, who employed as one of his assistant masters a young man representing as far as genius can the new educationally aspiring class for which England made so little provision, Mr. H. G. Wells.

for a learned clergy, ensured that New England and its colonies, though not the South, would be far in advance of old England.

Until the Reform Bill of 1832, the English government took no interest in or responsibility for popular education at all, and for a generation after that it took very little. Schools for the children of the poor were either mere private-adventure schools run for meagre profit or schools controlled by religious bodies. And these in turn fell into two great groups: those run by the Church of England and those run by the Dissenters. The central government began to give grants to schools meeting simple tests of efficiency; it moved on to the creation of a nucleus of an education office; and in 1870 the Gladstone government passed an act setting up school boards where the existing schools were thought inadequate by the local voters. The new board schools [10] were not free, nor was education compulsory. Twenty years later these two improvements had been secured, but other problems had arisen. Over a great part of rural England there were no school boards or board schools. In these areas the children of Dissenters were taught in schools which prided themselves on their "church" atmosphere although they could absent themselves from the specifically religious instruction. More serious, no non-Anglican school-teacher had any more hope of employment in these Church of England "national" schools than a Catholic or agnostic teacher would have in rural Georgia. On the other hand, in the towns where school boards had been established, "undenominational" religious instruction was given, a solution which suited the Dissenters since the points on which they differed from Anglicans were just those that were banned as "denominational." And as the school boards could call on the local

[10] It is revealing that although school boards have been abolished since 1902, a large part of the English middle and upper classes still talk of "board-school boys." They are unaware of the great transformations in English popular education brought about in this century. More excusable is the fact that Mr. H. L. Mencken, although he now knows in the fourth edition of *The American Language* (p. 241) that the council school has replaced the board school, still uses the other nomenclature of the abolished system.

taxpayers to contribute to the cost of the schools, the buildings were better and teachers' salaries in general higher than in the church schools, which had to rely exclusively on state grants and on voluntary subscriptions. The financial condition of the "voluntary" schools (which were mainly Anglican and Catholic) grew too bad to be borne and the Conservative government passed a great Education Act in 1902 which enabled the current costs of these schools to be met out of the local taxes, in exchange for the acceptance of some control by local bodies, no longer the school boards, but the county councils and other local authorities.

The great reform of 1902–3 was marked by that comparative readiness to ignore local vested political interests which makes so marked a contrast between England and the United States or pre-Vichy France. The 2,527 school boards were replaced by 328 education authorities, a very important rationalization of the system.[11]

At the same time power was given to the new education authorities to establish secondary schools, the courts having held that the old school boards had no such power.[12]

It thus came to be accepted that the state could and should provide secondary education, but the new secondary schools could not compete in prestige, in material resources in the way of buildings and sports fields, or in social amenities with the richer and more respected "public" schools. Nor did public opinion want from the new schools an acceptance of the duty of providing social, athletic, and, thirdly, intellectual nourishment or diversion for all or nearly all the adolescent young. There was now to be an

[11] Even the old school boards were, on the average, large, well-equipped administrative units compared with the typical American school districts. When all allowances are made for the great area of the United States, the 130,000 school districts represent a great atomization of the school system for which there has been no parallel in England in this century. The consolidation of school districts in some states has just begun to produce some of the results attained at one blow in England.

[12] This example of judicial review was, it is thought, deliberately provoked by an ingenious and resourceful civil servant who wished for a thorough reform. The courts spoke, but, of course, Parliament was there to reverse them, as it did.

approach to a system of *"la carrière ouverte aux talents,"* but the *talents* were underlined. Those who had only one or two talents were politely advised to spend them otherwise than in acquiring or failing to acquire more schooling, unless, of course, they had money as a substitute for brains. There was to be an educational ladder, but those who could not climb more than a rung or two without becoming dizzy were told to get down; the ladder was not turned into an escalator. In short, the new schools concentrated on what they could do with the resources put at their disposal, on teaching in the narrow sense of the word, on providing book learning. In that possibly too limited an endeavor they were and are far more successful than is appreciated by the "educated" public at home or in other English-speaking lands. The full appreciation of this achievement is confined to the schools themselves, to their educational rivals, the great public schools, and to the awarders of scholarships at Oxford and Cambridge. The standard reached by the pupils of quite small and very obscure local high schools might, if it could be made evident to complacent Americans and Scots, startle both of them into emulation.[13]

The main defect of the state school system (apart from the large number of things it does not do at all) is its very inferior physical equipment. The school buildings as a rule are drab, meanly functional; they represent the ideas of an age when education was doled out to the poor as a charity or as a necessary concession. The board schools that Sherlock Holmes saw as so many lighthouses in the darkness of London belong most obviously to the age of gas and hansom cabs. And in the great cities the old board schools are still the typical schools of the poor. In new suburbs, or where an enterprising education authority has taken its courage into its hands, things are better, but probably no English public buildings (ex-

[13] "Secondary education in Great Britain is now at least as good as it is or has ever been in any European nation, and it is much better than the typical brands provided in the Dominions and in the United States." (F. H. Spencer: *Education for the People*, p. 13.) For "Great Britain" I should read "England." Some of the intellectual weaknesses of the American high school are present in Scotland.

cept army barracks) are less generously planned than state schools.[14]

And if this is true of the old board schools, it is still more true of the schools erected by the churches. The schools maintained by Anglicans and Catholics were always poor by the standards of the board schools, and after the Acts of 1902 and 1903 it was the building and maintenance of the school buildings that was the main burden on the faithful.[15]

But the inadequacy of rural school buildings is not due solely to ecclesiastical poverty or niggardliness. It is also due to the poverty of rural life. To provide a rural equivalent for urban resources involves great financial outlay—and that for purposes not necessarily ranking high in rural priority lists.[16]

It is worth repeating that one of the main drawbacks to the class

[14] When a new girls' school was built on the outskirts of Oxford on the eve of this war, there was some local grumbling at its lavishness, especially at spending money on a pillared portico. This criticism was not based on architectural grounds, that it made the school look like a Southern manor out of *Gone with the Wind,* but on cost. Some local taxpayers definitely belonged to the school of thought of the apostle Judas in this matter.

[15] "If the school is a country school, it will happen oftener than not that it is a National School, built and maintained by a Church of England organization, semi-ecclesiastical and neo-Gothic in design, with an uneven, much divided playing-space, not even asphalted; and in a large majority of instances the school is quite unfit for most purposes except the actual confinement of children during a very large fraction of their daylight hours, and in winter for most of them." (Spencer, op. cit., p. 9.) The average English village school is not any worse and is usually better than the "little red schoolhouse" of American tradition, but there is no English romantic tradition of the "little yellow brick schoolhouse."

[16] Lord Raglan in a letter to *The Times,* August 18, 1942, sets out the situation in rural Monmouthshire. "In this county the rural school buildings are without exception old and obsolete in type, many of them containing only one classroom. Of 80 rural schools 11 have less than twenty and 45 less than 40 children on the register; in these no division into classes is possible." That is to say, in this county many of the defects of the single school-district of American rural states are reproduced without the same institutional excuse. It is probable that only in the pay, legal status, and, possibly, training of the teachers has Monmouthshire any advantages over Kansas or Georgia.

system in English education is the ignorance of the old "educated classes" of what has been done by the new educational system. Yet some of the achievements of that system have greatly and *obviously* increased the chances of a successful pursuit of happiness for the vast majority of the children of England. The exploitation of children, their filth, their ignorance, their exposure to crime and disease—these were among the chief charges brought against urban England, and especially London, by critics of English industrialism and English class structure. Here the improvement has been immense and is easily illustrated from the city of Oliver Twist and David Copperfield. A picture of the average board-school class of fifty years ago and the average county-council-school class today is striking. So is the experience of the army, the hospitals and the jails. The changes are not all for the better, but most of them are; and the school system is the single biggest force for good.

The work of the schools in civilizing London was not confined to spreading literacy and keeping children off the streets where they were in danger of becoming Artful Dodgers or less well adapted, though equally antisocial, elements of the population. That squalor which visitors to London had long noted was combated with great success. Beginning in 1902, with a campaign against ringworm, the cleanliness of the children became one of the concerns of the school. The statistics of such unpleasant but important incidences of London child life as being flea-bitten showed striking gains on this front. Between 1908 and 1926, children returned as "badly flea-bitten" fell from 30 per cent to 3.7 per cent. In 1913 a third of the older girls at school were suffering from lice in the hair; by 1928, only 8.5 per cent.[17] Of course it was not only the work of the schools. The rise in the general standard of living, and the growth of social services not connected with the

17 "It is of much interest to note that this rise in percentage as regards cleanliness stands in close relation with the marked decline in the prevalence of tuberculous disease of the glands of the neck in school children." (*New Survey of London Life and Labour,* Vol. I, pp. 211-12.)

schools, played their part. The growth of public health services, of which the National Health Insurance system of 1911 was the most striking example, helped. But the basic credit goes to the schools and to the school-teachers.[18] And it is hardly necessary to emphasize for anybody who knows the life of a great industrial city from some point nearer than Beaconsfield or Horsham how important this increased cleanliness is. No democratic school system can begin to work if the mothers of clean children live in terror of what their children may bring home from school. And even the most socially ambitious lower-middle-class mother in England is more worried by fleas than by accents.[19]

The new and *really* public education system in England has serious defects or, at any rate, inconsistencies. The church authorities (Anglican and Catholic) control appointments to teaching jobs that are wholly paid for out of public funds, and this angers the purists (of whom there are some) and the anti-clericals (of whom there are more). There is a steady decline in the number of church schools, and many Anglican leaders are, privately at least, convinced that the attempt to keep alive a national system of church schools is doomed to failure and that a compromise that would give the parson and the convinced Anglican school-teacher right of entry to a common school system would be preferable to

[18] "The cleansing scheme which played so great a part in this beneficent revolution was at first very unpopular with parents, and great patience and tact were required on the part of the teachers and nurses, as well as the strong support of the Council before the opposition could be overcome." (Ibid., p. 212.)

[19] "In less than one generation the death-rate for children has been reduced to about two-sevenths of its former dimensions, whilst for all ages up to 20 it has been reduced to about one-half. The reduction has been greater among children than amongst adults, and the improvement diminishes rapidly among those old enough to have missed at school even our present partial efforts to see that children are well nourished and are kept healthy. The improvement is, of course, due to a complexity of causes: but among them, school medical care and school feeding are very important." (Spencer, op. cit., pp. 253-4.)

the waste of money and zeal on the dwindling assets of the voluntary system.[20] These Anglicans feel, too, that the doctrinal points on which the clergy insist are matters of indifference to most of the Anglican laity, if not to the Anglican faithful. There is a chance, therefore, that the primary educational system will be unified by the adoption of the "secular solution"—roughly, the system that has prevailed in America since Catholic opposition drove undenominational "Bible"—that is, Protestant teaching—out of the public schools. Such a unification of the school system would increase the general efficiency, especially on the side of buildings and the training of teachers.

Whether the system of training teachers is a good one depends on the relative optimism of one's views of human ability. The English elementary schools, with 150,000 teachers, are the basic problem. If these teachers are all to be university-trained, it is argued by the pessimists, *either* the universities will maintain their standards and there will be too few teachers *or,* in order to produce enough teachers, they will be forced to lower their standards. Therefore, it is argued, the specialized training college which accepts the ineluctable fact that most people are not very clever and that not very clever people can yet do very useful work is the necessary solution. But even if one accepts this view (as I do), it does not follow that even not very clever people do not benefit by association in universities with much cleverer people, and still less does it follow that clever people in universities will not benefit by association with dull people, although as long as higher education is so much an affair of money, the second problem cannot be re-

[20] The number of Catholic schools rises slowly. The example of Scotland shows that this easily identifiable minority member of the national education system can be taken into a system of state control, while keeping its religious character. Of course, if Catholics were as numerous as they are around Boston, Massachusetts, new difficulties would arise. But their comparatively small numbers make a satisfactory if inelegant solution possible, as their small numbers would do in Kansas or Georgia if the people of Kansas or Georgia were as indifferent to lay and Protestant zeal as the rulers of Scotland and England are.

garded as urgently needing attention. A separation of teachers into two easily identifiable classes, however justifiable on paper, has the disadvantage—not a trivial disadvantage in a country like England—of seeming to mark the elementary-school teacher as an intellectual proletarian. And that mark will reflect on the schools in which he teaches.

A more urgent problem is that of making secondary education available to far more of the able boys and girls born to poor parents, even if that means denying secondary education to the dull boys and girls who are often born to prosperous parents. Although there have been great improvements in recent years, the race, except for the *very* clever boy or girl who is also lucky in health and in the health of his parents, is still to the prosperous. It is at the break between elementary and secondary education that the greatest wastage occurs. But in the secondary schools the dice are still weighted against the poor boy and girl, too.

Only 6.6 per cent of the boys and 3·6 per cent of the girls leaving secondary schools enter universities.[21] Most of them go to the new universities, but a high proportion of their most talented pupils are creamed off for Oxford or Cambridge. More than half of the scholarships at Oxford and Cambridge colleges go to candidates trained in grant-earning schools, and these candidates themselves came, in the proportion of over two thirds, from elementary schools where they paid no fees.[22] It should be noted, of course, that the pool from which these candidates are drawn is about five times as large as the pool of "public school" candidates. The best of nearly half a million boys and girls in secondary schools got rather more than half of the highest academic prizes; the rest went mainly to the best of 75,000-odd boys and girls at "public" and "good" private schools. But it would be very rash to infer that the public

[21] To these might be added those entering training colleges, since if they were in the United States (and Scotland), these future teachers would largely enter universities as part of their professional training. Of boys 1.9 per cent and 7.7 per cent of girls enter training colleges.

[22] At the other end, more than half of the candidates who get "firsts" at Oxford and Cambridge come up from grant-earning schools.

schools were four or five times as fortunate in the ability of their pupils or in the efficiency of their teaching as the secondary schools. Even if we assumed that the Oxford and Cambridge colleges never made mistakes and never allowed social bias to affect their judgment, even unconsciously, it is by no means certain that the boy and, still more, the girl of poor parents can afford to go to Oxford or Cambridge, scholarship or no scholarship. What is evident is the intensity of competition that is involved in the distribution of Oxford and Cambridge scholarships among the boys and girls leaving the secondary schools in any one year. They win less than five hundred scholarships; as the average school life is about five years, these five hundred scholarships (or less) have to be allocated among the most ambitious boys and girls out of 100,000! This is, indeed, the survival of the fittest, an educational version of the history of the "froward Homunculus." And like that lucky survivor, a successful boy or girl, thinking of school-fellows whom ill health, selfish parents, bad luck, or other accidents debarred from competition at the one or two opportunities open each year, might murmur (if self-critical):

> *Shame to have ousted your betters thus,*
> *Taking ark while the others remained outside.*

On the other hand, it must be remembered that the English attitude, even when most "democratic," sees in democracy rather a selective than an equalizing force. The English educationist, like Thomas Jefferson, sees a good educational system as producing smaller and smaller groups of the really talented (the type Jefferson called geniuses), rather than one spreading roughly the same kind of education over as large a number of people as possible. Too close an attention to what the public appears to want seems dangerous. As Mandell Creighton, the great scholar bishop, put it: "If you plunge enthusiastically into the task of supplying the popular market, you lose the capacity for raising the popular standards." And this selective view is less resented in England than it might be elsewhere. The working-class parent whose child fails to win a scholarship does not (however great his regret may be) usually resent a competitive system, though he may regret that there are not more prizes. He does not insist on a system of general education which wipes out the difference not only between rich and poor, but between talented and dull. He does not welcome schemes of "practical" education that may, in fact, be more useful to the average boy if there is any implication in them that the exceptional boy of poor parents is to have his chances of the same education as the rich boy diminished. There is no necessary connection between such a system of "practical" education and a limiting of the opportunities for normal higher education for the sons of the poor, but the conservative sponsors of such schemes do not always succeed in making this clear.[23]

One example of this attitude is the comparative readiness with which local authorities provide funds enabling clever boys to take up scholarships in Oxford or Cambridge. There is a good deal to be said against this system. It deprives the new universities of the most able students whom their local area produces. It costs a good deal of money that might go to providing cheaper university education for more, rather than highly expensive education for comparatively few. But the talented poor boy is thought to be entitled to the best.

Of course, the drawbacks are seen later; not all boys uprooted

[23] In general, the public tends to think of the Conservative Party as being more stingy in educational matters than its rivals. I believe that the decision of the Conservative majority of the London County Council to cut out school prizes in the economy crisis of 1932 helped to destroy their majority at the next election. It is normally only Conservative local authorities who try to evade paying the national minimum salaries to teachers. But no Conservative local authority has stopped paying its teachers altogether or has shut down its schools, as has happened in several American states. And even if they wanted to do so, no government, however Conservative, would permit them to do so. But it is natural that a party none of whose leaders have any direct knowledge of or private interest in the state schools (through their own children or the children of their friends) should be lacking in tact in dealing with an educational system of whose services they never think of making use.

from their class and section profit, notably, by their sojourn in
Oxford and Cambridge. And it helps to make the official ruling
class more uniform in background, which is not all to the good;
also it makes the faculties of all universities too uniform in academic training. Yet the quasi-monopoly of Oxford and Cambridge
has its good as well as its bad side. It prevents one type of provin-
cialism, if it fosters another. In every institution of higher learning
in Britain, a large proportion of the teachers have had a university
training that, whatever its other faults, has not been marked by
local prejudice or patriotism. Oxford University is not in any sense
the local university of the southwest Midlands nor is Cambridge
the university of East Anglia. Their graduates bear a national, not
a local brand.[24]

Whatever may have been the case fifty years ago, there is no
longer any plausibility in the view of English education as divided
into a minority of schools and universities for the sons of the prosperous, and a miscellany of private schools run for profit, and
inadequate schools, supported by taxes, for teaching the minimum
of literacy to the children of the poor. The system is much more
complicated than that. The new secondary schools, like the new
universities, have come of age. The public schools, like Oxford
and Cambridge, are merely the most conspicuous members of the
aggregate of educational institutions. And it may well seem that
the position of the public schools requires no further discussion.
Yet the amount of interest, hostile or friendly, well informed or
simply romantic, that these schools excite shows that their present

[24] With all due allowances made for the size of the country, the American
university system caters more than is altogether healthy to local standards
and clientele. Even Harvard and Columbia are not national universities in
the sense that Oxford and Cambridge are. "Although there is a fairly even
distribution of Ph.D.'s over the entire 'market,' the graduates of any given
department tend to congregate in the immediate region of their home
university. In 1939, 46 per cent of the teaching Ph.D.'s who had received
degrees between 1926 and 1935 were teaching in the region where they
had done their graduate work. Thirty per cent were still in the same state."
(W. B. Hesseltine and Louis Kaplan: "Doctors of Philosophy in History,"
American Historical Review, Vol. XLVII, No. 4, pp. 783-4.)

and future role is of the highest importance to the English democracy. And in such a discussion it is almost impossible to avoid an amount of indignation or enthusiasm that no educational system can justify.

To read and listen to some of the critics and apologists of the British public-school system, one would think that English history began around 1840, when Dr. Arnold's example at Rugby began to be taken up all over England. That the English ruling class was the envy of Europe, for its success, long before the public school in its modern sense was born, that alone among the great feudal states England was transformed by an oligarchy, not by an absolute monarchy, that the survival of the independent corporation (of which the public school is a minor example) is far more important than compulsory games or prefectorial authority in giving its peculiar tone to English society—these simple truths are neglected. If one were to take this argument as seriously as its authors do, we should be forced to think of John Milton worrying because he went to St. Paul's, not to Eton or Harrow, worrying still more because he became a master in a private school, and feeling ill at ease in the presence of such of his colleagues in the government of the new Republic as had been at good boarding schools. We should have to wonder at the stupidity of William Pitt and William Wilberforce, who refused to send their talented sons to Eton, for different and good reasons. If the modern public-school system were as important as is usually thought, we should be forced to wonder if that product of unreformed Eton, Shelley, would not have had a healthier, more English outlook if he had gone to school fifty years later and had become a sedate, normal old Etonian man of letters like Swinburne or Aldous Huxley. In short, we should have to think a lot of nonsense, and that this compulsion is felt by so many shows that the public-school system is psychologically important and a serious matter of national concern for that reason.

It is still true, though less true than it was a generation ago, that in most departments of English life the leading figures are men who have been educated at a "public school." This is true of politics, literature, the bar, less true of science and industry. And yet not only is it impossible to define a public school with any close accuracy; it is impossible even to list them. The vagueness of the term "public school" becomes evident on reflection, and the difficulty of estimating the importance of the public-school system—or of its products—becomes intimidating.[25]

Most schools which are admitted to be "public schools" are boarding schools, but there are some undoubted public schools which are wholly or mainly day schools. Since so much emphasis is laid on the effects of living in a community, it is notable that some of the effects of a public-school education can be got in a day school *if* the day school is rich and famous enough. More than that, the prestige value of education at such a school is greater than that of education at a marginal public school. The great day public schools do better what they set out to do than the poor boarding schools do, because they get brighter pupils and better masters—and that is largely a matter of money. And so there are students of the English educational system who reduce its proud system of moral and intellectual grading to a coarse monetary standard. "The true category of public schools, it is argued, consists of the 37 schools with fees of over £150 a year together with a few others. In other words, they are all boarding schools and all expensive."[26] This definition, however crude it may be, has at least the merit of bringing to the surface some questions tactfully hidden by the standard definition which makes any school whose headmaster is admitted to the Head Masters' Conference a "public school," and the products of such schools "public-school men." If the wide definition of "public school" is accepted, there are

25 "When we remember the importance attributed to public schools, some being of opinion that they hand on to successive generations all the best traditions of our race, and others viewing them with anything but favour, it is remarkable that we should be wholly ignorant as to the number of pupils who either benefit or suffer from them, as the true state of the case may be."—A. M. Carr-Saunders and D. Caradog Jones: *Social Structure of England and Wales*, second edition, p. 117.

26 F. H. Spencer, op. cit., p. 181.

about 150 of them and their old boys are a fairly representative sample of the upper- and middle-class male. With due allowance made for different national ways of doing things, more than half of Congress comes from much the same social strata as do the families of the boys at the 120 marginal schools. And it is more or less a matter of accident that some schools are not so classified and also a matter of accident that a boy goes to a marginal "public school" or to one just outside the pale.[27]

That the vast majority of the children of the rich should go to these schools is not, in itself, of the first importance. Their economic superiority has many other results than this educational one. More remarkable in England is the degree to which the children of the not very rich go to the same schools as the rich and *never* to those attended, perforce, by the less prosperous section of the middle class. This has helped to unify the government and ruling class. The chief civil servants, managers, lawyers, doctors, journalists, tend, in varying degrees, to share the background of the wealthy. So, on the whole, do the politicians even in the Labour Party, if we omit from consideration the trade-union leaders. It is this domination of English life by "the old school tie" that is the chief complaint against the public-school system.[28] It is still true

[27] A boy who for any reason cannot enter his father's old and quite indubitably "public" school may enter a school which makes no claim to being public at all, but has geographical or financial or intellectual advantages, rather than try his luck at a doubtful public school.

[28] Two able comedians, the Western Brothers, are more responsible than anyone else for making the proud wearers of old school ties self-conscious. Only the most famous school ties, above all Eton's, are still worn with easy pride. A school tie that may be a sign of status in one region may be of no importance or quite unrecognized in another. The number of ties is so great, schools, colleges, and athletic clubs have so glutted the market, that all but the most famous serve merely to identify their wearers to other old Greyfriars boys. And no tie, no matter how impressive, is compensation for doubts about the accent. The gaudy colours of one good and fairly new school which are the same as those of one old, famous, and unpopular Oxford college are more widely worn in America than in England. But that represents fondness for the colour scheme, not a usurpation of title.

that the old boys of the public schools dominate English life, even where that domination is not the result of a simple superiority of economic status. Yet that domination is weakening under the competitive attack of the new schools.

"In 1898, out of the fourteen men who were the permanent Heads of the principal Departments (Treasury, Home Office, Foreign Office, War Office, Colonial Office, India Office, Admiralty, Scottish Office, Board of Trade, Board of Education, Local Government Board, Post Office, Board of Inland Revenue, and Board of Customs) ten had been educated at one or other of the five following schools: Eton, Harrow, Winchester, Rugby, Charterhouse. At the end of 1938, the same five schools provided only four out of the fourteen." [29] Authority in England often speaks with an exotic accent and with a genuine ignorance of the realities of the life of the receivers of orders. And the public schools, as far as they make mutual understanding difficult, are responsible for the cleavage. "This two-class division in English society means that public life is administered by people who, quite literally, know next to nothing at first hand, about the life of the public, are not even conscious of their own ignorance, and tacitly assume that they are typical English men and women." [30]

And because of the great role that intonation plays in English

[29] Dale: *The Higher Civil Service*, p. 193. Statistics showing a predominance of one educational type over another are not in themselves conclusive. This can be illustrated from the United States. Of the six men elected to the presidency in this century, only one was not a college graduate (Harding), and of the other five, four went to "smart" colleges (two to Harvard, one each to Yale, Princeton, and Amherst). In the list of the fifty-five most important men in Washington given by Mr. W. M. Kiplinger (*Washington Is Like That*, pp. 434 ff.), forty-four are college graduates and five more attended college but did not graduate. Of the six who did not go to college at all, two were not born in the United States. Of those who went to college, thirteen went to Harvard—as did the President of the United States, who is treated as *hors concours* and is not one of the fifty-five. It would be easy but rash to make assumptions about American democracy based on these figures.

[30] T. H. Pear: "Psychological Aspects of English Social Stratification," *Bulletin of the John Rylands Library*, Vol. XXVI, No. 2, May-June 1942.

speech, the success with which the schools impose a common speech on their products is the most important non-economic difference in English life. The dropping of the "h" is now quite rare; bad grammar is no more common among the products of a secondary than of a public school, but the fatal Cockney vowels and the corresponding stigmata in other areas of England make many successful men uneasy and unsuccessful men embittered, men who would not have that cause of irritation or resentment in Scotland or the United States. Nor is this all. It is true, though hard to believe, that it is very often possible to tell how an Englishman will speak before he does speak, even though his dress does not mark him off as poor. There is a manner which the public schools give which the average climbing Englishman finds it hard to imitate—which would not matter if he did not wish to imitate it. As more and more public-school boys are forced to compete, often unsuccessfully, with other boys, this difference in manner breeds resentments which may sour a man or keep him a good radical.[31]

The hold of the public-school system on the English mind is revealed in its literary aspect, the school story. This is a purely English phenomenon. All literatures have stories of youth and

[31] "Of speaking, considered as a means of social communication, 'speech-melody' is perhaps the subtlest characteristic. By varying it, emotional relationships are established with others who understand our language. This proviso must be remembered. Mr. Priestley recently broadcast a short play. It contained only meaningless letters of the alphabet; the melody on which they were 'sung' carried their significance. Since intimacy or 'distance,' friendliness or enmity, interest or boredom, command or prayer, deference or disrespect are expressed by speech-melody, it is not surprising that social differences are emphasized by the way in which words go 'up and down.' This is well known to self-constituted judges of good manners, especially those who, on the basis of a brief interview, recommend candidates for posts.

"The auditory 'aspect' of speech is perhaps more important than the visual accompaniments, facial expression, gesture and posture. Possibly the comparative absence of facial expression and gesture from the speech-behaviour of the English 'ruling classes' is a sign of social stratification observed particularly in officers in the fighting services and in some school prefects."—T. H. Pear, op. cit.

adolescence which may include some account of formal education. But they are not like the classical English school stories which are marked by the acceptance of the values of adolescence; the author is not explaining the kind of man he is by telling us the kind of boy he was; he is treating the boy as an end in himself, his own final cause. In this willing return to the standards, the joys, the achievements of adolescence, the author and the reader reveal something charming or irritating about the English mind; its simplicity or sentimentality, according to taste. There are almost as many English school stories as there are English detective stories, and from *Tom Brown* to *Mr. Chips* they are marked by an acceptance of the four or five adolescent years, which in most other countries are remembered with distaste, as the most important years of life. That the public-school system should achieve this for its own sons is miracle enough, but far more astonishing is the success with which this literature is sold to boys and girls who have no first-hand experience of the system at all. Yet the annual crop of public-school stories finds markets far wider than those provided by the old or present or prospective public-school boys.[32] And it is

[32] The most remarkable example of this general interest in the system is provided by the long life and success of *The Magnet*. This was the most successful of a series of weekly boys' papers. Its never ageing heroes were boys at a public school, Greyfriars. Although most English boys, at some time or other, have read of Harry Wharton and Billy Bunter, the main market was in areas and classes where entry to a public school was not even a dream. Without jealousy or rancour tens of thousands of boys destined to be labourers or machine-tenders read of the very different lives led by the boys of Greyfriars school. It is true that school life in the ordinary sense, class-room japes and hard-fought cricket matches, provided only part of the materials for this endless epic. The boys were allowed to leave school and visit Texas and central Africa and spend a good deal of their school-time foiling American gangsters and Italian spies. But it is noteworthy that these standard boys' adventures were somewhat arbitrarily fitted into the framework of a rather out-of-date picture of public-school life. In the years before this war careful observers noted a decline in the popularity of this type of boys' magazine. Its cricketing and football heroes could not compete with young aviators in the affections of a machine-minded generation. Yet *The Magnet* continued to flourish and it was the object of an able attack in *Horizon* by Mr. George Orwell, who naturally regarded this

not this general inexperienced public that buys the fictional attacks on public-school life, the books by old boys that show up their old schools. The increased demand for books or plays of the *Loom of Youth* or *Young Woodley* type is more interesting as illustrating the growth of the critical spirit in the public schools themselves than in the general public. The common reader prefers the romantic world of the *Fifth Form at St. Dominic's* to the latest brilliant revelation of the sordid sex life of St. Benedict's. The problems of the public schools interest a far smaller body than do its more than twice-told tale of victory snatched from defeat on the cricket-field, or villainy unmasked in the headmaster's study. And contemplating this mass vicarious enjoyment of the romance of a system whose prestige is based on the exclusion of the mass of the people from its benefits, the revolutionary, as so often in English history, must be tempted to throw his hand in. But being English himself, romantic, tenacious, stimulated by opposition, and often a public-school product, he continues manfully fitting the English people to his pattern.

Yet what no popular protest has done (perhaps because there has been, in fact, no popular protest) is being done by a falling birth-rate, by rising taxes, by a changing social structure. The public-school system is not really old and its heyday is over. It no longer fits all needs or the most important needs of the ruling class, because that class is now millions strong politically, and if the ruling class economically is very small, that means that most public-school boys do not belong to it. The public schools served their purpose best when the need for a system of assimilating the newly rich and newly powerful to the older national tradition was greatest, when it was in danger of being swamped by the mere numbers who sud-

---

sexless, classless, uncritically patriotic narrative as clouding the social consciences of the proletarian boy. The author of the thirty-year-old cycle, Mr. Frank Richards, answered Mr. Orwell with great ability. Immediately after it made the pages of *Horizon*, *The Magnet* (and its companion papers) died. That its owners should have chosen to sacrifice this type out of their numerous boys' papers to the paper shortage is possibly significant.

denly emerged into the upper classes. But not only the need but the means were then most abundant. There was an increasingly numerous class of prosperous parents whose existence made it safe to found new schools, as well as expand old ones. (Some of the most successful public schools are younger than most American state universities.) There was in an expanding Empire, in an expanding commercial system, in an optimistic nation and world, room for the boys trained in the public schools to fit that world. Nor was this all. There was faith in abundance, in the rightness of the world, in its progress in a definable direction. The standard schoolmaster and the standard parent knew what they wanted; the father paid the school to make his son a member of a fairly defined class, with suitable ideas inside a wide but not unlimited range of tolerable variations on a basic theme. In that age Clifton and Rugby could afford to have an obstreperous radical as headmaster because Percival's ideas were merely extravagant; they were not "un-English." Cormell Price, Kipling's headmaster, had friends who were far from sharing the Imperial orthodoxy of the boy or the man. But the school system partook of and contributed to the stability and confidence of the golden last years of Victoria's reign.

Today the case is altered. There are fewer newcomers to be assimilated.[33] The free incomes to be spent on the education of a family is badly eaten into by income tax. To belong to a class which "can't" send its children to a secondary school means in many cases to belong to a class that cannot afford to have a child, or more than one. The old quasi-monopoly of the civil service, the professions, the press, is gone. The products of the secondary schools are effective competitors, as were the Scots a generation ago.

The results are already visible. After the last war came the last spurt of the old system. Old schools expanded; new schools were founded. The men who had done well out of the war wanted to make gentlemen of their sons. But the cotton profiteers of Lancashire, the shipping profiteers of Cardiff, have been thinned out.

[33] Eton this year has accepted the sons of two new peers, one Scottish, one Canadian, both prominent "new men." But Eton is a special case.

More important, they have not reproduced in numbers adequate to justify the optimists who built new schools, new boarding houses, new swimming baths, or new science laboratories twenty years ago. There is a shortage of boys and so of fees.[34] The schools that have shown the first signs of collapse have not been the most expensive, but the marginal schools. As a rule they have no endowment or a small one. As a rule they draw their boys from families with fewer financial reserves than the families that send their sons to Eton or Charterhouse. They are the schools for whose survival the richer classes have least motive to make sacrifices. It is these schools that have begun to disappear or to amalgamate with other schools, usually on terms that show that the poorer school has had to accept the terms of the richer. Thus when Kipling's old school, the United Services College, amalgamated with Haileybury, the new scale of fees was that of Haileybury, probably a good deal more than many of the parents whose boys went to the smaller school will be able to pay. As long as this economic pressure continues, the public-school system will contract, losing units whose main fault is lack of endowments and the comparative poverty of the families they serve. Competition for survival is competition for boys and competition for boys with fully solvent parents. The church, the army, the professions, the traditional providers of public-school boys of ability and character, will be less and less able to afford to send their boys to such schools—or to have the boys to send. Two changes in the apparent trend of English society can reverse this process. One is a rapid increase in the number of free family incomes of £1,000 a year and upwards; and the tax system makes this change very unlikely. And no more likely is a change in the social habit that limits the size of families, since one motive for that limitation is the competitive standard of living, of which English education is one aspect. Only by a change in social values

[34] One marginal school raised quite a large sum of money after the last war to build a memorial chapel. The whole school plant, including the chapel, was recently offered to the highest bidder. The money spent on the chapel might, as endowment, have kept the school going.

which, incidentally, would destroy much of the prestige of the public schools can those schools escape the contraction that has already set in.

One alternative solution is no real solution. It is argued by many conservatives as well as by public-school masters that the true remedy is to make public-school education available to all talented boys. But if this prescription were applied literally, the public schools would be flooded by boys from poor homes. And the main service of the schools in the past has been the social assimilation of the sons of the new rich, not of the old poor. That the ablest boys of the country should be educated together in boarding schools, that this privilege should be granted to all boys who meet the tests regardless of their parents' income and be denied to all who do not meet the tests regardless of their parents' income—this is a scheme that, on paper, is practicable. But it is not a scheme for saving or reforming the public schools. It is a scheme for creating a new type of school: a boarding school that does not reflect the profoundly inegalitarian character of English social habits. Such a school system would be revolutionary indeed. I shall believe in its practicability when I see one of its old Etonian sponsors sending his son to a good but obscure public school, just on the edge of the system, out of admiration for the character of its headmaster and the sterling qualities of the boys it produces.

Yet among many more or less conscious defenders of the *status quo* who wish to make the English social system safe for the public schools by admitting a few poor boys at state expense, there are genuine reformers who think that the public schools have something, for all their faults. It is not the art of leadership; that art requires more rigorous and selective training than the public schools give, and a great many defenders of the public schools are really defending not the claim of those schools to produce leaders, but the claim of the total educational system to produce people willing to be led. The number of natural followers, though large, is not now identical with the poor. And nothing is more disconcerting to a boy accustomed to think himself a leader than to find himself face to face with a lot of people who have not been accustomed to regard him as a leader. Some of the undoubted physical superiority of the public-school boy is due simply to better food, better doctoring, better housing, all consequences of the economic superiority of his parents, of which his public-school education was another consequence. But in their emphasis on health and physical energy the public schools did a public service. And as Dr. A. D. Lindsay has pointed out, even a month of good food, regular hours, and well-designed exercises does more for a poor boy than years of "leadership" training in clubs and other institutions that do not give him the physical stamina that the public school gets. More free, healthful holidays for all poor boys is probably of more national value than the admission of a handful of the cleverest of them to the public schools.

But the merits of the public school are not supposed to be physical. They are supposed to be more; they are supposed to reside in something called character. And there is something in this claim. In such a case subjective prejudices are the only evidence and there is something in the alleged character-training of the public schools. (There is not so much as its devotees believe; otherwise the vast non-English world that hasn't got public schools would be in even a worse mess than it is.) First of all, there is the internal solidarity of the system, which, like the clannishness of the Scot, is not altogether a bad thing.

Captain Grimes of *Decline and Fall* has testified to the permanent value of a public-school education; those who have passed through the same ordeal never let one another down. But there is another and more dignified sense in which public-school products stick together. They expect and are usually right in expecting that the full rigour of the game will be tempered by habits of consideration and moderation, habits learned in a society in which life could be made difficult for the majority if the free activity of the natural individualist were given free play. So, instead, life is made intolerable for the totally uncooperative individualist. This habit of restraint, of abating the full rigour of the game, makes life more agreeable. College teachers sometimes find that boys who have not been disciplined by the community life of a boarding school are very hard to handle in the first year or so at Oxford or Cambridge— unless, indeed, they display an unnatural docility, which is equally distressing. In a society in which these co-operative habits are expected, so individualistic a public-school product as Mr. Churchill has noted the degree to which the internal harmony of the Royal Navy was upset by the unscrupulous vigour of Lord Fisher, who neither practised nor admired the public-school virtues. The Royal Navy needed one Lord Fisher, but not more. And it is to be noted that his indifference to the code did not keep Fisher from the highest rank nor prevent his having his own way.

It is probably true, too, that the public-school product is more careful of financial probity than some types of climbing middle-class boy. His friends and rivals and enemies have made him less ready to try to be too smart, to sail too close to the wind in business or private life. And it is true, I think, that a good many Englishmen take to government service because of the unsporting atmosphere of business. But more take to it for another good reason. The public-school boy is a bad salesman of himself or of anything else. He expects, foolishly, that his merits (many of which the great world sees as defects) will be appreciated, as they were by his fellows and even by his masters. This is a weakness; the world is the salesman's oyster. But there are enough salesmen in the world—at least enough—and the shyness, pride, or diffidence of the public-school type is attractive, even if it is a national luxury.[35]

And before coming to any final decision on the merits of the

[35] Where the worst side of this refusal to try to make a good impression is seen (apart from its dangers in dealing with foreigners of all kinds) is in the manners of young women who have been sent to the English girls' schools which imitate the great boys' schools or to smart finishing schools. A girl who doesn't mind appearing sulky or indifferent is no asset to the world, and the shopping voice of many products of Roedean or Wycombe Abbey is one of the most distressing sounds on earth. Fortunately, most English girls get over this stage, but those who don't recruit that large class of formidable middle-aged women with whom England is too well supplied. There ought to be a law about it.

public-school type we ought to be sure that there is a type. Who is the typical Harrovian, Lord Baldwin, Mr. Churchill, or Pandit Nehru? Who is the typical product of Winchester, Sir Oswald Mosley or Sir Stafford Cripps? Who is the typical Rugbeian, the late Neville Chamberlain, the Archbishop of Canterbury, or Professor R. H. Tawney? Who is the representative old Etonian in public life, Professor J. B. S. Haldane, the leading intellectual of the Communist Party, or Captain Ramsay, who is now entering his third year of captivity as a suspected Fascist? It is the smaller, poorer schools that produce the types whose only support to wavering self-esteem is the memory of the few years in which they were shut off from a world which does not appreciate their merits.

The sad fact is that no modern system of society has yet provided opportunities for the development of the talented on absolutely equal terms. In Nazi Germany and Soviet Russia there are obstacles that do not exist in America and Britain. In America and Britain there are obstacles that do not exist in totalitarian societies. Above all, in Western democratic societies there is the great obstacle of poverty, the great asset of wealth. Poor boys get less good chances of formal education than do rich boys. This is true in America as it is in England. "What are the requirements for getting into, staying in, and graduating from some kind of college in the United States? . . . The factor chiefly determining the length of education is the income of the student's father. . . . A study in Kansas revealed that a majority of superior high-school graduates were not in college. . . . In general, collegiate status means economic status." [36] What is true of Kansas is true of Kent. What is different is that probably the average boy has a better chance in Kansas of getting a good college education, whatever the economic status of his parents, than has the average boy in Kent. What is almost certainly true is that the very brilliant boy has a better chance of getting a first-class college education in Kent than in Kansas, if by first-class we mean Oxford and Cambridge and take

[36] Robert M. Hutchins, in the *Saturday Evening Post*, August 15, 1942.

them as the equivalent of Harvard or Chicago or Columbia.

The English educational system reflects and reinforces the inequalities of the economic system. But it also runs counter to them. It weakens the hold of mere wealth, which is a good thing. It fosters native snobbery, which is a bad thing. And it reflects the unsystematic and highly individualistic character of English life. Indeed, there is no system. There are at least two. One, the newer, may swallow the older. But it may not. A curious symbiosis may result in a country where even more than in Ireland the inevitable never happens. If for once the inevitable is going to happen, the public schools are doomed.

English Religion

OF ALL ENGLISH INSTITUTIONS, none is more English, less to be interpreted in general terms or judged by general standards than the Church of England. Its very status as "by law established" is almost impossible to describe or to justify. Modern liberals, brought up, for the most part, to regard church establishment as an anachronism or an outrage, may well wonder at the continued existence of the Establishment. They may plan to disestablish and disendow and, while planning this great revolution, will find that their object is also the cherished dream of eminent Anglican divines who, far from thinking that the Establishment is the strength of the Church of England, think it a fundamental weakness.

"The Church of England as by law established" is a fine and apparently clear statement, but what does it mean? Or, rather, what does "establishment" mean and what is establishment? The Establishment and the Church of England thus linked by law are neither of them easily described. To begin with the Establishment. What does the state do for the church? It does not, as is widely thought, pay the church money. There has never been a concordat between church and state such as those made between the Pope and Napoleon, the Pope and Hitler. In such bargains the secular power, in return for some degree of control of the church, pays out of the national revenue some or most of the expenses of the church, and the clergy are a special type of civil servant. The English state does not pay anything to the English church nor are the clergy state servants. The income of the church is a corporate income which the state helps the church to collect as it helps other corporate institutions—hospitals, colleges, and the like—to collect theirs. But the state does more; it collects some of the income itself, turning over the net proceeds to the church, but this is a limitation of church power, not a privilege.

The erroneous view that the Church of England is directly a beneficiary of the state, is fostered by the existence of the Ecclesiastical Commission. The Commissioners are appointed by the "Crown"—that is, by the Prime Minister—and they control most of the real estate owned by the Church of England. But that real estate is the "private property" of the church, and were that property sold and the proceeds invested in securities, the Church of England would be no better or worse off, morally at any rate. Nevertheless, it is probably true that by being a great landowner the church finds itself in positions that weaken its spiritual authority. Thus if it leases property in London for ninety-nine years, it has no means of preventing the temporary owners of that property from turning some houses into brothels or slums.[1]

And, as a great landowner, the church, through the Ecclesiastical Commission, is in the position of having to drive hard bargains. A great corporation cannot make special concessions and many a pious Anglican has been on the edge of unkind thoughts after argument with the Ecclesiastical Commissioners on questions of repairs and the duties of lease-holders. But, all the same, the Estab-

[1] It is true that a century ago the church, like other property-owners, was not very tender-minded about slums. But the church was no worse a landlord than were great noblemen or Oxford colleges. Under the shadow of the Christ Church of Pusey and Lewis Carroll lay some of the worst slums of Oxford, and New College at a not very remote date spent on not very successful ornament funds that might have been used to rebuild local slums. Such conduct today would seem unsocial even in the case of a college dedicated to St. Mary Magdalen. "We are all Marthas now," as Sir William Harcourt might have said.

lishment of the present Church of England is not financial; it is moral.[2]

The Church of England is still for most Englishmen the national and proper way of rendering to God the things that are God's even if that belief involves another: that Cæsar is to determine what things are God's and what his. The state, in theory, does lay down what the Church of England believes and how it shall conduct its public services and administer the sacraments. The church, on this theory, is a branch of the civil service; its articles of faith and its modes of public worship are set out as schedules to Acts of Parliament. Only the most old-fashioned and unrealistic lawyer

[2] These truths are obscured in the public mind by the question of tithes. These are charges on land. They represent the mediæval view that a tenth of the fruits of the earth was payable, in kind, to the church. At various times in the past and present century they have been reduced in severity and commuted to money. Some owners of land, at various times, redeemed the tithe—that is, made a capital payment. Other owners did not. The difference in status, in pure economic theory, ought to be represented by a difference in the price of the land. To some extent it is. Like all other burdens on land, tithe is bitterly resented when prices fall as they have been doing in recent years; the English farmer feels like the Iowa farmer in such matters, and the grievance of the English farmer against the church is even more lively than that of the Iowa farmer against the Vermont banker. For the banker, in fairly recent times, did lend money, while it is a long time since the church's services were as valuable to the average farmer as tithe would suggest. The landowner, naturally, would in most cases like to see tithe abolished. In most cases, but not all. For tithe is not specifically payable to the church at all. A great deal of it is payable to laymen or to corporations like Oxford and Cambridge colleges. Thus the Russell family, when they got Woburn Abbey as their share of the loot of the monasteries, also got the great tithes which had been payable to the abbot. This share of church plunder is payable to the present Duke of Bedford, not to any parson. A great landowner or an Oxford college may receive more as tithe on land they do not own than they pay as tithe on land they do own, and some of the tithe they pay in one capacity, they pay to themselves in another. To abolish tithe may be an excellent thing, but if the abolition does not take the form of confiscating the tithe revenue for the state, it will be simply a way of making a large present to landowners who have been lucky enough not to have redeemed their tithe. The Church of England might be less unpopular with farmers if this were done, but the community at large has rights as well as farmers and parsons.

now believes that this picture has any real relation to the facts. The relation between God and Cæsar is more complicated than that. For if there was ever a time when the Church of England was willing to allow the state to determine its belief and practice, that time is long past. As a not totally unkind critic said, the troubles of the Church of England in modern times are due to the fact that in its old age it has got religion.[3] A series of revivals of old and preachings of new doctrines have made it impossible to say what is the central doctrine of the church or what is its practice in public worship. Theological positions hard to distinguish from those of Rome, Constantinople, Geneva, are all held with impunity. The barest minimum of ritual is soundly Anglican as is a profusion of ornament that drove, so the famous story runs, one lady to regret the simple worship of the Church of Rome.

The official thirty-nine Articles of Religion of the Anglican Church were designed, or have been found, to be patient of explanations. They can be affirmed (in some sense) by almost every type of Christian. To the Anglo-Catholic, they may be the "forty stripes save one"; to the modernist, something to be swallowed rather than accepted. But we have moved a long way from Tract XC, and the grievance of acceptance of the Articles is purely a clerical grievance and not, it seems, a very lively grievance even for the clergy.

The case of the Prayer Book is very different. The Prayer Book is far more a mark of Anglicanism than are the Articles. By insisting on the formal ritual of Archbishop Cranmer, the Anglican Church insisted not only on a mode of worship that was abandoned by the other Reformed Churches [4] but, in practice, on a mode of public worship by the laity that is far more ritualistic than that commonly practised in the modern Catholic Church. A prayer

[3] I am, of course, aware that it has always had religion and that, as Professor Sikes and Canon Smyth have shown, even in the dullest days of eighteenth-century torpidity there was more evangelical zeal and work than used to be thought.

[4] I am aware that the Wesleyans and other reformed churches have service books, but they do not play anything like the pre-eminent part assigned by Anglican theory to the Book of Common Prayer.

book is not the same as *the* Prayer Book. Had the whole Anglican communion effectively insisted on the uniform use of the Prayer Book, it could have been claimed, with some justice, that Canterbury rather than Rome had effectively secured uniformity, reverence, and continuity in the public prayers of the laity. And it could also be claimed that the admirable English of the Prayer Book had quietly influenced the minds of all sorts and conditions of men who were hardly conscious of what it was that had coloured their views of how God should be worshipped. The old Anglican was not perplexed by temporary innovations and the fancies of parsons or the fashions of the time. The *Pilgrim's Progress* was not Holy Writ nor the eloquence of any modern century a substitute for the traditional prayers of the church. And the idiosyncratic and self-willed English mind needed such a discipline. As long as uniformity was fairly generally observed, it received it. But with modern times, with the revival of factions within the Church of England, the old, dull, disciplined days were over. Sung Mattins (some hold) concealed the beauties of the Prayer Book from the congregation and the obvious obsolescence of some parts of the Prayer Book became apparent to the critical, a powerful if not a large body.[5]

[5] "Yet I do not think that a boy, especially if his education is directed towards the study of words, can hear every morning, from his tenth to his eighteenth year, the measured and formal English of the Prayer Book without submitting his mind in some degree to the discipline which this Prayer Book enjoins. The collect for the week; the prayer for all sorts and conditions of men; the State prayers; the general thanksgiving. I took these things for granted, and never thought that they might be moulding my mind. Yet, even then, I assumed that the purpose of 'this ancient school' was 'that there may never be wanting' persons qualified for 'the service of the Church and State.' Not a word about 'business'; not a word about the life-jobs of those figures, who, term after term, faded out of the lower and middle reaches of the school to serve neither church nor state, but someone's bank or someone else's warehouse. Here we were, in the centre of London, at the ganglion point of high capitalism, the tallest pyramid in the modern competitive system; we continued, calmly and without self-consciousness, to use the terms describing an English society which was beginning to disappear even before a sixteenth-century merchant

More serious was the adoption of a kind of congregationalism by the clergy. Evangelicals had long neglected some parts of the Prayer Book. And their subtractions were held to justify additions by others. Short of the use of the Ordinary of the Mass in Latin, there were hardly any extremes in alteration which the very "High" clergy did not permit themselves. Anglo-Catholic divines, like Bishop Gore, might insist on the Prayer Book, and the Prayer Book only, as the worship of Anglicans, but this Chillingworthian doctrine was defied by many of the most zealous clergy.

The laity, too, were less attracted or repelled by the variations in the Prayer Book than by the splendour or poverty of ritual. Any visitor could see that there were great differences in the conduct of public worship at Holy Trinity, Brompton, and All Saints, Margaret Street. Not so many noticed whether All Saints or St. Albans or, for that matter, Holy Trinity rigidly followed all the prescriptions of the Book of Common Prayer, week-day and Sunday alike. The educational effect of a common liturgy was lost. The Book of Common Prayer ceased to be a norm, and, in ritual as well as in doctrine, the Established Church ceased to stand for anything defined.[6]

The difficulty—indeed, the impossibility—of defining the doctrine or practice of the Church of England irritates the Erastian lawyer like Sir William Harcourt and the exact theologian whether he be Anglican or non-Anglican. All are appalled by the toleration for incompatibles that is the genius of Anglicanism. To treat Christianity thus is very English; to treat Marxism thus, as Mr. Bertrand Russell has pointed out, is also very English. The legal establishment of the Church of England is a public recognition by the English state of a vague historical respect for Christianity and, still

had founded our school. I do not think that this point ever occurred to the Merchant Taylors' Company."—E. L. Woodward: *Short Journey*, pp. 19–20.

[6] The Episcopal Cathedral in Glasgow bears (1942) a notice affirming that "prayer-book services" are held within. It is no longer a guarantee of anything that a church is in communion with Canterbury.

more, for a very old, traditional English institution called "the Church." Before the Reformation the central Roman authority might impose order and doctrinal coherence. But once that control was removed, the absence of any English appreciation of the attractions of consistency, of the repellent character of anomalies, made it certain that, whatever form organized religious life took in England, it would not be coherent and consistent as it was in the Europe of Geneva or the Council of Trent. The establishment of a church which offers not the doctrinal and ceremonial *table d'hôte* of the other communions, but a varied *à la carte* service in both respects, is hard to justify. But only too intelligent Englishmen, seeing the Church of England from too close at hand, can think that its representative role is over or that it can be either disregarded or swept to one side. "C. of E." may be a very meaningless term. The Church of England may only be the church that the majority of English people stay away from. But they want it to be there to stay away from; it is their spiritual home whenever (which is not very often) they feel they want one. They would not be at home in a more functional institution, in a church which knew its own mind and followed out to their logical conclusions the generally accepted premises of its doctrines. Such a church would be, in one sense, a more respectable institution, but it would be very much less an English institution. No doubt the vagueness of Anglicanism has contributed to the evasiveness of English thought in more than theological matters. No doubt the vagueness of the national mind has affected the church. But whether the Church of England bred the English mind or vice versa does not matter.

Before the Roman came to Rye or out to Severn strode,
The rolling English drunkard made the rolling English road.

Some time later in English history the same defiance of Euclidean geometry produced the Church of England.

It is possible to hold that all that keeps the Church of England together is the fact of establishment, which gives what little coherence there is and which gives, in addition, a prestige that the church, as a church, would not otherwise command. While the Anglican Church had a legal monopoly of higher education, of political position, when its privileges were enforced by laws which kept Dissenters and Catholics and Jews in their place, this view had some plausibility. But the church today neither has nor wants such privileges.[7] During the past century, the legal privileges of the Anglican Church have been reduced to very little, until today a large body of its active members and leaders see establishment not as an advantage but as a disadvantage. The Church of England has some rights in the school system. And the King is by custom a member of the Church of England in England and of the quite different Church of Scotland in Scotland and, by law, a "Protestant" everywhere. The old legal pre-eminence of "the Church" is reflected in other ways. For example, the college chaplains of Oxford and Cambridge colleges are Anglicans, as are the college chapels.[8] The aristocracy in England are almost entirely Anglican or Catholic.[9] This social pre-eminence of the Anglican Church has extended from its aristocratic laity to the clergy themselves. Their social rank rose all through the nineteenth century and is only now falling again as the clergy become recruited, more and more, from the lower middle and upper working classes.

That the English parson in the age of Swift or Fielding was a kind of superior domestic is true; that Mr. Collins was probably

[7] What bishop today would waste his time, as did the learned and saintly Christopher Wordsworth, fighting to keep the title "Reverend" off the tombstone of a Methodist minister in a churchyard?

[8] This need not mean much; least of all uniformity. See Brittain and Manning: *Babylon Bruis'd and Mount Moriah Mended.*

[9] There are, of course, great Presbyterian houses in Scotland and a number of Nonconformist peers of recent creation in England. But although there was at least one peer of reasonably ancient creation who was a Moslem, and all other religions may well be represented in the peerage, for all I know, the national passion for religious eccentricity in the aristocracy fights a losing battle with the national passion for snobbery when it is a question of belonging to an unfashionable form of Christianity. According to Mr. G. M. Young, the return of the Willoughby of Parham family to the Anglican fold in the eighteenth century ended the last of the great Puritan nonconforming houses.

representative of a good many parsons of the age of Jane Austen is also true. But the English parson in modern times became a kind of equal of the squire, ranking above the doctor and the attorney. He had, in many cases, been to the same kind of school. He might, especially if the living he held were a good one, be a member of a great family. A friend of Newman's, the Reverend Samuel Wood, was a great-uncle of the present Lord Halifax. He might also be a sporting parson, orthodox, popular, but profoundly unprofessional by the standards of Rome or Edinburgh, as was another clerical member of the same family.

It was roughly true that the policy of the Church of England in that happy nineteenth century heyday was to put a "gentleman in every parish." This ideal, though more practicable than that of putting a saint in every parish, was beyond the resources of the church. A poor gentleman can exist, but he cannot remain a gentleman in a representative capacity if his income definitely declasses him. And the resources of the church were not adequate to giving to all the incumbents of parishes a gentleman's income. Nevertheless, the gentility, real or presumed, of the parson had some social advantages. In an inequalitarian society like that of England the levelling tendencies of the Christian faith must always cause difficulties. Where the clergy are the uncontested dispensers of means of grace and cannot be replaced, their spiritual authority may cover their social inferiority although, as Innocent III found out, the untamed feudal noble could square a good deal of anti-clericalism with a conscience that had a genuine horror of unprofitable heresy. So a priest in a Catholic country need not be a gentleman in any sense of the word so long as his priestly prerogatives are unquestioned. And in a rigidly organized Presbyterian society the authority of the church may cover the weak social or economic position of the clergy.[10] But England was not Scotland or Prussia and the

[10] It should be noted that in Scotland most though by no means all of the "good" families have drifted in the last two centuries away from Presbyterianism to Episcopalianism. (This has had good results as well as bad for Scottish Presbyterianism.) Without agreeing with Charles II that

choice was not between some form of clerical independence (or, if you like, tyranny) and a tamed Erastian church, but between one form of Christianity adapted to a society highly conscious of social distinction and another. Between German Lutheranism and Anglicanism it is not hard to make a choice. The parson was given a more independent position by the abuse of his "freehold"; by the lack of system in church organization; by the great social position of the bishops, which resulted from their large incomes and great houses.[11]

Quite apart from any general levelling tendency (and such exists in England) the special social prestige of the Church of England is not what it was. But for the officially-minded who like to know where they are, "Church" is nice and "Chapel" doubtful and this social ranking extends to all aspects of English religious life. More people than would admit it or are conscious of it are of the mind of the sergeant major,[12] who classified his recruits into "C. of E.," "R. C.," and "fancy religions." The only change they would make would be in putting "R.C." definitely under "fancy religions." But this customary precedence is very little based on law; it is based on the normal English attitude to organized religion in his own country. The Church of England is the *normal* form of religion; even the Dissenter who dissents from its claims, like the earlier Nonconformist who refused to conform to its practices, admits, by his protest, its predominant place. An Anglican bishop, even in a city like Liverpool, where his Roman rival has more adherents, is by national custom the chief representative spokesman

Presbytery is no religion for a gentleman, there is a sense in which a kind of Anglicanism may seem to be pre-eminently the religion for a gentleman to whom gentility is of fundamental importance. On the other hand, Christianity in any fundamental form can hardly seem to be a religion for a gentleman in the usual sense of the term.

[11] When the first Archbishop Temple sold the country estate of the Archbishops of Canterbury because he did not think that, in modern times, an Archbishop of Canterbury had any business parading as a great landed magnate, he was anticipating as great a change in the role of the Archbishopric as the marriage of Cranmer and Parker portended.

[12] i.e., Top sergeant.

of the Christian viewpoint.[13] And without any legal sanction in modern times, the Church of England is thought of as being the Church of the Empire, a cause of disillusionment to pious Anglicans when they go to Canada or Australia and discover the strength of their Roman and "Dissenting" rivals.

This prestige of the Church of England may be a result of past legal privilege and may owe something to the present connection with the state, but it is possible that a disestablished Church of England, provided it stayed united, would keep this kind of hold on the English people as the Church of France did when it was disestablished in 1905. For it should be remembered that in organization, if not in doctrine, the Church of England has been far more changed in the last century than it was at the Reformation. Its finances have been reformed; not enough, perhaps, but reformed all the same. Its bishops are no longer opulent feudal magnates, representing the distribution of wealth and power that suited the England of Henry VIII.[14] The creation of new sees in the nineteenth century, the increase in income tax, the rise in the standard of episcopal duty that has been accepted since Samuel Wilberforce set the example in the diocese of Oxford, these have all made bishops very different men and officials from what they were in the days of Dr. Proudie of Barchester. A century ago a bishop appointed to a really good see could leave a quite impressive fortune

[13] *Who's Who* carries this principle to an extreme. Although Catholic bishops in Ireland are certainly far more important than bishops of the Church of Ireland, and are legally in exactly the same position, they are entered in *Who's Who* under their proper names, not under the names of their sees. That honour is reserved for the bishops of the disestablished Church of Ireland.

[14] "Few changes in our modern England have been more remarkable than that in the character of the Bishops of the Anglican Church and the way they are regarded. Forty or fifty years ago they were usually rich, dignified, and rather indolent magnates, aristocratic in their tastes and habits, moderate in their theology, sometimes to the point of indifferentism, quite as much men of the world as pastors of souls. . . . The revival within the Church of England began from below, and reached the bishops last." —James Bryce to Thomas Hughes, *Life of Bishop Fraser*, pp. 357–8.

to his children. Today he less often has children, and certainly cannot leave them a fortune out of savings from his salary. Among the qualifications that make a man episcopal timber today is a private income that will enable him to bear the burden of such white elephants as Farnham Castle, or other "assets" of the old order that have now become liabilities.

Despite his archaic costume, his official precedence, and, in the case of the old sees, the tenancy of a "palace" that recalls the golden days of golden stalls and the state of great landed magnates, the modern bishop is not a rich or an idle functionary. Promotion to a bishopric is often, in fact, what it has always been in theory, a call to greater labour, reluctantly accepted. Probably at few periods in church history have the words *"Nolo episcopari"* been uttered so often so sincerely as in modern England.[15]

Yet it is in the method of nomination to bishoprics that the connection between church and state survives in its most important aspect. Since the time of Henry VIII the nomination to this great spiritual office has been in the hands of whoever effectively disposed of the state patronage—in the hands of Charles II, in the hands of Lord Palmerston. The King or the politicians who chose the shepherds of the Anglican flock could be of any religion or none. A Lutheran background, in the case of Prince Albert, a fondness for Presbyterian ways and men in the case of Queen Victoria, submission to the Evangelical views of Lord Shaftesbury in the case of Palmerston, a very outside point of view in the case of Disraeli, High Anglican principles in the cases of Gladstone and Salisbury, all affected the character of the episcopate in the second half of the last century. Of the nine persons appointed to the office of Prime Minister in this century, three were Presbyterians, one a Baptist, one a Unitarian; and the Anglican orthodoxy of the re-

15 I was once present when the future of an eminent divine was being debated. His learning, his good looks, his admirable manners, his good business habits, the reasonable orthodoxy of his religious views, all were discussed and admitted. But, it was added, he could not be made a bishop. He had "no pastoral zeal," and that, it was somewhat reluctantly admitted, was now necessary in a bishop.

maining four was not, in every case, above reasonable suspicion. Yet there is abundant evidence that, in making these appointments, modern Prime Ministers, whatever their origin, have shown a strong sense of responsibility. None has behaved as Disraeli did in candidly making appointments to help his party at an election.[16]

Yet there is, at first sight, something distasteful in the thought of spiritual office so bestowed. For although Prime Ministers do not make scandalous appointments, they do make appointments that it is unlikely would be made by any "free" church. Chosen by an indirect democratic plebiscite, for reasons that have nothing to do with church questions,[17] with no certainty that they will have either knowledge or interest in this field, Prime Ministers may impose chief pastors on very reluctant flocks. The see of Hereford, for instance, has more than once been used by Prime Ministers to show their indifference to mere local clerical and lay opinion. Where appointments have involved apparent approval of certain types of religious views, a Prime Minister has seemed to some to be, in effect, extending the limits of tolerable variation in doctrine. And when some appointment has annoyed an important section of church opinion, the resentment of lay nomination has found expression in threats to exercise the rights of the church, rights preserved by the "election" of a new bishop by the cathedral chapter. In form the Prime Minister merely nominates a candidate to the chapter, but in effect the so-called *congé d'élire* is only permission to elect one person who is named.[18]

[16] It should be remembered that patronage, the modified English version of the spoils system, was just being abolished in Disraeli's times. His attitude, though a little scandalous when looked at from the side of the angels, was not particularly novel or scandalous from the side of the practising politician.

[17] This was one of the flaws in the argument whereby John Richard Green tried to justify the system by a parallel with the popular election of St. Ambrose as Archbishop of Milan. Mr. Gladstone might be the people's choice as much as St. Ambrose was, but he was not chosen to find a modern Ambrose for the see of Winchester.

[18] I have simplified the procedure, but I have not, I think, distorted its meaning. The *congé d'élire* is, in effect, like an American primary. The

No effective resistance has ever been made to this system, although the possibility of a clerical revolt had, no doubt, had a limiting effect on the choices made by Prime Ministers, who in modern times always consult the Archbishop of Canterbury and are thus in a position to know how much the Church of England will stand.

Yet, seen from the outside, the nomination of bishops by a lay authority has its advantages. It does, in fact, result in making bishops of men who would be very unlikely to reach that high office were bishops elected by the laity, or the clergy, or by any combination of the two or any method practised by other branches of the Anglican communion.

It can be argued that the representative character of an Anglican bishop is, in part, derived from his secular origin. Because he has been chosen by the lay power, he is more likely to think in a non-clerical fashion of the problems where the lay and clerical points of view are in conflict.[19] The qualities that appeal to a lay Prime Minister may be very valuable qualities that do not appeal to the minority of zealous laity. A bishop so appointed may be able to defy the sectarian opinion of the faithful.[20]

---

electors of Texas will by the time this book has appeared have elected Mr. O'Daniel to the United States Senate. But they will have had no real option. By winning the Democratic primary, Mr. O'Daniel has been given the equivalent of a *congé d'élire*. For the electors of Texas to vote for the Republican candidate (presumably there is one) would be as revolutionary an act as for a cathedral chapter not to vote for the candidate named in the letters missive of the Prime Minister. They would not, of course, be subject to the penalties of præmunire. It might be pointed out to uncritical admirers of Magna Carta, that one of the chief grievances against King John, and one the charter was intended to put an end to, was royal nominations to bishoprics. "Back to Magna Carta" is a possible battle-cry for the enemies of this system today.

[19] It is, I hope, unnecessary to say that by "clerical" I do not mean "religious."

[20] Another form of patronage which might be but is not now used in a simple political fashion is that of nominations to regius professorships. In Oxford and Cambridge and in the Scottish universities a number of the most important chairs are "regius"; that is, the professors are appointed by "the Crown," which in England means the Prime Minister, in Scotland the Secretary of State for Scotland. In the past, politics of a kind played

An Anglican dignitary, in such cases, is far more free than leaders of the "free churches" who cannot go too far ahead of their flocks. An American Methodist bishop who had expressed doubts about the wisdom of the "experiment noble in purpose" would have been a hero, and yet if no American Methodist bishop has ever had doubts on the wisdom of constitutional prohibition, the political wisdom of that bench of bishops must be very low. A Catholic bishop in a region like Brooklyn really "cracking down" on Coughlinism would be a parallel to Charles Gore criticizing the Boer War in Joseph Chamberlain's good city of Birmingham, or Dr. Hensley Henson, not yet a bishop, denouncing the profiteers of the Putumayo atrocities by name in Westminster Abbey. More instances could be given to support the view that if we are to give any meaning to "fearless," other than noisy statements of views already known to be popular (the meaning the word has acquired in the cheap press), the high Anglican clergy are today at least as fearless as the ecclesiastical leaders of any part of the English-speaking world. And some of these Anglican leaders would not have been chosen by any "democratic" methods of election.

---

some part. Thus it is believed that had the Liberal government been defeated a little sooner than it was, Lord Acton would not have been made Regius Professor of Modern History at Cambridge by its Conservative successor. But direct political rewards are rare in this field. I know of only one case and that not very recent. It was widely believed that a very active politician was given a regius chair in a Scottish university in recompense for his effective services as an election agent for a cabinet minister. Whether this be so or not, the professor of whom the story was told became, in the not very long run, world-famous in his own field of medicine. And, as in the case of bishoprics, the outsider's view is sometimes more objective than the domestic view. But there are, of course, drawbacks to the system. In 1870, when Glasgow University had some of the greatest names in the British academic world on its roll of professors, the official academic chief of the future Lords Kelvin and Lister and the two Cairds was Principal Barclay. "He was without any particular literary or scientific distinction and was commonly reported to have received his appointment from the Crown because of the presence of mind he had shown in the management of a boat by which he had saved the precious life of one of its ministers" (John Henry Muirhead: *Reflections*, p. 27).

[7 1]

There is another advantage in the nomination of bishops by politicians. The Church of England is rent by internal ecclesiastical politics. The appointment of bishops from the outside can be used by a prudent lay politician not only to keep the balance true within the church, but to remind the clerical combatants that they are members of a technically united body. Thus the variations in doctrine and ritual that might well be associated with the changing party positions of successive Bishops of Truro are not without their educational value. A nomination of a well-known party leader (in the church sense of "party") is not necessarily a triumph for the local section of his party in his new diocese; that party has not just carried an election and is not necessarily much benefited by the arrival of a bishop who has been appointed by a Prime Minister who has had other motives than the desire to promote true Catholic doctrine or to score off ritualists.[21] And the bishop, once enthroned, has *usually* settled down to the job of being a father in God to all the faithful, no matter what their ecclesiastical colour. In this the bishop is, of course, profoundly English. He acts in the spirit of Bishop Sanderson's preface to the Prayer Book of 1662 and avoids the "sundry inconveniences" that arise from the attempt to remedy evils that may have arisen from things "advisedly established."[22] This respect for vested interests, emotional as well as material, makes the good bishop, although possibly a bishop who serves the church as a semi-secular rather than as a purely religious body, chiefly concerned to declare the faith once delivered or to be delivered to the saints. A Bishop Gore in one direction, a Bishop Barnes in another, may not accept this limitation of their functions, may take an un-English view of the importance of intellectual clarity and insist on definitions ("no evident necessity so

[21] It is not a real solution of the problem of keeping party spirit within due limits to accept what is, in effect, a geographical limitation of parties. The Protestant Episcopal Church of the United States lays more stress on the "Protestant" in Richmond (Virginia) than in Fond du Lac (Wisconsin). But what of the Virginian member who moves to Wisconsin?

[22] I take this citation from Dr. Hensley Henson's admirable *Church of England.*

requiring" such action in the eyes of their brethren), but they are not typical of the man whom the Prime Ministers normally call to the episcopal office.

The connection with the state is important in another way. For twenty-six bishops are members of the House of Lords.[23] As the House of Lords has over seven hundred members, the twenty-six bishops would be a tiny minority *if* the lay peers took their legislative duties seriously. But they do not and the bishops may often be a numerically large as well as intrinsically weighty section of the actual working upper house. It is less and less common for a bishop to take much part in mere or pure politics, but in questions with a moral content, questions of moral legislation (for example, drink, gambling, and the like), or questions affecting the treatment of natives in the Empire[24] they have a concern. In

[23] The two Archbishops of Canterbury and York, the Bishops of London, Durham, and Winchester are members by right. The remaining bishops become members by seniority of their appointment to their sees. This curious system has a very English origin. When it became evident in the nineteenth century that there were not enough bishoprics and that those that existed were often in the wrong place, Parliament reluctantly agreed to tamper with the work of Theodore of Tarsus, Lanfranc, and Henry VIII. So new sees, beginning with Manchester, were created. But the change was not to be used to increase the clerical membership of the House of Lords, so, with respect for the rights of the archbishops and the three historically most important episcopal sees, all claims were lumped. This means that a bishop may have to wait a long time before he enters the House of Lords. The Archbishops always and the three *ex officio* bishops usually have been bishops before, so that they come to the House of Lords with some episcopal experience. (The present Bishop of Durham went straight to the episcopal bench in the Lords.) The other bishops have years of utterances on public questions bottled up before they get an official platform to express them from. The pedantically-minded among historians still lament a system that may leave a Bishop of Lichfield outside the House of Lords and put a Bishop of Bradford into it.

[24] The Church of England is now a great missionary church with more first-hand knowledge of all parts of the British Empire than any secular body. And among its missionaries have been some of the most zealous defenders of the rights of the natives, men like Bishop Weston and Archdeacon Owen. The English bishops, in such cases, may be spokesmen for a great unrepresented body.

mediæval language, the post of "keeper of the King's conscience" was entrusted to the Lord Chancellor, who in modern times is a great lay official and judge.[25] But in a non-technical sense the keeper of the national conscience is now more often the bench of bishops in the House of Lords.

But a church is not a mere matter of bishops. What of the lesser shepherds and what of the flock? Here it is important to notice one effect of the theory of establishment. The Church of England claims to be the church of the whole English people. In modern times it admits that there are large dissenting bodies, Methodist, Romanist, Jewish, and others, but these, even if lumped together, are still a minority of the English people. And, it is held, the Church of England has the cure of souls of the rest. So it is under obligation to provide means of worship all over the country; in regions where there are few Anglicans; in regions where there are few inhabitants. No more than a Post Office can it refuse to provide service in remote or unprofitable regions in order to concentrate on those fields that are white for the harvest. This means a maldistribution of resources that is not necessarily discreditable. There are sixteen thousand clergy (not all of them doing parochial work), so that if the man-power of the Church of England were evenly distributed over the whole country, each parson would have to look after three thousand people, which of course reduces the pastoral office to a formality. So the rural parson is underworked and the town parson overworked, and the fiction that the Church of England is a church serving all the population is not at all plausible in a big industrial city in the Midlands, whatever surface truth it may have in an agricultural area like Lincolnshire or in central Oxford.[26]

The Church of England has never had in modern times as many

[25] At present Lord Simon (Sir John Simon).

[26] It is significant that the illustrations to Dr. Hensley Henson's book are all taken from the countryside or from the old cathedral towns. There is no illustration of church life in the places where the great majority of the English people live, the great new industrial areas.

bishops or as few parish clergy as it has today, and the bishop has kept his place as a national figure better than the parson has. The system of choosing men for given parochial or other posts loses its attractive simplicity as soon as we descend from the high plateau where bishops and deans are made and live.[27]

Lesser patronage is no longer a simple matter of nomination by a Prime Minister. The Prime Minister continues to nominate to some ecclesiastical posts, but the Lord Chancellor nominates to more. Other officers of the Crown (for instance, the Chancellor of the Duchy of Lancaster) have other jobs to give away, and so have the Universities of Oxford and Cambridge and the colleges which are part of those universities. So far, so comparatively good; clerical patronage is administered by public or semi-public bodies with, on the whole, a due regard to decorum and piety.[28]

But most patronage is private; it is in the hands of private land-owners. In the Middle Ages pious landowners often gave the right to take the profits of a parish to an abbey, whose abbot thus became the rector and who put in a vicar who did the work and received a stipend which was less, possibly much less, than the income of the parish. At the Reformation other landowners took their lands away from the suppressed abbeys, but forgot to give back the great tithes to the parsons who did the work of the parishes. Thus, in England, the average parish priest is a vicar and not a rector, and it is usually

[27] Deans of the great cathedrals may be much more like characters out of Trollope than any modern bishop can be. Of course, Trollope, for all that he was a Liberal, would have been astonished at the Bolshevik enthusiasm of the present Dean of Canterbury (Dr. Hewlett Johnson) and, despite his robust view of popular literature, he might have been a little puzzled by the ease with which Dr. Inge, when Dean of St. Paul's, combined the careers of Paul Elmer More and Mr. Westbrook Pegler and had enough time over to fulfil the duties of the great office once adorned by John Donne.

[28] It has been my experience in Oxford and Cambridge that the difficulty today is to find candidates who can afford to accept the average living. I have been told that on the list of possible nominees kept for the use of the Lord Chancellor some names (and the most favoured) gain attention because they are marked off by the letters "WHM" which being interpreted stand for "wife has means."

a safe guess that a vicar or a perpetual curate is less well off than a rector.[29]

The old untrammelled days of nomination at what was practically the good pleasure of the patron are over. So are scandalous nominations and sales of nominations. The great grievance now is the characteristically English one of "party trusts." Instead of the great magnate nominating a kinsman whose call was more to the temporalities than to the spiritualities (and thus raising the social standing while lowering the spiritual tone of the clergy), the right to "present" to vacant livings is vested in trustees. These trustees buy up, with funds they have been given or left, vacant rights of presentation. They are associated with parties within the church, especially with the extreme "Protestant" parties. Their object is to make sure that, in as many cures of souls as money can buy, the Gospel truth, as they see it, shall be preached and no Romish doctrines or practices be tolerated.[30] The patronage system is being more and more limited, and it is its approaching extinction that accounts for the current zeal of the purchasers of presentation

[29] Sometimes more than the great tithes were acquired by the new class of hard-faced men who did well out of the Reformation. The Russells got all the assets of the Abbey of Woburn and sometimes styled themselves lay abbots of that great foundation. The present head of the family, the pacifist Duke of Bedford, has ceased making any contribution to the support of Woburn parish church. Its incumbent receives none of the spoil of the abbey, not even the lesser tithes. The Russells have usually been strongly Erastian and anti-clerical in their views, but this cannot be attributed solely to the fact that, like so many other great families, "their hands are dripping with the fat of sacrilege" as (unless my memory fails me) Mr. Lloyd George vividly put it apropos of the eminently clerical Cecils.

[30] It is a matter of controversy whether the "Protestant" trusts are worse in this respect than the "Catholic." But they are better provided with funds and as it is true that the extreme old-fashioned Protestant view is held by the least impressive section of the Anglican clergy, the nominees of the Protestant trusts tend to have less personal prestige. The ecclesiastical position of the great Lord Shaftesbury is probably that which appeals least of all to the religious mind of today. (It is the leader of this section, Bishop Chauvasse of Rochester, who has rushed to the defence of the bankers.) Here the dead hand of Victorian wealth and piety is heavy on the living church.

rights. But in the combination of religious ends and very worldly means, the trusts are among the most English of institutions. And yet they are in some ways un-English. The blind respect for vested interests, which the free hand given to these trusts exemplifies, is in a way reminiscent of the immunity given to American educational foundations since the decision in the Dartmouth College case, over a century ago. No English or Scottish college or foundation has any such immunity from the amending hand of the law. Oxford and Cambridge have both reformed themselves and been reformed from outside. But there are many parishes in England whose pastors are chosen for them by trustees determined to see that in the age of Karl Adam and Karl Barth, Maritain and Reinhold Niebuhr, Cadoux and Needham, the intellectual standards of the *Speaker's Commentary* and the religious spirit of the Ecclesiastical Titles Bill shall be preserved. The Church of England as a body may amend and explain, but inside it, these ecclesiastical strongholds of the past still hold out, buttressed by money against the spirit of the age.[31]

And, once appointed, the Anglican incumbent is almost as much his own master as is the bishop. He holds the "parson's freehold" and, short of very scandalous neglect or misbehaviour, he is secure for life. This permits, of course, the ill-fitted parson to keep his job long after his utility is gone. It even permits the scandalous parson too long a run for his money, or his patron's money. It also allows the saint to go his own way without adjusting his view of life to the wishes of an unsaintly congregation. It is unlikely that this legal

[31] Another example of the dead hand which is able to affect contemporary practice is the Lord's Day Observance Society. English sabbatarianism is not dead, but it is less living than it would be, had it to depend on current income to pay for its campaigns. The universities may be held by some to be in the same class. But neither Oxford nor Cambridge insists today on the literal teaching of what was orthodoxy, religious or academic, in the past. The Bampton lecturers are allowed to go beyond Mansel. And the Gifford lectures on natural religion in the Scottish universities have been given, in one case at least, by an avowed opponent of "natural religion" in its ordinary sense (Karl Barth).

guarantee of the right of the parson to do what he likes with his own will last much longer. That it has lasted so long is part of the English conservatism which marked the old establishment.[32]

Bishops appointed by politicians, parsons appointed by private individuals who may not be either resident or absentee landowners with some interest in the peace, or even in the religious well-being of a parish, but legal agents of a long-dead zealot; how can such a church have a hold on the English people? It is easy to ask the question, but harder to answer it; yet the parson has a hold, or, if that is too strong a word, he is at one end of a rope that, however slackly, binds, or till recently bound, the English people to the English Church.[33]

[32] "The position of an incumbent in the Church of England would be, if they knew of its wild licence, the envy of foreign tyrants. In 1914 an incumbent who conformed to a minimum of legal observances, who refrained from murder, notorious evil living and conspicuous drunkenness, could do pretty much what he pleased—that is, in principle. In practice, as had been proved by a long succession of technical lawbreakers, he could, if he were enthusiastic, devout, hard-working and beloved, ignore the legal minimum required of him, and turn his parish church into a colourable imitation of a Papist chapel or a dissenting meeting-house."—R. Ellis Roberts: *H. R. L. Sheppard*, p. 86.

[33] The national character of the Church of England is illustrated by the fact that it is the parson, not the priest or minister, who is the traditional butt. He appears in ludicrous roles on comic postcards, being scored off by the village drunk. He is a classical figure of the mildly humorous drawing-room ballad ("I was a pale young curate then," or the other which tells of the clerical philanderer who is now "a vicar in the North Country at a salary three times greater"). He is the hero of the joke about the curate's egg and the hero of *The Private Secretary*. There can be no doubt what denomination ordained Mr. G. S. Melvin, or unfrocked Mr. George Robey. The Anglican clergyman is also the hero of innumerable ribald, unprinted jokes. A touchy and thoughtless person once complained of this fact and was admirably answered by Mr. St. John Ervine. Anti-clerical jokes are common in all countries. And they must be directed against the traditional representatives of religion. In France that is the *curé*, not the *pasteur*; in England it is the parson and not the priest. This merely proves that, as André Siegfried said, the *curé* is part of the furniture of French life as is the parson of English life. And for that reason there was wisdom as well as humour in the jest of a friend of mine at the time of the famous

"I have never seen, heard, nor read, that the clergy were beloved in any nation where Christianity was the religion of the country. Nothing can render them popular but some degree of persecution." So wrote one of the most eminent if not most representative of Anglican divines, Dean Swift, and the readiness of the English people to laugh or sneer at their established pastors is partly due to the fact that it is quite a long time since the Church of England has been persecuted, or even thought it was. It is nearly a generation since F. E. Smith declared that the Welsh Disestablishment Bill had "shocked the conscience of every Christian community in Europe." Even the boldest rhetorician today, on his way to high legal preferment, would have to find some other means of proving his stout Church-of-Englandism than oratorical flourishes like this. The church may be impoverished; what old Scottish divines called the "crown rights of Christ" may be affronted by an Erastian Parliament, but the parson is not linked to his people by any bond like that which unites the Irish priest or the Nonconformist minister, by a memory of wrongs suffered in common. A few sections of the Church of England have more recent memories of suffering than the Civil War of three hundred years ago provides, but in the main, until very recent times, church and state in England have lived more like bickering spouses than like passionate lovers or deadly enemies.[34] Indeed, the neutral observer of the relationship between church and state in England is sometimes reminded of Mr. Dooley's observation that, in the Archey Road, when a man

---

and scandalous trial of the unfortunate Rector of Stiffkey: "This trial has done more to endear the Church of England to the English people than anything since the trial of the Seven Bishops." Scandals in the Church of England are public property, not the private mortifications of private sects.

[34] The Anglo-Catholic party keeps green the memory of its Victorian confessors. And it is possible that if the lively, riotous days of Lowder of London Docks could return, or a few priests like Green of Miles Platting spent a year or two in jail in defence of what they took to be orthodoxy, religious zeal (at least as it is understood in Belfast) would revive and the churches be filled again, with worshippers as well as rioters.

and a woman find that they can't go on living together, they go on living together.

Yet there are moments when the strain seems about to become intolerable. Thus the House of Commons has twice recently refused to sanction changes in the Prayer Book asked for by the constituted authorities of the church. The majority of English members of Parliament were willing to give the church what it wanted, but a minority of English members aided by members from Scotland (where a different church is established) and Wales and Northern Ireland (where no church is established) refused to permit the cloven hoof of Rome to be inserted in the doorway of a church which the most vociferous orators never entered anyway. The result was a solution of a type not uncommon in ecclesiastical politics. The church went its own way; the bishops had no effective means of putting down "Romanism"; but the Protestant feeling of the British, if not of the English people, was satisfied. To a large section of the practising and believing Christians in the Church of England, the rites and doctrines condemned by that unimpressive version of a church council, the House of Commons in a religious mood, were essential and sacred. They refused to give them up, no matter how much that might annoy stoutly Erastian divines from Paisley or Portadown. So, in effect, the state washed its hands of the matter, leaving the battle to be fought out, inside the church.

But what constitutes being "inside the Church"? It is easy to exclude Presbyterians, Catholics, Jews, Christian Scientists, but what is the position of the occasional conformer, of the Englishman who stays away from the parish church and not from another rival place of worship? Apparently this unwillingness to submit himself to the discipline of church-going gives this not untypical Englishman a special right to insist on having his way. It is, on this view, the duty of the Church of England to be ready at any moment to provide for the religious needs (if such they can be called) of persons who are only in any degree either churchmen or Christians, because *some* relation to the church and to Christianity is part of the make-up of any decent Englishman.[35] It is the prevalence of this view and the unconscious arrogance that often accompanies it that irritates the minority of the English people to whom the English Church is part of the Christian Church. For a church that meets the demand of this simple "Church-of-Englandism" most certainly does not meet the needs of the devout believer.[36] Less than ever in these days when the whole Christian conception is threatened, and by more than argument, is the conscious Chris-

[35] This view was very candidly expressed by "A Soldier" in a letter in the *Spectator* (July 31, 1942). "Like all my relatives that I ever heard of I was baptised and confirmed into the Church of England, and all of us expect, in due time, to be married and buried according to its rites. . . . I often intend to go to church and succeed in getting there a dozen times a year, when I enjoy and believe myself to be edified by the old liturgy, especially the Psalms, Lessons and Collects which high-falutin' parsons gabble and mutilate. I hate parsons' antics, high or low church. . . . To be honest I should admit that I am much more an Anglican churchman than I am an orthodox Christian." This is surely a very advanced form of what Gladstone called "the Erastian theory that the business of an Establishment is to teach all sorts of doctrines and to provide Christian ordinances by way of comfort for all sorts of people, to be used at their own option" (*Life of Bishop Wilberforce*, Vol. II, p. 353). The new view seems to be that the customer is always right, even if he is hardly a customer at all.

[36] Many persons brought up outside the Church of England have been astonished (and often irritated) by the phenomenon of "Church-of-Englandism." It is over fifty years since Augustine Birrell allowed his normal urbanity to be overclouded by his Scotch and Dissenting ancestry and training. "Church-of-Englandism is far too robust, too secular-minded, to care a rap about the opinion of bishops and divines, who are but necessary evils, only to be defended when attacked by low-minded Radicals and vulgar Dissenters. It is the external church, the bricks and mortar, the ivy-mantled tower, nestling in the valley hard by the 'Blue Boar,' the chiming of the bells on a Sunday morning as they fall on the ears of men walking in an opposite direction, that appeal to these stalwart sons of the Establishment. . . . To men of this mould, to cease to belong to the Church of England is to be a renegade from the national flag, to go over to the enemy. Church-of-Englandism is the religion of England, and it is the duty of every Englishman to belong to the English religion. What that religion is doesn't matter, and is perhaps uncertain. But, whatever it is, it is a moderate, decent religion which leaves you alone, or which you can leave alone if so minded."

tian minority in the Anglican Church disposed to make concessions to the Laodicean majority to whom the Church of England is, like cricket, part of the English background. Indeed, the acceptance of so vague a religion as this seems fraught with danger to the more concrete religion of the zealous minority which now realizes fully that it is a minority and that in the old sense England is no longer a Christian country.[37]

The Christian cause in England is not represented solely by the Established Church. For all the passion of the English people for social conformity was not strong enough to control the national individualism in religion. And one of the great dividing lines in English life, one whose effects are not yet exhausted, was that between "Church" and "Chapel." That line was theological (for each Nonconformist body broke away on some specific point of doctrine or practice), but it was also, as has been said, social. And it was political. For to the Nonconformists the Church of England and the Tory or Conservative Party were aspects of the same intolerant, exclusive attitude in religion and politics. Only the Wesleyans preserved, until well into the nineteenth century, the Tory politics of their founder. All the other dissenting bodies (and ultimately the Wesleyans) were Liberals or Radicals. The converse was not equally true. There were Anglicans who were Liberals, but it was an anomaly that Mr. Gladstone in his progress from High Toryism to Radicalism never abandoned any of the High Church principles he had learned at Oxford. He led, in his old age,

[37] "While the humanistic religious sentiment which expresses itself by the catch in the throat at the last Evensong in the old School Chapel, the community singing of 'Abide with me' at a torchlight tattoo, and the standing to attention during the Two Minutes' Silence, can be utilised by totalitarianism, a religion which speaks of redemption by the incarnate Son of God, which offers mankind the sacramental means of union with the eternal life of the God-Man Jesus Christ, and which makes the perpetual representation of His atoning Sacrifice its essential act of worship must be the declared enemy of all who see in the state the be-all and end-all of man's life."—Humphrey Beevor: *Peace and Pacifism*, p. 207; cited in T. S. Eliot: *The Idea of a Christian Society*, pp. 84–5.

a party whose clerical leaders had little in common with him except basic Christian faith, then a less effective bond of union than it is now.[38] It is probable that Nonconformity reached its height of political power, was most representative of the temper of the English people, round the beginning of this century.[39] Its hold on the middle and working classes was still strong. Its political principles seemed relevant to the problems of the time. Its moral and political optimism seemed justified. It was united, while Anglicanism was divided. It knew what it knew and what it believed. It was no longer hampered intellectually by the educational disabilities of the days of Anglican privilege, and its own internal divisions into rival sects were no longer so bitter or weakening as they had been. But in the generation that had passed since the great Liberal landslide of 1906, one of the greatest changes in the English religious and social landscape has been the decline of Nonconformity. Partly that decline has been due to the general weakening of the hold of Christianity on the English people; partly it has been due to the comparative irrelevance of the peculiarly Nonconformist (as apart from Christian) view of the contemporary world and its problems. Be the causes what they may, the decline is a fact and an important fact.

The decline of the power of Nonconformity in England has undoubtedly weakened a link between the English and American peoples for which there has been no substitute. The common tradition of evangelical religion, the common belief in conversion, in

[38] High Churchmen tended to become Liberals as a protest against the favour shown by Disraeli to the Low Churchmen and, still more, as a protest against the ritual prosecutions which he, driven to it by Queen Victoria, made possible. G. W. E. Russell, who was both a Radical and a High Churchman, attributed some of the Liberal success in forlorn hopes like Brighton at the election of 1880 to good churchmen voting against the author of the Public Worship Regulation Bill. Other Anglo-Catholics later went "Christian Socialist." Gore's background, of course, like Lord Halifax's, was Whig.

[39] I have heard it stated, on what authority I know not, that the great Liberal Parliament elected in 1906 was the first since the time of Charles II most of whose members were non-Anglicans.

the literal inspiration of Holy Writ, the common taboos (even if they were more rigid in America than in England), all provided a common ethos. Moody and Sankey were almost as great figures in England as in the United States; the common stock of hymns and of devotional books was drawn on with hardly any sense of national difference. The "Council on Interchange of Preachers and Speakers" may have been optimistic, in the present, when it declared that "English religious books are more widely read in America, and *vice versa* than any other literature. The language of religion is almost the only language of both countries which does not require re-interpretation." [40] But it certainly was true a generation ago. And if it is not true today, the chief reason (after the decline in the importance of organized religion in both countries) is that English Nonconformity has changed more than has American Protestantism.

For a generation past, Nonconformity has been losing its influence over the working classes. In this it is repeating the history of the older Dissent which, by the eighteenth century, was overwhelmingly middle-class. The Wesleyans have followed the Independents and Presbyterians. Their flocks today are not at all proletarian. Nor are the pastors. Just as the Church of England is going back to the condition of the eighteenth century, with its parsons drawn from all ranks of society, with the sons of workmen serving side by side with the sons of professional men and even of the aristocracy, so Nonconformity is going back to its eighteenth-century condition. No member of a Nonconformist chapel is likely to have been at Eton, and only one Nonconformist minister is the son of a peer. [41] But it is also unlikely that many members of Nonconformist chapels should be on the dole, or that their ministers should be drawn from as poor families as now supply so many par-

[40] Quoted in R. H. Heindel: *The American Impact on Great Britain, 1898–1914,* p. 40. Professor Heindel is rightly sceptical of the contemporary truth of this judgment.

[41] His father is a millionaire and a new peer. Whether there are any third-generation Nonconformist peers would be an interesting subject of inquiry.

sons to the Church of England. There is no reason to be unduly surprised at the view expressed by the former Bishop of Durham [42] that the average minister is now of a higher social rank than the average parson.

This development has more than social importance. The minister is at least as likely to have had a good formal education as the parson and to have had that education at a recognized public institution of learning.[43]

The consequences to relations between the two countries are serious. There *is* an interchange of ideas and persons between the leaders, Anglican as well as simply "Protestant," *at the top*. The Archbishop of Canterbury has given the Gifford lectures at Glasgow University; Dr. Reinhold Niebuhr has given the Gifford lectures at Edinburgh University. British divines are easily made at home in Union Seminary or the University of Chicago. But there is no lively demand in England for the old-fashioned hell-fire, fundamentalist preacher of the type still popular in such different American cities as Los Angeles, Minneapolis, and Forth Worth. Men who are great public figures, cultivated by politicians and lavishly reported by the press in their home towns, are, when they come to England, either ignored, or are the guests and the stars of small and decaying sects. They discover to their pained surprise that English Nonconformist leaders are more likely to be on terms of sympathetic understanding with learned Jesuits or Dominicans than with the heirs of Moody and Sankey. Only in Wales, Cornwall, and the Highlands, or in the most strait sect of the Low Churchmen of the Anglican Church, is their language still spoken

[42] Dr. Hensley Henson.

[43] Readers of Mrs. Oliphant's *Salem Chapel* will appreciate the difference between the status of a minister who has had a brilliant career at a denominational college unknown outside his sect and one who has had a brilliant career at a modern university or at Oxford or Cambridge. Today one of the regular theological professors at Cambridge is a Nonconformist, and the Nonconformist colleges at Oxford provide some of the greatest ornaments of theological learning in the university world. Dr. Micklem is no more a character out of *Salem Chapel* than he is a character out of *Mark Rutherford*.

in the theological sense. Indeed, Welsh (and even Gaelic) would be a more useful introduction to the life of the old-time religionists in Britain than is English.

It is true that the moral principles may still seem the same. But they will be less rigorously held in England. It is likely that leading English Protestant divines would be less surprised both at finding themselves at a Catholic meeting and at being offered cigars than were the American divines who met this year to discuss rural problems.[44] Although the "social gospel" has made a great deal of progress in America, to the extent, some would say, of replacing the Gospel, the old view that personal faith and personal morals (the latter mainly in the form of "thou shalt nots") are the sole business of the church is far stronger in America than in England.[45]

The political responsibility of the churches in England is seen very largely in economic and political terms. Views about the "profit motive," about the future of international relations, the terms of peace, the organization of the world, these are the themes of church discussion in England. And they are less the themes in America. English heresy trials are in the future as likely to be over the nature of interest as over justification by baptism; the banker may soon be the typical sinner whom a Christian may have to be told that he has to forgive, rather than the brewer or the bookmaker.[46]

[44] See *Time,* October 19, 1942.

[45] I deliberately say "England." The Celtic fringe is more American and less progressive than England in these matters. According to the new chief of the Baptist Church in Scotland, the Reverend T. A. M'Quiston, the chief problems facing the church in war-time appear to be the danger of allowing "secularists to infringe upon the sanctity of the Lord's Day," the permitting of "privileges for the drink traffic, the gambling fraternity [and] the cinemas" (the *Glasgow Herald,* October 20, 1942). Mr. M'Quiston would be at home in Knoxville, Tennessee.

[46] The indignant bankers who write letters to *The Times* complaining of the harsh words of the Archbishop of Canterbury would be better advised to claim, rightly enough, that they are the representatives of the publicans of New Testament times. *Verb. sap.*

And in the great current controversy over war and peace the emphasis in American Protestantism has been on the degree of sin or innocence involved in taking part in war, rather than on the social problem of the community and war. When an English minister says that there "must be no more war," he is more likely to mean that society must be organized to prevent war than that he will free himself from all share in the common sin by refusing to aid the war effort. The American pacifist minister is still, very often, at the stage of saving his own soul. If the world imitates him, the problem is solved; if not, so much the worse for the world. He is not his brother's keeper, except in matters like prohibition and other sumptuary laws. For it is, to an outsider, a surprising fact that men who do not think that justice or humanity is worth fighting for are (or were) ready to use the secular arm to impose a taboo on alcohol. If the non-pacifist clergy ought to repent the lives lost in this and other political wars, the pacifist and prohibitionist clergy should repent the gang wars their zeal bred and fostered. And if they reply that war does not bring justice or humanity, still less does prohibition bring sobriety.

This war is an experiment as noble in purpose as the eighteenth amendment was and whatever the claims on our respect of the Christian pacifist who does not want the aid of the secular arm for any real or alleged moral purpose, the position of that not uncommon type, the Christian pacifist who wants the power of the state to be used for *his* ends but for none that he does not think worthy, is not so easy to defend. And it finds fewer defenders in English church circles than in American, not because the English divine is by nature more clear-sighted than his American brother, but because some grim political truths are more clearly seen in a London that has known the *Blitz* than in a Chicago that has only known the massacre of St. Valentine's Day.

But the movement of American Protestantism is probably towards the English emphasis on collective religious responsibility, away both from the unconscious anarchy of some modern attitudes and from the emphasis on Biblical orthodoxy that is still so strong in American evangelical religion. Whether this means that the Protestant churches will play a bigger or smaller role in the future than in the present is another question.[47] But at the moment a more important fact is that the role of the Protestant churches as a common link is less important than it was a generation ago. In both countries the role of organized religion is less important and the differences in the national view as to what organized religion is *about* are probably greater, at this moment, than they ever have been or are likely to be in the future, when the natural evolution of American Protestantism has brought it nearer to the new English pattern. The American small town, home of the old-time religion, has no real counterpart in England and less of a counterpart on the religious side than on any other.[48]

[47] We learn that in "Middletown" growth in church congregations has been roughly in proportion to the growth in population. But the growth has been among the marginal, unintellectual, poor sects and is in part accounted for by immigration from the South (R. S. Lynd and H. M. Lynd: *Middletown in Transition*, p. 297). The same phenomenon might occur in a growing London industrial area, drawing a large part of its new population from Wales. It has occurred in Detroit as well as in Muncie.

[48] One thing that they still have to some extent in common does not make for mutual friendliness. One of the toughest survivals of the old English religion is Sabbatarianism. Since in the seventeenth century the Hebrew Sabbath was imposed on the Christian Sunday, negative observance of the Lord's Day has been to a great many English-speaking Protestants what not eating fish on Friday is to a great many Catholics, all the Law and the Prophets. So the American soldier stranded in an English small town on a Sunday will find no substitute for the ever-open drug store, for the movie house, for the amusement park. The majority of the inhabitants of these towns are giving no other indication of their belief that Sunday is a sacred day than their negative support for the legal closing of all homes of public relaxation (except the places where booze is sold). The effect, on an American soldier, is less likely to be an admiration for the staunchness of English religious principles than profound irritation with a people that has the folly to have such laws and has not the enterprise to break them. It is then that he wishes himself back where

> You can pick the morning gloria
> Right off the side-walks of sweet Peoria.

As for having to spend a wet Sunday in Glasgow or Holyhead, that is enough to make the American wish himself in a reasonably good peni-

Shocked by the paganism that is pretty widespread in England, shocked both by English hypocrisy in some spheres and by the absence of it in others,[49] the common Puritan tradition that does still bind Temple (Texas) and Wolverhampton (England) may seem to the American to have lost all its power. He will be wrong; in great crises it still has power, but it is not what it was in the days of Henry Ward Beecher, or Spurgeon, or what it still is in Atlanta or Des Moines.

The decline of the power of Nonconformity has had important consequences in the political field—important and, on the whole, unfortunate. The division of the English bourgeoisie into two groups, "Church and Chapel," had deplorable cultural results. English Nonconformity in the days of its power was not, æsthetically, an attractive spectacle, and its emphasis on comparatively minor matters of conduct distorted its view of the national life and weakened its hold on the working classes. It was often negative; it was often smug. But at its worst Nonconformity was a protest against, as well as a victim of, English snobbery. When the economic and other power that the squire and the parson then had is reflected on, there is something heroic in the ugly, poor, and now neglected chapels that can be seen in so many English villages in East Anglia, Somerset, and other strongholds of the old Puritanism. The last great peasant revolt of English history was the Monmouth Rebellion against James II.[50] It is as the scene of the martyrdom of

_____

tentiary, for in Scotland and Wales he cannot even get a drink, and in Glasgow, a city rather bigger than Cleveland, the stern moralists of the City Council have reluctantly allowed four cinemas to open, three of them in the suburbs. It is, in fact, impossible to explain these things to Americans in the high moral terms that the natives of these islands command so easily.

[49] The recent public candour of Englishwomen in the matter of smoking, make-up, dress, language, etc., shocks a great many Americans whose standards are nearer those of Toronto than of the northwest district of Washington or the "roaring forties" of New York.

[50] I commend this thought to the Belloc school of historians. Their hero, James II, was the last King of England that any serious number of poor Englishmen thought was worth fighting *against*. It was the English La Vendée.

these humble and unlucky heroes that Taunton ought to touch the heart of anybody who likes the English people for what they are, instead of for what they might have been had English history been entirely different. We may assume without much risk of error that the average

Village Hampden that with dauntless breast
The little tyrant of his fields withstood

withstood him for his erroneous views of the next world, as well as for his tyrannical conduct in this. Religious dissent, accompanied by hardships that are serious but not demoralizing, is a good education in real radicalism. People who have had that training are not usually taken in by the easy sophistries that suggest that liberty is easy to get, easy to keep, and not worth any great trouble to keep or get. These people have made more serious sacrifices for their political rights than payment of poll taxes and are not tempted to believe that their duty (and an onerous duty) has been done when they have made the effort to register and vote. In a country where the weaknesses of English Nonconformity are present without the background of political and social handicaps, its political role is likely to be almost entirely harmful, so that nothing said in defence of the Nonconformist conscience in England should be taken as applying (without further consideration) to the United States, Scotland, or Wales. To be a minority, if not of active and convinced Christians, at least of the run-of-the-mill conforming Christians, to belong to bodies that were, in varying degrees, unfashionable, in a country where snobbery is the rival religion to Christianity, to be forced to accept companions, to go to schools, to conform to social customs below the social level which your financial status and education made natural to you, this was to receive a character-building education not provided in many public schools.[51] Non-

---

[51] A young woman, for instance, forced to go to a Sunday school which none of her normal schoolfellows attend and to take part in the social life of a chapel which has hardly any links with her normal social life has a training in the varieties of life in England.

conformity is, in this context, a more important phenomenon than mere dissent. To mark yourself out as peculiar is to show courage if bad worldly judgment. And that may be one important reason why the English Nonconformist, sharing almost completely the theological views of the Low Churchmen, has had far more interesting political views and has had a far more respectable intellectual record than the Anglicans who made the best of both worlds, by being "Church" and thus escaping social disabilities in this world and being "evangelical" and thus escaping damnation in the next.[52] The Nonconformists, whatever their natural temperament may have been, or the temptations of their economic status, were predisposed to sympathy with rebels.[53] Thus, they resisted the temptation to exploit the national anti-Catholic bias of the English people, since that involved, in modern times, hostility to Irish Nationalism; and the Nonconformists and the Irish had many common enemies—and some common principles.[54]

This alliance continued even after Nonconformist disabilities had become a less and less heavy burden and after the Catholic attitude on such questions as the drink traffic and religious instruction in schools had provided grounds for a political divorce.

The decline of political Nonconformity was probably inevitable. Not only was religious zeal growing more tepid, but the character of political problems was changing. As Anglican exclusiveness be-

[52] Politically the Low Churchmen were almost always Tories. And it is worth comparing the intellectual weight of their leaders, Sir William Joynson-Hicks or Sir Thomas Inskip, with such Liberal Nonconformist leaders as Sir Henry Fowler (Lord Wolverhampton) and Sir John Simon.

[53] Spurgeon was once asked, ironically, why he did not mortify the flesh by voting Tory at times. He replied: "I mortify it by voting Liberal. I'm a Tory by temperament."

[54] In this they set an example which the old English Catholics did not follow. They were too good Tories to be upset by the fact that their most vociferous political allies were as bitterly anti-Catholic as they were "loyal." So it was an eminent Catholic preacher that Arthur Griffith, the founder of Sinn Fein, described as "an English Catholic in Christian clothing." And it was the Anglican Archbishop of Canterbury (Dr. Davidson) who made the most effective clerical protest against the Black and Tan atrocities, not Cardinal Bourne.

came more and more anachronistic, as the weakening of the Christian position laid stress on what united rather than on what divided, the obvious course of prudence, the mere dissidence of dissent, came to seem a little silly. It was, in part, the pressure of Anglican privilege that had acted as a training ground for Nonconformist discipline. And, as the history of the French Radical Party shows, the survival of the verbal habits of a militant and underprivileged minority into easy and prosperous times is a strong test of character. It became more difficult for the Nonconformist who would valiant be to find what to be valiant about in the religious field, and the temptation to make the attainment of the Kingdom of Heaven in this world, by the aid of the law, the chief object of corporate activity was often succumbed to. Serious wrongs abroad, the cause of the Armenians, of the oppressed Indians of the Putumayo, of the Congo Negroes, of the Balkan Christians, and of the numerous more or less oppressed peoples of the British Empire, these attracted the genuine and admirable zeal of many. So did the deplorable habits of the English working man, his fondness for putting on horses, or into the purchase of what was technically called alcohol, his money that ought to have gone to keep his wife and children. So did other moral problems affecting private conduct. And it is easy, too easy, to sneer at the Puritan zeal of the Nonconformist clergy, especially if it absolves you in your role of Catholic intellectual or columnist from commenting on the life of really Puritan communities like Ireland or Quebec. But the regulation of (or meddling with) the lives of the poor is not a great cause such as the nineteenth-century radicals had at heart in their wars against slavery, or tyranny, or illiteracy, or religious intolerance. And the new major questions necessarily divided the Nonconformists, for the rich members of the community had or tended to have different views on regulation of wages and hours, or the role of trade unions, or the incidence of taxation, from those naturally held by their poorer brethren. The young men of Nonconformist origin and low economic status now tended to move into the nascent Labour Party as did Arthur Henderson. Other reasons brought about schism in the Liberal Party, and when, for the first time, a Nonconformist became leader of one section of that party, the day of its greatness was past. Mr. Lloyd George was not the chosen hero or leader of the old Liberal orthodox; he was Welsh, not English; and the Labour Party tried to take over the assets of the party which it had supplanted with such pride—and such unconscious prophetic self-judgment, as "the Official Opposition."

Among the assets whose transfer was attempted was political Nonconformity. The attempt was only partially successful, even when the necessary writing-down of the assets is duly allowed for. Once the old denominational link between Wesleyan millionaires and Wesleyan miners was broken, it was difficult to find a substitute for the connection. Religion can be the opium of more than the proletariat, and many old Radical families—and fortunes— quietly went Tory. This would not have mattered if the Labour Party had ever got beyond the stage of being the Official Opposition, but one result of the decline or alienation of political nonconformity from the Labour Party was that the Conservative Party had its not too difficult job made even easier. The bright young members of party congresses and readers of papers at intellectual week-ends might not care, but political work is done when not very bright and not terribly young people of indeterminate social class are moved. There are fewer people standing at street corners singing hymns than when I was a child; there are also fewer people at street corners singing the Red Flag.[55]

But it is not only that the Labour Party has failed to take over the assets that political Nonconformity provided for the Liberals;

[55] The older members of the Labour Party knew this. One of the most famous leaders of the party told me that he got elected to the local council for the first time in a district of London where he seemed, on paper, to have little chance. The working-class nucleus was too small to overcome the bourgeois impermeability of the middle-class region. But it was from one of the bourgeois areas that he got the votes that put him in. And, he discovered, those votes came from a Dissenting community of fairly prosperous people who had no strong views on Fabian Socialism, but did know a Tory when they saw him—and so voted for the anti-Tory.

no one has succeeded in doing what Nonconformity did: in giving a prosperous bourgeoisie a sense of duty and a sense of social obligation. For all the cant and hypocrisy of the Nonconformist conscience, it was a real conscience and, as I have said elsewhere, if hypocrisy is the homage that vice pays to virtue, it is real homage and better than no homage at all. If English public policy was driven to pay that homage, it was due more to the influence of political Nonconformity than to any other force. The businessman, doomed to smugness, to complacency, to the temptations of the market, was forced to pay some kind of lip service to general principles of morality and, what is more, to principles of political morality which otherwise he does not so much defy as ignore altogether. It is not evident that the Birmingham of Mr. Neville Chamberlain and the Federation of British Industries is, in this respect, an improvement on the Birmingham of Dr. Dale and John Bright. The defence of Munich as a good thing, as justice, as good business, as something worthy of the English people, would have been harder in the days when Liverpool theatre-goers rose to cheer when the line came in *Othello:*

> *The Turks are drowned,*

and men of every type and school in England combined to condemn the Turkish outrages in Bulgaria and the prophetic indifference of Disraeli.

The English middle classes have not yet found a substitute for the Nonconformist conscience. Many individual members have found it in Labour politics—and a high proportion of them are children of Nonconformist families. But, inevitable as it may have been, the decline of political Nonconformity is a national loss. It cannot find an equivalent in general Quaker toleration and charity; Philadelphia shows that Quakerism is not enough, perhaps because there can never be enough Quakers. And no other instrument than militant Nonconformity for making the thriving middle class conscious of general ideas and general principles has yet been found in England. It may be said, of course, that this does not matter, but observers of politics who think, after the experience of the last twenty years, that the failure of the Labour Party to get a real hold on the majority of this class does not matter are real political fundamentalists. In this class lies the block of voters which alone can give the Labour Party a decisive majority; the technicians who can make the transformation run smoothly; the potential Fascists who can turn the revolution into the counter-revolution.

Church and chapel do not exhaust the varieties of Christianity that deserve notice as part of the English scene. A few years ago it might have been worth while discussing the role of Buchmanism as the only current example of that American influence on English Protestantism which was so important in the nineteenth century. But since the outbreak of war the Groupers have not had the good or, at least, lively press they could once have counted on. They have not even continued their tactics of cashing in on one of the two or three most valuable publicity names in England, Oxford.[56] The ambiguous war role of Dr. Buchman may have something to do with this. Many of the best hotels have been taken over by the government of Britain or house more interesting guests. And it is possible that the discovery that in "Moral Re-Armament" the military metaphor was so often purely metaphorical that it has further depressed the market in this once promising issue.

The iniquities of the Bishop of Rome have been common form in England for four centuries, and Gladstone was right, in his time, in stressing the fact that anti-Popery was one of the few basic articles of English faith. The good old violent days are over. Lewes no longer burns His Holiness in effigy with anything like the old zeal, and when an Ulster M.P. reminds the House of Commons that the Pope *still* has a bad name in Portadown, the House is more amused than impressed; and when Lady Astor sees fit to attack the Master of the Rolls (Lord Green) as a Papist, it is taken as one more proof that Virginia will out. The position of the Catholic

[56] It is a well-known but inexplicable fact that anything that happens at Oxford is news and that nothing that happens at Cambridge is.

Church in England (or, if it is preferred, the "Italian Mission," to quote a former Archbishop of Canterbury) is odd—that is, English. There is still a great deal of suspicion of Jesuit wiles (which may not be at all connected with the actual English province of the Society of Jesus). There is a suspicion that Catholic influence in the Foreign Office affects policy and there is irritation, not to put it more strongly, at the nostalgia of certain Catholic papers and individuals for the good old days when Mussolini was a combination of Augustus, Constantine, and Justinian. A generation ago there was a more serious conflict, since a majority of the Catholic population in England was of Irish origin and deeply interested in the fate of Ireland. Today not only is there a generation more between them and Ireland, but Irish grievances are hard to work up passion over in people who have been through the *Blitz* and whose local hero is more likely to be Brendan Finucane than Mr. De Valera. And Ireland, it must be remembered, is close to England, so that the Irish-English population, unlike the Irish-American population, knows a great deal about contemporary Ireland—knows, for example, how different it is from modern England or modern America. The Londoner of Irish origin knows that he would not be much at home in an Irish-speaking, agricultural, backward-looking Ireland after the model of Mr. De Valera's Eire. The Irish of Boston have no such opportunities for inspecting and disliking the Ireland run by their distinguished but untypical fellow citizens.

In addition to the Irish, there are Catholics of French, Italian, German, and Spanish origin, and from some points of view the Catholic Church is a collection of what the French anti-Semites call "métèques." But in another sense it is deeply English, far more English than the Catholic Church in the United States is American.

For the Catholic Church is, to use a phrase dear to Augustine Birrell, "the old religion." It is part of the historical background in a way that it is not in most of the United States. Mr. George Santayana in King's College Chapel, listening to the cool Anglican service and thinking that he, rather than the choristers, is really at home in the shrine of Henry VI, is a typical figure. The claim of the Church of England to continuity with the mediæval church helps to keep the Catholic side of English history alive. The Pope is part of English history; he may have been a bad thing, but there he is.[57] And not only is the Pope part of English history, but so are some of the great families that refused to follow Elizabeth into schism. For some of the *very* best families remained true to Rome and some very good families have since been reconciled to the Holy See. The reception of Roman Catholicism in the nineteenth century was helped by these two historical facts.

The fact that some of the greatest families had remained true to Rome was far from being unimportant in a snobbish country like England. It was less important than some ecclesiastics thought, but it was important all the same, that most of the blood of most of the Howards was Catholic, and although the exchange of an Earl of Shrewsbury for a Newman was a good bargain, even though the Earl was a Talbot, his secession was a loss. The old Catholic family was part of the English (and Scottish) background. Thus when Macaulay met Lord Clifford of Chudleigh in Rome, he was prepared not merely to meet a descendant of a member of Charles II's cabal, but a Catholic nobleman, a standard figure of the English landscape. It is true that Macaulay, like so many of his contemporaries, was deeply influenced in his views of British Catholicism by Sir Walter Scott and was disappointed when Lord Clifford did not turn out to be gloomy and Gothic like Lord Glenallan in *The Antiquary*, but, for all that, Lord Clifford was as much a part of Old England as a learned minister was of New England.[58]

---

[57] An odd example of the value attached to this papistical prestige is furnished by the soundly Presbyterian University of Glasgow. Although a large proportion of its alumni for four centuries past have been doubtless brought up to regard the Pope as Antichrist, the university, far from hiding the fact that it was founded by a Pope, flaunts it, possibly as a snub to the pretensions of the more recent municipal foundation at Edinburgh.

[58] Macaulay even found himself at home in that famous headquarters of the Counter-Reformation, the English College in Rome. He seems to have liked it largely because it smelled like Peterhouse. Although an almost

And there are parts of rural England which the Reformation has only formally affected. A generation ago an Anglican parson in certain parts of rural Lancashire was not as much an intruder as a parson in Connaught or a minister in some parts of the Outer Hebrides, but he was a bit of an intruder all the same.

In addition to the old Catholics and the immigrant Catholics, there has been, since the Oxford Movement, the convert. The list of converts to Rome is long and impressive. Newman and Chesterton are weightier names than Orestes Brownson and Heywood Broun. And it is mainly, though not exclusively, to the converts that the intellectual prestige of English Catholicism is due.[59]

Although the English Catholics are only a tenth as numerous as American Catholics, they are more important in English intellectual life than their co-religionists are in America.[60] Catholic ideas have more prestige than they have in America. The Catholic solution to present troubles is more in the minds of non-Catholics as a possibility than it is in America. And more is known of the Catholic attitude.[61]

Like the Church of England, the Church of Rome is part of the furniture of the English household, whether it is in the basement or in the attic or in the new functional, up-to-the-minute living-

---

excessively loyal Trinity man, Macaulay had enough general Cambridge patriotism to account this to the English College as a virtue. This example of an *odeur d'Angleterre* among the *parfums de Rome* should have interested Louis Veuillot.

[59] The most eminent of all Catholic apologists, Mr. Belloc, is not a convert, but he is not wholly English either.

[60] I have been convinced by correspondence with a distinguished professor at the University of Notre Dame that an earlier expression of this view was too dogmatic. But, with a few minor corrections, I think it is still true.

[61] It is possible that Catholic private life is less well known, as the leading Catholic novelists of the younger school do not give a very representative picture of English Catholic life. Neither Mr. Graham. Greene's *Brighton Rock*, nor Mr. Evelyn Waugh's *Vile Bodies* can be regarded as exceptions to this rule.

room. Dr. Inge may assert firmly that English Catholics are not English, but the Pope could tell him differently. And the difference between the Catholics in America and in England can be adequately illustrated by a true story. When the Anglicans of Liverpool planned to build a great cathedral, they employed a Catholic architect to adapt a mediæval Gothic cathedral to the needs of Anglican worship. When Cardinal Mundelein wanted a really American chapel for his new seminary outside Chicago, his architect was told to adapt a New England meeting-house to the needs of the Roman rite.

One Christian denomination deserves notice, although it is ostentatiously not English. But the Church of Scotland, from which three of the last six heads of the Church of England have come,[62] deserves note if for that reason alone. The Church of Scotland has even more serious claims on our attention than that. For the proximity in a small island of two different established churches, asserting different and incompatible views of the nature of the Church of Christ, while it has been an offence to theologians and an irritation to Anglican snobbery, has at least illustrated the almost (ancient) Roman tolerance of the British state. The political authority in the island of Britain may be held to affirm that the church in Scotland should be Presbyterian in government; in England that it should be Episcopal; in Wales that the state should have no views on this matter. And for the religious peace of the Empire it was a good thing that the legally equal position of the Church of Scotland forced some understanding of the

[62] Of the last six Archbishops of Canterbury, three have been Scotch Presbyterians by origin. Five have been from Oxford as against one from Cambridge. Of the five Oxford men, four have been Balliol men (two were also graduates of Glasgow University). The present archbishop is the son of a previous archbishop, and another was the son-in-law of a predecessor. Four had been headmasters of public schools. With data like these, it should be possible to predict the succession with some confidence, making allowance for the fact that the last three archbishops have had no children.

need for tolerance on intolerant Anglicans. Had there been more Anglican leaders like Archdeacon Strachan in Canada, or had they been more powerful, they might have driven English-speaking Canada into the arms of the United States and even driven French Canada too.[63] By being both established and non-Anglican, the Church of Scotland has taught a useful truth to many Englishmen of an Erastian type of mind who might otherwise have identified religious orthodoxy with parliamentary enactment. It is good for this type of Englishman to go to Scotland and find himself a Dissenter. But the Church of Scotland has had other utilities, too. Since it has been reunited, it has given the Church of England the example of a united national church freely determining its own discipline and doctrine. And as one of the traditionally important churches of Calvinist origin, it has linked British Protestantism with the most militant Protestants of the Continent. For the Calvinists of the world, Edinburgh ranks well after Geneva, but with Dort and Heidelberg and Sedan and other cities where the true doctrine has been attacked, defended, and expounded. In the Empire, Presbyterianism has been as great a force as Anglicanism, and David Livingstone has a place in the hearts of all British Protestants brought up with a sense of their duty to the heathen sitting in outer darkness. And, of course, the old connection between the Presbyterians of Scotland and the United States, between the Scottish universities and Princeton, is still important.[64]

In the national stock-taking that is going on during the war, there has been a revival of discussion of religion, if not a revival of religion. Many optimistic intellectuals have come to a belated recognition of the fact that there are such things as bad, not merely

[63] Strachan was, it should be remembered, a Scot, too full of the national *præfervidum ingenium* for the peace of Upper Canada.

[64] Woodrow Wilson got his first name (Woodrow, that is, not the suppressed Thomas) from a collateral ancestor, the famous librarian of Glasgow University at the end of the seventeenth century. This Woodrow was the historian of the Scottish Covenant, whence, it is possible, President Wilson took the name for the constitution of the League of Nations.

ignorant, ill-advised men.[65] The failure of optimistic humanism to
eradicate evil from the hearts of men, the failure of "education"
without any dogmatic moral bias to provide any reason likely to be
found convincing by the average man why he should follow certain moral codes and not others or none, the resistance of some
prominent European churchmen to Hitler, all have combined to
bring about a curiosity about the prospects of Christianity. And
this discussion centres on the alleged duty of "the church" to give
a lead in social matters and the alleged duty of the state to encourage the growth of a Christian society by educational reforms.

The Church of England, as far as the archbishops represent it,
gives a lead by protesting against the acceptance by the church of
the pursuit of wealth or, at any rate, money as the chief end of man.
If it be replied that modern society does not in fact accept the
pursuit of money as the chief end of man, the archbishops will
find a great deal of support for their view that little or nothing is
done to shake the conviction of the young that the advertising,
newspaper-making, business-adoring world in which he lives conceals very effectively any doubts it may have about the superiority
of the millionaire over the mystic.[66]

And in a world in which simple economic utilitarian calculation
has been proved to have far less driving power than its romantic
salesmen thought it had, the churches may be more in touch with
the movement of the world than the belated nineteenth-century
leaders of the old capitalist and Socialist parties. To believe that the
chief end of men is higher dividends or higher wages does not seem
so modern, so realistic today as it did around 1900.

How far that lead will be followed in religious terms remains to

[65] To the abandonment of the old habit of judging men may be at-
tributed some of the early propaganda successes of Hitler outside Germany.
Many Englishmen refused to see the evident fact that Hitler, Goebbels,
Himmler, and their like were *bad* men.

[66] I mean the poor mystic. Many millionaires and one or two mystics
have managed to take a contemptuous view of money. It doesn't matter
at all, provided you have enough of it. The Anglo-American invention of
the Mammon of Righteousness is still in good working order.

be seen. From the Christian point of view, the replacement of bankers by People's Commissars of Public Investment is not necessarily a great gain, if the commissars and the people seek first the kingdom of this world. Christianity may, indeed, be the most "this-worldly" of the great religions, but it is still less this-worldly than the world is.

Another view of the function of the church which is now being pressed is that it is to give meaning to life, to counter the scepticism of the young, their scorn of ideals, their lack of character. This doctrine is preached with a complacency that will annoy the young, if they ever get round to noticing it. One would have thought that only persons whose own austere upholding of the highest standards of political morality, in home and international affairs, was a national asset would be ready to lecture with such unction the generation that produced the R.A.F. Or, rather, one would think this if one did not know that England, a kindly country, is the game reserve where people of this type are protected by national good manners from the caustic and ribald answers they would get in, say, the United States.

But leaving on one side the mere preachers, the moralists have something to say. It is true that the experiment of an educational system without a strong dogmatic framework has yet to prove itself. Germany and Russia have shown that the dogma need not be religious in the ordinary sense of the term, but it is dogma, all the same, that prevents the young Russian or the young German from thinking or, at any rate, from saying that he owes nobody anything and that if there is any question of debt, he is the creditor. But there are two objections to the schemes of more or less compulsory indoctrination of the English young with Christian patriotism. First of all, Christianity is not so good an instrument for creating national dogmatic union, for eradicating individualism, as are Communism or Nazism. However it may be interpreted or adjusted, Christianity does insist on the individualism of duty, on the need of laying up individual treasure in heaven. It might be necessary, if Christianity really took, for the sponsors of revival to see that it did not take too well. They should all be made to read Dostoievsky's fable of the Grand Inquisitor before they build up a united, duty-loving, nationally-minded England on Christian foundations. For that kind of building the foundations may be sand. And any political structure into whose foundations Christianity, in any real sense, is built must necessarily be a house divided.

There is another objection. It is not at all certain that there is enough living, concrete religious faith to supply the demands made on it. If it is merely a matter of increasing the dose of vague, sentimental, thoughtless religiosity that colours the English mind, that is one thing and a thing not worth much worrying about. This is already provided for by the educational system. It could be increased without any great strain on the consciences of the typical teacher or the typical army officer.[67]

But what the reformers want is something more definite than that. They want to restore to all parts of the educational system that conviction of the importance of concrete religious belief that was exemplified in the founding of High Church schools like Lancing, Low Church schools like Dean Close. In the Anglican orthodoxy of Oxford and in the reaction of the agnostic intellectuals against that orthodoxy. They want college chapels in Oxford and Cambridge to be centres of definite religious life, which of course involves their being places worth staying away from as well

---

[67] Thus a vigorous critic of many sides of the existing educational system is quite ready to accept religious teaching of this kind, even when it is given by teachers who "not only have . . . ceased to take part in public devotions, but . . . are no longer Christians in the sense that they could, with unqualified belief, recite even the Apostles' Creed. They teach Scripture, and often Christianity, but they are formal and not active Christians. . . . On the balance, the present arrangements tend decisively towards the upbringing of reasonable, fair-minded, unselfish, kindly men and women; towards decency in fact. This may not be a specially religious result. It has, perhaps, little relevance to the great question of the relationship of man to God. It does, however, make this country, for all save the poorest class, the nicest country to live in."—F. H. Spencer: *Education for the People*, pp. 262–3.

as worth attending. But this program will break down the moment any attempt is made to apply it on a great scale. For there has not been religious unity in England since the seventeenth century; so that the specific religious content of a national system would have to be low. Nor is there present at this moment enough religious belief, even of competing kinds, that is lively enough to carry the weight of a new national religion.

To be thus sceptical is not to deny that religion plays a great part in English life. There is a widespread belief that "righteousness exalteth a nation" and there are great deposits of moral conservatism that can be drawn on by the churches in crises like the abdication of Edward VIII. Public morality still has a meaning, and the man in the street does not really resent the preaching of the parson, although he may not pay much attention to it.

As guardians of morals, the clergy, it is true, often seem to the laity a little lacking in proportion, and the Anglican clergy suffer from this fault as do their brethren in other churches and other lands. Nor are they always exempt, whether they be great churchmen or eminent, not to say professionally eminent, laymen, from the weakness that leads to the belief that fearless denunciation (with its accompanying publicity) is a good way of serving God and attracting the attention of Mammon. In England, as in the United States,

> *Smut if smitten*
> *Is front-page stuff.*

But they do not so often strain the toleration of the laity as the American minister tends to do. They have no such dreadful error in judgment as prohibition to explain away. It is true that a great many of the clergy of the Nonconformist churches would have liked to impose prohibition, but they did not succeed. It may not be their fault that they had no Bishop Cannon to live down, but it is accounted to them for righteousness all the same.

Even Christian belief, of a vague kind, still has a powerful hold on the emotions of the Englishman in the street. He is a theist; he has a vague belief in heaven, a very much fainter belief in hell. This is not what was called Christianity in old or New England a century ago. It is much more like the religion of Washington or Lincoln, even of Jefferson or Franklin, than the religion of Jefferson Davis or William Jennings Bryan or the elder Pierpont Morgan. But it is not a negligible force. Can it keep its strength as the older, orthodox religion declines in general authority? Unless the cruse of oil is replenished, must not the thin film of Christian belief and standards dry and crack? It seems likely. And as far as it is true that the English people have been the people of one book, the Bible, they are so no longer. It is only necessary to appeal to get the Bible read as literature when it has ceased to be generally read as the word of God. The English are now more a Bible-buying than a Bible-reading people. Fewer people than ever before in modern English history take the advice of the hymn:

> You should read it every day,
> It will help you on your way.

And if the "Bible and the Bible only is the religion of Protestants," the Protestant religion in England is in a bad way.

It would be rash indeed to expect much accurate knowledge of the Bible from the man or woman in the English street today. Biblical phrases live in common speech (along with phrases erroneously believed to be Biblical, like the motto of Broadcasting House: "And nation shall speak unto nation"). But the book from which they are drawn is less and less known, even in Presbyterian Scotland.[68] It would be convenient but deceptive to attribute the weakening of Biblical knowledge to the negligence of the state schools; it is far more widespread than such an explanation would account for.[69]

[68] Thus I find in an excellent thriller the phrase: "like Gallileo, cared for none of these things." Even those who do not confuse Gallio with Galileo would, in many cases, be hard put to it to tell us what Gallio cared for, or who or what he was.

[69] For some years in Oxford I made an experiment. I used to tell my pupils (nearly all of them from schools where the Bible was "taught")

It seems likely, therefore, that Christianity in England will for a generation or two to come, be the active religious belief of a minority and that minority conscious of its new status, of its duty not to bring about a revival of religion but of a reconversion of England. Outside that minority will be a large, emotional, respectable, and very English majority, who will have a vague reverence for religion, for Christianity, for Christian ethics. This vague reverence will not matter much at most times, but it will matter, if rash, brash, and ill-informed political leaders decide to get rid of this apparently superfluous lumber. Then sentiment if not faith may revive and clerks be again troublesome.

And in the crises of the last three years probably more Englishmen than knew it felt their patriotic stubbornness strengthened, as they contemplated the apparently invincible might of Nazi Germany, by the thought that "except the Lord build the house, they labour in vain that build it." And obviously the Lord did not build the Nazi house. In that solitary but not desolate hour they felt as it is put in the Book of Common Prayer: "There is none other that fighteth for us, but only thou, O God." And, that being so, they did not ask for peace in our time, which, at that moment, was Hitler's time.

---

the story of the Lord Aberdeen under whose very reluctant leadership England entered on the Crimean War. The Prime Minister's conscience was very much disturbed. Although he was a man of real piety, he refused to rebuild the ruinous church on his estate of Haddo. When he died, he left money in his will to his son to build the church. He explained his conduct by a reference to a famous episode in the Old Testament. Only one pupil ever spontaneously spotted the reference. About half did not follow it when it was pointed out to them. Readers may test their own scriptural knowledge themselves.

England as a Democracy

IN THE CITY OF LONDON there stands (or stood before the great raids) more than one warehouse whose rear wall is built upon the old Roman wall of London. Business goes on in buildings whose foundations and parts of whose walls go back to the days of Hadrian, when London was the greatest western city of the Empire that stretched to the Tigris, the Sahara, and the Upper Nile. But it would be rash to do business with the people using these buildings on the assumption that their command of arithmetical method was no better than that of their Roman predecessors. For hundreds of years the smartest businessmen in the world have been coming in to the City of London from Amsterdam and Paris and Frankfurt and Genoa and Smyrna and Boston, and the survival of Roman and mediæval foundations in the city has not prevented it from being the successor of Carthage and Venice. Many English political institutions are like these London warehouses. Under a mediæval guise, they are up-to-date, modern, and efficient instruments of democratic policy. In London, for instance, "the City" survives as an island of local autonomy, with its own police force, with its highly ornamental head, the Lord Mayor; but the real municipal government of London is the County Council, with its unromantically named Chairman. It is in the neo-classical County Hall, in time a twentieth-century building, across the river from the nineteenth-century Gothic Houses of Parliament, that the real municipal business of London is done. If you want to see a really complicated, unrationalized, historically explicable, but not defensible agglomeration of competing local government bodies, the place to go is not London but Cook County, Illinois. The mediæval lawyer, delighting in privileges and peculiars, would be far more at home in Chicago than in London.

The most indisputably English export to the United States (apart from the basic language) was the common law, but if you want to see the old common law in all its picturesque formality, with its fictions and its fads, its delays and uncertainties, the place to look for them is not London, not in the modern Gothic of the Law Courts in the Strand, but in New Jersey. Dickens, or any other law-reformer of a century ago, would feel more at home in Trenton than in London, where, despite the survival of wigs and miniver and maces, the law has been modernized, simplified, made more rapid and efficient; in fact, everything that is desirable except cheap.

The same archaic exterior covering modern interiors marks all aspects of English politics. Change anything except the appearance of things, is the favourite English political method. "Our Sovereign Lord the King" is addressed with all mediæval humility plus a coat of German court servility, but the King is much more a symbol than a power. The House of Lords still goes through its rituals with solemn disregard of the fact that it is now the weakest second chamber in the world. Only in this century was the most important English officer of state, the Prime Minister, given official recognition. The Imperial Parliament at Westminster has ceased to legislate for a great part of the Empire; formally it could undo what it has done, take back all that it gave in the Statute of Westminster, but of course it doesn't. Nor does it pass bills of attainder or confiscate property or deprive people of life or liberty without due process of law, except in very rare cases. But it can do all these things if it likes. For the law is not a vague, sacred body of unalterable principles, revealed in the decisions of a Supreme Court, but what is enacted in Parliament. And Parliament can enact what it chooses.

This is the first and most important difference between the English and American political systems, not the fact that one is a "monarchy" and the other a "republic." It could be argued by the pedantic that the presidency is a much more monarchical institution than the modern English kingship and that, by its acceptance of the unlimited power of sovereign people, the English parliamentary system is more republican than the elaborately divided system of the United States. But these are formal distinctions of the kind that the English mind dislikes making. A far more real distinction is that the English system is planned, with some degree of success, to make it easy to determine what general line of policy shall be carried out and by what persons that general line shall be translated into law and administration. For the period of the life of a Parliament, which is usually about as long as a presidential term, a known group of men have complete power in all important questions to rule England, to commit England to international policies and bargains, to do much or little to change England. More than once, especially in the post-armistice years, the commission given to the victorious politicians has been a commission to do as little as possible, but that is a positive commission all the same. It should not be confused with the situation in which the American people has given authority to a President to do one thing, to Congress to do another, and to the Supreme Court to prevent either Congress or the President from doing anything that is banned by that vague concept of unconstitutionality, or, to translate the term, what the judges don't like. In this case, no one in the United States may want the result that occurs when such a stalemate prevents the adoption of any definite course of action. The electors who (as in 1942) vote to produce a House of Representatives which it is very unlikely will co-operate with the executive with no second thoughts, do not wish to produce a deadlock. But exercising their rights as congressional electors to restrict some of the grant of power they made to the President in 1940, the American electors are behaving in a way in which the English elector never gets the chance to behave. He votes only for one member of Parliament [1] at one time. There are no local issues to confuse the issue, no chance to split the wishes of the voters into several different and possibly conflicting layers.

The result is of course an artificial simplicity. Issues and men do not fall into simple groups of black and white, but for the purposes of English politics it is assumed that they do. To reduce political issues to as few as possible, to reduce the influence of personalities to the few leaders on either side who will, if they succeed, be the government, this is what the English political system is designed to do. For democracy in England means the choice of a government with nearly full powers to do as it likes. Anything, however desirable, which makes this choice more difficult is frowned on. Thus third parties wither away because the English voter dislikes "wasting his vote," and it is, he thinks, wasting his vote to use it to return candidates, however popular, however eminent, however deserving, if they have no chance of real power. Only in a few areas is local tradition or personal prestige strong enough to outweigh this practical consideration. The willingness of the American elector to return to Congress men whose sole claims are local or personal strikes the English voter (or would strike him if he thought about it at all) as frivolous. A seat in the sovereign Parliament is not a reward for local services, or purely personal merit; it is a grant of a mandate to support (or oppose) a national government, concerned with national issues, too serious and too urgent to be complicated by the irrelevant loyalties and hatreds of Buncombe or Dutchess Counties.

It is obvious that a political system designed to put complete power into the hands of a few men whose exercise of that power is only restrained by public opinion and by a tradition of not pushing advantages to the uttermost is very different from a political system where power is deliberately divided; where little or no trust in the discretion of the legislature or the executive is mani-

[1] There are a few constituencies returning more than one member, but they do not affect the general picture.

fest; and where minorities (provided their geographical distribution is right) are given great legal powers to impede the action of majorities. And, on the few occasions when the English and American peoples are forced to notice that their systems differ, each thinks that the other's method of government is profoundly "undemocratic." And each, in his own terms, is right.

For the American is only in part using "democratic" in a political sense; he is referring to a national atmosphere and attitude that is almost indefinable, but which is also unmistakable. It is an atmosphere in which all forms of inequality (except economic inequality) are on the defensive, in which it is assumed, until it is disproved, that any man is as good as any other and that inherent differences in ability will not find their expression thwarted by artificial barriers. And even in the acceptance of inequality in economic levels, there is an American assumption (which may or may not be justified) that such inequality has or recently had a social justification. England is not such a country. It is a country in which inequality is cherished; in which even bodies whose existence is a protest against the more odious forms of privilege make their protest in remarkably unvociferous language.[2]

Not only is America more democratic than England in this sense, but the Englishman admits it and often thinks that such freedom from caste is a great moral and practical asset for the United States.[3] But in the political sense the Englishman, if he

[2] The National Union of Vehicle Builders has on its banner not only elaborate coats of arms of a feudal type but a Latin motto ("*Surgit post nubila Phœbus*"). Coach-builders have, of course, special relations with the luxurious upper classes, but in other lands that would not lead workers to adopt the emblems of aristocracy. The Nine Elms branch of the Associated Society of Locomotive Engineers and Firemen has for its motto a sentiment most admirably describing the attitude of the English trade-unionist: "Men who suffer an injustice with the power to remove it deserve not compassion but contempt" (Sir Walter Citrine: *British Trade Unions*, p. 40).

[3] The belief that in England all the forces of society are organized to make it difficult for an "outsider" to rise embitters the memory of their native land for a good many emigrants.

understood American politics (which he doesn't), would think England more democratic than America, for American constitutional law and practice are designed to minimize inequalities between states, between sections, between majorities and minorities, between individuals, while English practice (there is little law) is designed to give full effect to majority opinion—although there is no greater inequality than that of mere numbers.

The apparent docility and self-distrust of the English worker should not be taken too seriously. It is often the fruit of a realistic if cynical acceptance of the fact that progress is not made, in fact, in great jumps, and that it is foolish to throw away the crust of minor but tangible gains for the loaf of perfect equality which can be seen in the water. The English worker has, he thinks, made more progress, made more substantial gains, than the worker of any other European country, and if the comparison with the United States and, still more, with New Zealand is not so favourable, the Englishman knows that he and his rulers are not exploiting the same natural resources as are the Americans or New Zealanders.[4]

This apparent resignation naturally arouses the somewhat contemptuous surprise of the observer from another democratic country, France or America or Scotland, where an insistence on equality is the basic democratic attitude. And it is true that, as Chesterton put it, the English working man is less interested in the equality of men than in the inequality of horses.[5]

[4] The great economic prestige of the United States suffered a blow from which it has not totally recovered when English emigrants, caught in the economic blizzard of 1929, found that "America the Golden" was so backward, not to say brutal, in her attitude to the victims of the trade cycle. The survival in American *mores* of the rural attitude that unemployment was a matter of ill-doing was a shock to a thoroughly urbanized society.

[5] "An aristocracy of wealth is the only kind he recognizes, he is too material-minded to be an equalitarian. He compromises and goes all out for liberty instead of equality. To be free is a much hollower achievement than to be equal; but it is possible of achievement, and engenders self-respect and saves face. And he is given as much of it as possible. 'Freedom'

But although the Englishman is not enamoured of equality, he has a real passion for liberty and law. *"Dieu et mon droit"* is the motto of more than the King. And law as a guardian of liberty is respected, although the general English respect for law and order is fairly new. Law today is not thought of as something that has come down from heaven, but as the result of the continued expression of the will of the English people; and the making and alteration of the law, the continued exercise of an authority derived from the people's will, is what the Englishman means by democracy. The technical means whereby this will is expressed is the sovereignty of Parliament, and Parliament, in turn, is expected to transfer the active exercise of that power to a small group of its own members called the Cabinet, chosen by one of its own members, the Prime Minister. Under all the feudal trappings and elaborate procedure lies this simple assumption, that the majority of Parliament represents the majority of the people,[6] and, as the people cannot exercise direct power, no more can Parliament, so that the decision what laws are to be made, altered, and repealed, as well as the practical business of administration, is the business

---

is recognized as something to which every Englishman is entitled. If only a man is brave enough on any given occasion to 'stand up for his rights,' he will receive no injury when it comes to the point—the soldiers will not touch him, and the authorities will admire him. He is content to be free to obey the law. But the law must give him scope. And it does give him scope to indulge in the most dignified and the most telling of all forms of action—the Strike. Possessing this, he wants to leave all general political ideas aside."—J. S. Collis: *An Irishman's England,* pp. 138-9.

[6] The present distribution of seats, made after the last war, is out of date and Parliament is not fairly representative. Although there are (except in Ulster) no permanent vested interests in gerrymandering such as exist in Manhattan or the rural districts in most Eastern states, the electoral system is obsolete. It has been calculated that the change in less than a million votes in the area around London and one or two other big towns is enough to turn the Opposition into the Government. All over the south of England the evenly distributed Liberal and Labour minority is almost as effectually deprived of representation as the Republicans in the Solid South. But it is doubtful whether in any recent election the general will of the English people, that this party and not that should govern, has been thwarted.

of the Cabinet, as long as the House of Commons supports it. And the House of Commons is organized on a party basis to secure that such support will be given. It is only in the rarest circumstances that a House of Commons elected to support a government overthrows it. Normally it is a general election, in which the people shows that it has changed its mind, that turns the Opposition into the Government, with powers that are unlimited by law, however much moderation in their use is enjoined by custom.

It is this basic difference in the function of Parliament and of Congress that explains and justifies the great difference in the English and American attitudes to Members of Parliament and Representatives and Senators. Parliament is a more important institution in the English system than Congress is in the American, because it does not have to share its powers with a President or a Court over which it has no direct control. But Members of Parliament are, as a class, less important than Members of Congress because the Members of Parliament are expected to give away most of their powers to a small group, while no one expects a Congressman or a Senator to be a mere voting machine, which is what a good private Member of Parliament usually is. The English voter is primarily choosing a Prime Minister, and that primary function is far more important than the secondary functions that a Member may carry out if he wants to. In doubtful areas, where the margin between the parties is normally small, it pays a Member to have a private hold on the loyalty of his electors as well as the public hold which he gets from being the regular candidate of the locally dominant party. The few hundred votes he may pick up on his own account, by being helpful over pensions, local government issues, local charities, local sports, are valuable. If he is good at showing voters over Parliament, or arranging that a deputation can see a Minister to express some local grievance, he is a more useful candidate to his party than if he was simply a good party man who is never in the way and never out of the way, who votes when asked and does not ask to speak. The perfectly silent, perfectly docile, perfectly unambitious Member would be the ideal of the Whips if such Admirable Crichtons had election-appeal. But, unfortunately, the type of orator who is eloquent at home and willingly silent in the House of Commons is extinct. The type of speaker who is admirably equipped to answer questions at public meetings [7] is usually the type who insists on asking questions in the House of Commons and not the nice prepared, co-operative questions which the Minister is eager to answer, but the nasty, prying, awkward questions that force the Minister to let the cat out of the bag, or to indulge in such palpable evasions that general and, from the government's point of view, unhealthy curiosity is aroused. The gallant fighter of doubtful battles in the constituencies is seldom the modest violet when he is elected. He wants publicity; he may have causes or hobbies to advance; he wants office; he is a nuisance, but he is also an asset.

What the party machines really like is shown by the kind of candidate they provide for the safe seats which even the dullest, most docile, least photogenic candidate cannot lose. The Labour Party may, under pressure, give one of its safe mining seats to a party intellectual like Sidney Webb or to a party leader like Ramsay MacDonald or Mr. Dalton, but left to themselves, the local Labour parties very humanly use these seats as rewards for faithful service to the trade-union movement. The superannuated union agents vote straight, so what more is wanted? A lot more is wanted,

---

[7] "Heckling," the badgering of a candidate by questions, is, or was, one of the most entertaining aspects of British democracy (it was at its highest level in Scotland). It was also one of the most usefully educational aspects of the system. When Lord Palmerston or Asquith went down to their electors and answered questions put to them by the local dialecticians, they were both learning and teaching. Quick, apt, and even honest answers have won votes on such occasions. The increase in the size of the electorate, the decline in the number of close contests, the domination of the electorates by women who do not heckle though they do vote, all these changes have reduced the importance of this profoundly democratic institution. I think, too, that the habit of Labour Party zealots in Scotland of substituting noise and catcalls for questions was not helpful to the institution or to the Labour Party.

but why should any particular district have to put itself out to provide the raw materials for national leaders? The local party leaders cannot see their duties in this matter in any very different light from the primary electors in many American states who may choose Senators for all sorts of reasons except those affecting the competence of the Senate to carry out its most important duties.

But more revealing is the way in which Conservative members for safe seats are chosen. Even more revealing, for the Conservative Party is normally the governing party; it has far more safe seats, and they are far safer. You may convince the electors of a mining division like Seaham Harbour that it is their duty to turn against the Labour Party to save their country from financial ruin, but nothing would make the voters of Bournemouth turn against the party of Lord Baldwin and Mr. Chamberlain. So the Conservative nomination is in such places as identical with election as the Democratic nomination is in Texas. The first result is that a great many seats are sold. It is true that in theory and in history books the sale of seats ceased with, at latest, the second Reform Bill (1867). It is true that since the passing of the fifteenth amendment (1870) it has been unconstitutional to deny the right of citizens of the United States to vote "on account of race, color, or previous condition of servitude." The truths are of the same kind, only Americans, being irreverent people, do not put on so good a pretence of believing them as the English do.

The first requisite of a would-be Member of Parliament in many English districts is that he should have money in his purse and should be willing to give quite a lot of it to the local Conservative Association. The safer the seat, and the less normal party expenditure is called for, the higher the price of the nomination. As Lord Dundreary says, it is one of those things no fellow can understand. At least, no right-minded person. Low-minded persons may be inclined to reflect on the truth that the safer a bet, the worse price you get from bookmakers. Further reflections on this state of affairs is impeded by the English law of libel, but the fact is that a good many Members are in Parliament because they could afford to make handsome contributions to the local party funds and for no other reasons at all.[8] That such transactions were politically immoral, that the Central Office of the Conservative Party tried to keep the more outrageous transactions from being completed, that there were regular threats from indignant and indigent young Conservatives that if something wasn't done about it, they would do something pretty dramatic, did not affect the vitality of the system. That is, the local Conservative bosses are in the position of state legislators before the direct election of Senators. They can give away a seat to a distinguished statesman; sometimes they do, but they don't like it.[9]

The veterans of the trade-union movement passing the evening of their days in Parliament, and the Conservative gentlemen occupying the best seats that money can buy,[10] do not, of course, provide the governing class. The Cabinet and the auxiliaries of the Cabinet have other claims on the public attention than the possession of surplus funds. But the fact that seats are so safe means that run-of-the-mill Members have nothing to do but vote. This is a basic contrast with Congress. No district is so safe that a completely do-nothing member is possible. The district or state may never

[8] The *Evening Standard,* which, like all Lord Beaverbrook's papers, is often entertainingly un-English, used to publish the current prices of safe seats. These revelations should have made the faces of the vendors red, but as many of them were in the liquor business, they were probably red as it was. There was no sign of a break in the market as occasionally occurs in America when a reform administration is in the offing. This suggests that no serious danger of reform was felt by the market-wise businessmen interested in this commodity.

[9] Neither did their American prototypes. Mark Twain's Mr. Bigler in *The Gilded Age* reacted just like the Conservative Association of, shall we say, Eatanswill. "I tell you what it is, gentlemen, I shall go in for reform. Things have got pretty mixed when a legislature will give away a United States senatorship." But Mr. Bigler was frightened before he was hurt. His English brethren are neither frightened nor hurt.

[10] The Conservative Members for the safe seats are not all elderly. The essential condition of membership being money, and young men with money of their own or who have married rich wives and who have political ambitions not being unknown, there are some young members for safe seats, but there are not many.

return anything but a Democrat or a Republican, but even in the few states where there is no direct primary [11] a would-be Senator or Congressman has to face, as a rule, keen competition from within his own party. He cannot afford to fall asleep at the switch. He must do a great many local political chores which take up his time and energy. These chores may not be of great interest to the American people as a whole, but they are of importance to the voters who send the politician to Congress. He can afford to neglect the censures of the metropolitan press like the Irish M.P. who, when asked if he had seen what *The Times* had said of him, replied: "No and I don't care. What does the *Skibbereen Eagle* say of me?" It is a very rare member of either house who can afford to neglect this part of his congressional duties, as more than one eminent politician has found to his cost.[12] But not only must a Congressman or Senator do odd jobs, he must or, at any rate, he usually does do real jobs as well. The claim of experts like Mr. (Robert) Luce that Congress takes its legislative duties seriously and performs them well is justified. When the lack of public interest in their labours is taken into consideration, when the lack of public discrimination is allowed for, when the penalities of defeat for re-election are assessed, it is surprising that Senators and Congressmen work as hard, as competently, and as honestly as they do. The American voter, in fact, gets a better Congress than he deserves.[13] The English voter often gets less from his member than

[11] The unsatisfactory state of the nominating machinery in England may justify an attempt to adopt the primary system, since it is the ease with which a small clique can give away the nomination that is the secret of the present racket. To give the voters a voice in the choice of candidates is, in many parts of England, the only way of giving the voters any real political power.

[12] Mr. Tinkham of Massachusetts was not like most Congressmen, but he was very exceptional.

[13] The Senate might consider erecting a statue to Ross of Kansas, who, at the known risk of complete political and financial ruin, voted for the acquittal of President Andrew Johnson. It is obvious that the voters of Kansas did not deserve Ross any more than the voters of Nebraska deserved Norris.

he deserves to get; he, in some cases, gets nothing but general support for a Government or an Opposition, but, after all, that is the basic duty of a member. Anything more is a work of supererogation.

The House of Commons has, however, a further function to fulfil and one of the greatest importance. It is a kind of electoral college combined with a national convention. But it cannot do its work as an electoral college—that is, in effect, choose the Prime Minister—unless it has already done its work as a national convention. It must have something to go on in its work of putting the seal of success or failure on the aspirant to Cabinet rank. And the House of Commons cannot do this job well if its membership includes fewer and fewer of the politically ambitious and able young men of the nation. Every instance of a safe Labour seat given for irrelevant services rendered, every case of a Conservative seat sold, every disillusionment of the young and hopeful politician tells, in the not very long run, against the efficiency of the basic English political institution, Cabinet government. And no one looking at the recent House of Commons can have much doubt that they have not been representative of the abilities, the energies, and the views of the young men and women of this country. The Conservatives are supposed to show more courage than the Labour Party in giving young Members a chance to develop their talents in minor office, but the Conservatives have to exercise their choice among the Members of Parliament the present system gives them. They may pick the best of the runners, but there may be very few of the entries who are even plausible imitations of Derby winners. The American locality rule, perhaps, works even more effectively to keep first-class abilities out of Congress, but no one suggests that only in Congress can governing talent be found.[14]

Here again the decline of the Liberal Party has had unfortunate consequences. That party had a good many safe seats, but they

[14] Only one President elected in this century had ever served in Congress (Harding); only one serving Senator has ever been elected President (Harding). Only one member of the present Roosevelt Cabinet has ever served in Congress (Mr. Hull).

were not as safe as the standard Conservative or Labour safe seat is. It was usually necessary in order to induce a Scottish or Welsh constituency to accept an outsider that he should have serious claims on the respect of the voters. There was no equivalent of the automatic ratification of the choice of the local Miners Union or of the Conservative Association. So Asquith and Morley and Churchill and Gladstone and Trevelyan and a score of others were accepted and returned by electors who would have gagged at—well, their name is nearly Legion. Young men of great abilities were brought into Parliament in each great Liberal triumph or given an early opportunity to show their abilities. Compare the new members of 1906, the last great Liberal triumph, with the new Labour men of 1923 or 1929 or the Conservative rank and file of 1918, 1924, 1931, 1935! The Liberals did practise, to a respectable extent, the policy of a career open to talent; the two parties which since the last war have shared the basic responsibility for the government of the country have put ability, originality, and youth very far down indeed in their list of priorities. And if a monument to this policy is required, look at the present House of Commons.

In the choice of candidates, considerations of "availability" play some part. On the whole, it is probably a handicap to be either a Jew or a Catholic, although Jews and Catholics play a reasonably large part in Parliament. In a few constituencies it is convenient to the party managers if a good Jewish or Catholic candidate wins enough of his friends to offset the losses he may cause the party among normally loyal party members. But as a rule the Jewish or Catholic candidate has to be stronger than the run-of-the-mill candidate of his party.[15] But he need not be much stronger.

[15] The only Conservative candidate to lose a seat in Scotland in 1918 was a distinguished soldier of a great local family who was a Catholic. His son and nephew-in-law are both very distinguished soldiers in this war. It would be interesting to see if the son suffered his father's fate. A more odd case is the refusal of the Conservatives to renominate the popular head of a great Catholic family in Lancashire because he was a Catholic. It may be hazarded that an influx of Orange voters of fairly recent Irish origin had something to do with this ostracism.

But religious availability in the representative English (as apart from Irish, Scotch, Welsh) constituency is not very important. All religions are represented in all parties and in all districts. The old racial blocks of voters, mostly Irish, are dissolving and even Liverpool and Glasgow have now far fewer citizens who vote on opposite sides, as a means of refighting the Battle of the Boyne, than they had a generation ago.

An English Member of Parliament has recently recounted the reaction of a young American visitor to the House of Commons when he learned that an M.P. need not live in the area he represents. "But that's undemocratic," was his comment. And from the American point of view it is *undemocratic*, for, to the American, "democratic" has a flavour of equality to be produced, if necessary, by legal restrictions on political choice. But to the Englishman "democratic" has the flavour of a means of ensuring, as far as possible, that the general direction of public policy shall be in accordance with the will of the people and that the will of the people shall have as few obstacles as possible put in its way by law or custom. So that the custom whereby the electors of an English parliamentary division have complete freedom of choice (outside the small class of persons legally disqualified, a class whose chief members are peers, undischarged bankrupts, and lunatics). Any person eligible to sit in Parliament is eligible to sit for any part of the United Kingdom. The voters can shop around. But the American voter is by law, and still more strictly by custom, forced to patronize his "naborhood store" and if that has only run-of-the-mill or even less attractive statesmen to hand, well, they go to Congress to represent the voters of the sovereign state of Winnemac. The "locality rule" and still more the spirit behind it are one of those barriers to Anglo-American understanding that are almost impossible to climb. To an American, custom that debars any person not a resident in a district to represent it in Congress seems democratic. To the Englishman, it seems highly undemocratic since it limits the free choice of the voter; it seems silly as well. To the Englishman, to limit the elector's choice this way in the name of equality or democracy is like limiting the choice of the owner of the Yankees to players normally resident in the Bronx. Such legislation would be democratic in the sense that it would improve the chances of other baseball clubs in the World Series, but it would not provide as good a team, anywhere, as the Yankees produce, thanks to their liberty of choice. And the English government is always playing in the World Series and must not have its hands tied.

The freedom of choice of the elector does emphasize, in the public mind, the primary role of Parliament and it matters little whether there is no locality rule because Parliament has such prestige, or whether Parliament has such prestige because it is not absurd to pretend that it does contain most of the potential governors of the realm.[16]

Although the prestige of politics is not what it was, it is still great and the Mother of Parliaments could not be what she is, the healthiest member of her now dwindling family, if politics were not an amusement or an avocation that had a great power of appeal to the average Englishman.

"The average American seems to take it for granted that any one who is keenly interested in politics and who is associated with active political work is of necessity ambitious to hold public office."[17] This dictum is perhaps less true than it was twenty years ago, when Mr. Coolidge could declare that "the business of the United States is business" and let it go at that with pretty general approval. But it is still true that active, practical work in politics undertaken by people who have no wish for or no chance of office, or even of power, is much more common in England than in the United States. The long domination of practical politics in the

[16] Two of the leading members of the present government had no political position until they were made ministers. But although Sir John Anderson and Mr. Ernest Bevin do not owe their national position to their parliamentary position, they have both to be in Parliament all the same. A locality rule would have kept them out of Parliament, which would thus be weakened, not strengthened.

[17] Nicholas Murray Butler: *Across the Busy Years*, Vol. I, p. 366.

United States by the spoils system may have led to the identification of politics and jobs, but however that may be, it is common in England for men and women who want nothing from the politicians (who, in any case, have not got much to give away) to do a great deal of the work done in America by the regular organization but not, as a rule, done there by anybody else at all. They get out the voters; they keep alive the local party organization; they pay party dues; they are the public opinion of the party. This type of citizen is commoner in the Labour Party and in what is left of the Liberal Party than in Conservative ranks, but he exists there, too. And his place is taken to some extent by the normal organization of English upper- and middle-class life. The justices of the peace, the local notables, the members of hospital boards, the members of county councils, are, without any formal organization, the Conservative "machine." But in all ranks of society, in both sexes, there is a lively interest in politics and a readiness to take real trouble to make the party effective or to influence the policy and personnel of the party that it is hard to parallel in America.

Of course these zealous party workers are not a majority or even a numerically large section of the population. But they are numerous enough to affect the political thinking and voting of the great majority of citizens whose political duty is, they think, done when they have voted or grumbled or written a letter to the editor. Pure idiocy, in the Greek sense, complete indifference to politics, complete absence of political views, even silly views, is fairly rare in England.[18] The convention, as far as it still exists, that deprecates political discussion in English social circles has its justification, not in the fact that politics are a boring subject, but in the belief that they lead to rows—which is, alas! probably untrue. The same con-

[18] I can remember the astonishment and naïve sense of scandal which I experienced when on my first visit to the United States, in 1925, I found that many of my Harvard friends had never voted, never intended to vote, had no interest in politics at all, and were yet instructors in history, economics, etc. I found it hard to believe that young men who took no interest in the politics of twentieth-century Massachusetts were likely to be sound guides, whatever their learning, to the politics of other lands and other ages.

vention in American society seems to me to arise from the general belief that, except to a few professionals or cranks, politics are dull.

The general interest in politics is not, of course, an unmixed blessing. It accounts for the existence of a large number of crank societies, for the abuse of the national habit of judging other nations by English standards, of regarding the political life of the world as an endless prize-giving with certificates for good conduct being issued from London or Manchester to gratified political children. This is the side the non-English inhabitants of the world see and naturally resent. What they do not see is the permanent organization of English public opinion to criticize British internal and external policy, the fostering in the Englishman's mind of that belief that what his country does is his business, the preparation of the man in the street for the acceptance of duties, not in a spirit of blind obedience but of critical loyalty to the community. The role of the Member of Parliament who does not get office quickly or who does not make his mark in opposition is discouraging. He has not the automatic opportunity to achieve power and so interest in his job that comes to the Congressman who is lucky enough to get elected after his party has been a long time the minority and so badly provided with seniors occupying all the important committee posts. Thus the Democratic landslide of 1932 and the new Republican gains of 1942 make the career of a new member more interesting than it would be in England, save for the most exceptional newcomer.[19]

A young man with his way to make in the world finds it hard to

[19] When the Labour Party became the official Opposition in 1922, most of its Members of Parliament were newcomers, so that men like John Wheatley were able to create important parliamentary positions for themselves at once. But this is unusual. More common is the experience of Lord Wedgwood. "The enthusiastic arrive, bursting with energy, and the cold tap of reality chills their heart. 'What can we do if we have no chance to bring in Bills or move resolutions?' I once said in despair to John Morley. 'The function of the private member,' coldly replied the sage, 'is to popularize in the country the policy of his Party.' "—*Testament to Democracy*, p. 27.

have to wait for ten or fifteen years before his political career has any of the stability or rewards of a profession. So Parliament, partly for the reasons discussed, is far more full of rich men than is good for it. But the experience of France has shown that wealth will find a way even though it is not permitted or encouraged to appear in the forefront of the political scene. And the domination of English political life by the wealthy reflects what was, until this war, the national scepticism of the safety, or desirability, or practicability of profound changes. In that sense it was democratic; it was what the people wanted; although that may be no consolation to a spectator who does not identify majority rule with the good ordering of the state.

But, it may be objected, even if we admit that the English people wanted and deserved the government they got, there are important elements in English politics that are not even formally democratic. There is the Crown; there is the hereditary peerage.

The position of the monarchy is very difficult to describe. First of all, the contrast between the facts and the fiction is so striking that it breeds excessive scepticism. Because the King obviously has a position very different from that imputed to him by the language of the law, by the royal initials on postal equipment or by the emphasis on "His Majesty's Ship," the office may be too complacently reduced to one of mere representation; the English King may be thought to survive like a King Archon in Athens or a Rex Sacrificulus in Rome as a kind of national powerless medicine-man, whose title is still used because of atavistic superstition. The English invention of the constitutional monarch, which was for a short time the most widespread form of government in the history of the world, has proved to be less exportable than it seemed towards the end of the nineteenth century. So the accompanying theory that made of the constitutional king a mere hereditary embodiment of national power can now be discarded. No king is merely that, although hereditary monarchy is one of the most effective methods of securing that religious awe for the political form of the state which appears to be indispensable. It can be secured in a republic by encouraging a very conservative reverence for the form of the state. The worship of the Constitution by the American people; the reverence for its priestly interpreters, the judges of the Supreme Court; the truly Roman deference to the will of "We, the People of the United States," expressed in the sacred constitutional text; these are admirable solutions for the problem of finding a republican substitute for the more spontaneous reverence of mankind for a hereditary ruler. But the institutions must have real power; they must not obviously be mere devices to provide, with as little expenditure as possible of true power and true prestige, a cheap substitute for the divinity that once hedged a king. It is not wholly an accident that the only governmental system which collapsed altogether under German conquest was the French Republic, in which the problem of giving dignity to the governmental system and encouraging reverence in the governed was not so much badly solved as declared not to exist. Parliament and President were swept away; the one office not deliberately made weak and cheap, the rank of Marshal of France, alone had any power of serving as a rallying-point. You cannot beat something with nothing, or replace the traditional reverence for the King, which is an inheritance of all European peoples, with something so lacking in emotional appeal as a mere political system without dignity. No king was found to play the Pétain.

There can be no doubt that the English monarchy has a power of expressing and representing national emotion that may be above rational explanation. The English kingship is, from one point of view, very old. King George VI is a descendant of Alfred the Great and of William the Conqueror, as well as of even more remote and less certainly historical figures in the Celtic background of Scotland. The kingship is woven into English history as it is woven into the history of all old European peoples. But, in another sense, the English kingship is new. The House of Hanover is the first of those dynasties brought in to lend respectability to a new political system, to provide a façade for the drab structure of English politics. George I had some hereditary claims, but not too many; he was a foreigner, but not a complete foreigner; he was not a cipher either. And the modern monarchy has become more national, more intimately a part of the national life, while losing, at the same time, its more dangerous powers and so its graver temptations to offend the nation's pride or prejudices.

That there has been a great change in the character of the monarchy since the eighteenth century is obvious. The office held by President Roosevelt is more like the office held by President Washington than the office held by King George VI is like the office held by King George III. There have even been great changes in the office since the time of Queen Victoria. It is true that the recent boom in plays, stories, anecdotes, and even serious studies of the role of Queen Victoria has concealed the fact that she lost most of the political battles she fought, and that if she was a great woman or a great ruler, we are going to be at a loss to describe St. Joan or Peter the Great. It will not do to confuse the roles of Peel or Gladstone with Victoria's. Peels and Gladstones are rare; women like Queen Victoria are not rare, only they are not queens. But Queen Victoria did represent a royal attitude, if not a royal power, that is dead today. Even more dead is the attitude of her son, Edward VII. For he had not his mother's industry or good sense and he took most seriously just that part of the royal function that, in the not very long run, has least future, the role of chief of "society." As "society" becomes less and less important, less and less unified, as far as it provides the monarch with standards of behaviour, standards of life, with the public opinion of his immediate circle, it weakens the monarchy. No monarchy that takes the court too seriously, that forgets that a king is too exalted to be a snob or even to be socially discriminating, is safe or powerful for long. And because King George V did not give the impression of being smart and because most of his tastes were common, he was as important in the history of the monarchy as his grandmother. For she, while she reluctantly and often unconsciously gave up her most important political powers, preserved autocratic habits that in modern times would have made her profoundly unpopular. (After all, she was only uncritically worshipped when she was very old and when English complacency was at its worst.)

The abdication of King Edward VIII revealed, in a flash, the true position of the monarchy. "Loyalty" was not the blind, undiscriminating, unshakable adhesion to one sacred individual, designated by the mystical choice of hereditary succession. It was a much more rational, critical, and, politically, healthier emotion. The King held his crown on tacit conditions, one of which was that he should represent, publicly, certain standards of conduct which his subjects expected to be respected if not obeyed. The bewilderment of the unfortunate monarch, led astray by the language of solemn adulation to which he had been accustomed, was natural. The solemn humbug of many of the leading actors in the tragicomedy was nauseating. But survivors of the old Whig tradition might have smiled, grimly, at this sudden revival of the contract theory. It was (despite Mr. Bernard Shaw) the King of England, not Mr. Stalin, who held his job at very brief notice. Such persons as believed in the language of the Court Circular and, still more, in the language of court journalism were naturally shocked. Such persons as could not forbear from imputing to the monarch great designs and formidable powers were distressed; the type of historian and political writer who thinks that King Edward VII had great diplomatic power and designs also often thinks that King Edward VIII had great social powers and designs. But the English are a moderate, reasonable, and, in politics, eminently practical people; their attitude to their nominal hereditary ruler is the despair alike of the doctrinaire republican and the doctrinaire royalist.

Until comparatively recent times this fact was concealed by the survival of a curious phenomenon called "loyalty." This had two meanings, one important and unfortunate, one irritating but unimportant. To be "loyal," in English speech a generation ago, meant one of two things: it meant preferring English interests and sentiments to the interests and sentiments of your own country, or it meant a highly uncritical, superstitious, and verbally servile devotion, not to the institution of the Crown, but to the royal family, a devotion extending from the monarch to the most remote Princess of Hohenstiel-Schwangau who had been taken into the royal cousinhood by Queen Victoria.

The first type of "loyalty" was an aspect of a decaying imperialism. To a naïve Englishman of the great Victorian age, there was nothing comic or outrageous in describing Parnell as "disloyal." That Irishmen or Cypriots or Canadians had a duty to be "loyal" to England that was more imperative than their duty to be loyal to Ireland or the Greek community or Canada was an absurd doctrine widely believed in even by intelligent Englishmen. And in places like Trinity College, Dublin, or Toronto, they found Irish and Canadian allies.[20]

The arrogance of the old Victorian attitude to "loyalism" has pretty completely evaporated except in the most backward quarters. It is, in any case, rather difficult to justify the loyalist in, say, Cyprus, who is so enamoured of the beauties of British rule that he refuses to think of himself as a Greek without, incidentally, justifying Quisling and his fellows.

But "loyalty" had another meaning. It meant loyalty to the throne; it was set against Whig tepidity or republican irreverence. Lord Palmerston, Lord John Russell, were lacking in loyalty; Mr. Joseph Chamberlain in his early days was positively disloyal. It was even considered that Mr. Gladstone, for all his reverence for the throne, was disloyal in not giving in to Queen Victoria's whims. There was a time, and a not very remote time,

[20] Arthur Griffith, the founder of Sinn Fein, put the distinction very clearly. An Irishman who defended the union with England on the ground that it was good for Ireland was a good if misguided Irishman. The Irishman who defended the union because it was good for England was a traitor or what the English called a "loyalist." It should be noted that the Ulstermen are far too sensible to be real loyalists. They refuse to sacrifice any of their real or alleged interests to English needs. Their first duty is to Ulster.

when political duty for millions of men was summed up in loyalty to one hereditary ruler, who might be remote, who might be mad, who might be a foreigner, but who was, nevertheless, the Lord's anointed. So Italians and Frenchmen and Flemings as well as all kinds of Spaniards felt that their political duty was obedience to the imbecile and impotent last of the Spanish Habsburgs, Charles II, Duke of Burgundy and Milan, Count of Flanders, and King of the Two Sicilies as well as King of Castile, León, Aragon and Lord of the Indies. But those days are gone. The belief that it is to a family and not to a nation that loyal service is due is dead. A really legitimist war in the old sense, men fighting over the rightful succession to the crown, is an inconceivable phenomenon today. Even the Carlists of Navarre are partisans of a cause as well as of a family. And in Greece, where the question of republic and monarchy has played a great part, it was not mere devotion to the hereditary succession of the eldest son that made the enemies of Venizelos defend the cause of George II.

In England the case is hardly worth arguing. The origin of the title of the House of Windsor, the kind of hold it has acquired on the public affections, the terms on which that hold continues, all these make a political relation very unlike that defended by the dwindling legitimist parties of Europe who refused to recognize the revolutionary work of Napoleon, Bismarck, Lenin, Hitler. The foreigner may be taken in by words, but the relationship between the English King and the English people is a relationship far more modern and far better fitted to the needs of the times than the obsolete language and the obsolete trappings of the court suggest.[21] The first utility of the monarchy is the provi-

[21] "This difference of temper in respect to loyalty to the dynasty, or even to the State, as between the English and the German people, appears in the main to be a short-coming on the English side. The English fall short in point of self-sacrifice and abnegation for the sake of dynastic politics and the advancement of the reigning house and its patrician bureaucracy. By contrast with the naïve patriotic solidarity of the German people, the allegiance of the English might even be called a mitigated insubordination rather than loyalty tempered with self-interest. Yet it is more a difference

sion of a centre of emotional unity that *has* to be provided. This in a revolutionary state, can be done by the Leader; in Russia, by the combination of the legend of the Revolution, its leader, his successor, and the whole Russian past in one emotionally most powerful attitude. In a strongly established republican state it can be provided by institutions. Americans, gazing with reverential awe on the sacred texts of the Constitution and the Declaration of Independence in the shrine in the Library of Congress, are being subjected, at a more dignified and more rational level, to the same emotion-building experience as the Englishman moved by a royal procession.

But the monarchy fulfils another and possibly more important role. It is the sole legal link between the various dominions (England being a dominion herself). It is possible that a substitute for that legal link could be found in some treaty formula. It is a little more difficult to see how a substitute is to be found for the emotional link that the Crown does, in fact, provide. "Influence is not government," said Washington. But influence, not government, is all that holds the British dominions together, and influence is far more easily embodied in a person than it is definable in a formula. "The mystic chords of memory," to quote the famous phrase in which Lincoln, at Seward's suggestion, appealed to the South in his first inaugural, are more easily made to vibrate by a man than by a text.

It may be and has been argued that these advantages are too dearly bought. If important political powers are put in the hands

---

in degree than in kind. The English appear to have lost something in the course of these centuries, which the Germans have retained or even re-enforced,—something in the way of an habitual abandon of deference to the majesty of the State and the pretensions of the sovereign. There is less devotion in the habitual outlook and temper of the English. There is, no doubt, a good and serviceable residue of the honorable obsequiousness still left in the frame of mind habitual among the English; but it has the appearance of having been left over, in some sense by oversight, and even what there is left over of it is subject to a limit of tolerance imposed by an afterthought of self-interest."—Thorstein Veblen: *Imperial Germany*, pp. 103–4.

of one man simply because he is the eldest surviving son of his father, this is, indeed, undemocratic. If these powers are held, regardless of the will of the people, which may have changed since the accession of the monarch, that is, from the point of view of an English democrat, a contradiction of the basic principle that all governments derive their just powers from the continuing consent of the governed.[22] The abdication crisis showed that the continuing consent can be withdrawn, and recent English political history has shown that the political powers of the Crown are not fundamental or decisive. The most important royal office is that of nominating a new Prime Minister. But it very seldom happens that the King has any choice. The leader of the party victorious at the elections is designated for the office by the voters as directly as the next President of the United States is designated to the electoral colleges of the states. For the King to have a real choice is as rare as for a presidential election to be so indecisive that Congress has to choose.

In 1923, when the illness of Bonar Law and the split in the Conservative Party made it uncertain who was the obvious successor, George V did choose between Lord Curzon and Mr. Baldwin. But it was hardly a choice of persons. It was the application of a constitutional principle. The King decided—and rightly decided—that a peer who could not speak in the House of Commons was incapable of meeting the basic condition of eligibility to the office of Prime Minister, that of securing constant and loyal support from the House of Commons. King George decided a question of categories, not a question of persons—and, in his de-

[22] It is not quite so clear that it is undemocratic in the American sense. For not only did the American people tie its hands by accepting a constitution that, in many things, enables the will of the minority to prevail, but the political role of the Supreme Court involves the survival into a totally different political situation of the will of a past majority, expressed in the election of the President or Presidents who nominated the effective majority of the Court. Thus should the New Deal be overthrown in 1944, the Supreme Court which Mr. Roosevelt has nominated, will remain in office and power for quite a long time, as the Harding-Coolidge-Hoover Court survived until about 1938.

cision, showed that he had noted the increasingly democratic temper of the age. The second instance in which a royal decision was apparently important was the choice, in 1931, of Mr. Ramsay MacDonald as the head of the new "National" government which followed on the resignation of the Labour government of Mr. Ramsay MacDonald. But any other decision would have been a real royal usurpation. For Mr. MacDonald had become Prime Minister in 1929 because he could command a majority of the House of Commons, not because there had been a great national plebiscite in favour of the Labour Party. There was no Labour majority, as such, in the House of Commons.[23] The House of Commons was no longer prepared to support a Labour government. It was prepared to support a MacDonald government. These two obvious facts were not ignored by King George V. His only reason for not acting on his knowledge would have been a conviction that behind the House of Commons that wanted a new non-Labour government under Mr. MacDonald, there was a country that wanted either a continuation of a Labour government without Mr. MacDonald, or a National government without Mr. MacDonald as Prime Minister. But the subsequent election showed that the country and the King were of one mind. And to protest against the decision of the King is to move perilously near the French republican doctrine that the sovereign people is only sovereign when it wants what you want.

As a hereditary political force the monarch is weak, and if it be admitted that, somehow or other, emotional reverence for the form of the state must be provided, the English monarchy provides it in a less conservative form than the American Constitution.

But the monarchy is not the only hereditary political institu-

[23] The Labour Party had more members than the Conservatives, but to get a secure majority it needed Liberal support. More people voted for Conservative candidates (that is, for continuing Mr. Baldwin as Prime Minister) than voted for Labour candidates (that is, for making Mr. MacDonald Prime Minister). But more people voted against Mr. Baldwin than voted for him.

tion in the country. There is the peerage. And the peerage is the political aspect of a class, the nobility, whose intermingling of social and political pre-eminence is the unique English contribution to the solution of a problem that complicated the evolution of every great European state. On the Continent the solution generally adopted was the preservation of the economic and social privileges of the nobility in return for a complete surrender of political power. The Prussian Junkers thought they had made, and had made, a good bargain.

Und der König absolut
Wenn er uns den Willen tut.

But the King of Prussia had, in fact, the power of political decision, of peace and war. He could not easily tamper with the privileges of the nobility, but he did not need to pay much attention to their judgment. The English nobility was not content with a compromise like that accepted by their Continental brethren in France, Germany or Russia. Nor were they as narrowly arrogant as the closed aristocracies which had seized power in the Italian republics. Disraeli's comparison of the great Whig houses to the Venetian oligarchy was too flattering to the Venetian oligarchy. For in the great days of Whig rule, and even in the twilight of the Whigs, theirs was a real public spirit and theirs a practical sagacity that paid them well and yet did the state some service.

Even today the memory of that golden day survives in the assumption that certain great officers like the Viceroy of India and, in the days when the Governors-General of the Dominions were still chosen in London, the representatives of the Crown in Canada or Australia had to be hereditary peers.[24]

But the great days of the peerage are over, all the same. The

[24] The only instance in modern times of a Viceroy of India being chosen outside the ranks of the hereditary nobility was the nomination of Lord Reading (Rufus Isaacs). Lord Reading was the first Marquess of Reading, a "new man." Lord Halifax was a commoner when nominated to India, but he was heir to the Halifax title. He was, of course. made a peer in his own right before he sailed for India.

seven hundred peers no longer represent a known and identifiable governing class, a recognized list of the "good, the wise and the rich" whom the English people should and did look up to with reverence. In a century or less the change had come.

One of Disraeli's more than ducal dukes was (as a duke could then well afford to be) a decided radical. He was in favour of abolition of all the privileged orders—except dukes. Dukes were a necessity. In the great days of the English aristocracy dukes, whether a necessity or not, were great figures indeed. They were the richest class in the world. They were also a powerful political class, owing some of their power and prestige to their wealth, but having much more power and prestige per thousand pounds a year than mere millionaires.[25] They were revered for their wealth and for the fact that its origin was not too recent. They accepted into their charmed circle, not of course on terms of equality, all the talents, brains, beauty, wealth. They were generally Whigs, like the Duke of Omnium. (The Tories were not the smart party any more than the royal family was in the smart set, *ex officio*.) The great "Revolution Families" were taken almost as seriously as they took themselves, and their frequently repeated vote of thanks to themselves for having "saved us our freedom, religion and laws" was echoed with a genuine, unbought "hear, hear" from the solid middle classes.[26]

In the nineteenth century, even more than in earlier ages the English aristocracy showed a statesmanlike readiness to admit

[25] Although the Astors and Vanderbilts had already risen to challenge the pre-eminence in opulence of the Dukes of Bedford and Devonshire, Bret Harte in "Lothaw" makes the English hero wealthy beyond dreams of American avarice. It should be noted, however, that the original of the Lothair who was the original of Lothaw was a Marquess (of Bute). His great wealth made him, for exemplary purposes, as good as a duke.

[26] Macaulay, when visiting Naples in the forties, noted with surprise at such stupidity even in a Spanish Bourbon, that the King of Naples neglected to cultivate "so great a man as the Duke of Buccleuch." The Duke's greatness was purely ducal; he belonged to that class of "the great" known to the eighteenth century, but rapidly declining in the later nineteenth.

newcomers who by talent or wealth strengthened the ruling class, a wisdom which marked them off from the pedigree-ridden and politically frivolous aristocracies of Europe. The envious Continental nobilities learned that not many English noblemen had many unblemished quarterings to show, but, like the House of France, the English peer was above the narrow prejudices of the *Almanach de Gotha*.[27]

The school system helped the assimilation; so did such expensive sports as racing, which required a constant hazard of new fortunes; so did intermarriage with the older families. The constant need for party funds made it possible for the fountain of honour (the chief whip of the party in power) to find ways of persuading the Prime Minister that such and such a cotton magnate or ironmaster deserved to be ennobled. And in a generation or so, the accent dropped, the "h's" acquired, the quiet change from Nonconformity to Anglicanism, from Liberalism to Toryism, safely made; the second or third peer was as fine an old English nobleman as if his ancestors had come over with William I or William III, had pleased the eye of Elizabeth or of Charles II.[28] The peerage, in thus taking over so many of the new rich, in serving, like the public schools, as a great assimilating force, per-

[27] There were several convents for which the French princesses were ineligible because of that mésalliance of Henri IV with a banking family (the Medici). And a British ambassador at Vienna, a century ago, found that his wife was not of adequate rank by Habsburg standards because she belonged to a great banking family, too. I hasten to add that I am aware that, in comparatively recent years, the *Almanach de Gotha* did not apply the full rigour of the social law, admitting people like the Prince de Borodino despite the anguish of people like M. de Charlus.

[28] This is not always understood even by exceptionally well-informed Americans. I have heard an American of a Main Line dynasty express his sympathy with the sad case of a nobleman who had been forced to let his castle to the American. The Philadelphian was saddened at the thought that Lord X was reduced to this; he hardly felt at home in the castle. I could have soothed him by pointing out that his own ancestors were important figures in eighteenth-century Pennsylvania when the peer's ancestors were Lowland farm labourers. The distressed nobleman's grandfather, indeed, had been a successful ironmaster who would have been thought a

formed a useful function, but one that was harder and harder to make romantic. The skill with which English "county society" took in the newcomers was a tribute to its political good sense. The rise of Silas Lapham or, at any rate, of his family would have been much faster in London or the home counties than in Boston.[29]

The peerage as a political order in the state, and the nobility as a social class into which all the rich who cared to pay the price in cash and effort duly entered, were not identical bodies, but they overlapped, so that the public attitude to one group was transferred to the other. To the man in the street it was a matter for occasional wonder that there should be lords sitting in the House of Commons. He was told, if he inquired, that they were Irish peers or bearers of courtesy titles. When the Irish Free State was set up, the Irish peerage began to disappear as a political body, for the official whose duty it was to arrange for the election of Irish peers was abolished, and thus the theoretical rights of this not very impressive body are vanishing in a characteristic English way.[30]

---

rough diamond in early Pittsburgh. But the coal mines, the blast furnaces, the company towns, were now in the distant past (round 1850, that is), and the castle was as far away from the source of the now diminished family fortune as was compatible with its being in the same country.

[29] One consequence of this marriage of new wealth and old ways was unfortunate. The millionaire who had made his fortune in Leeds or Glasgow felt no obligation to Leeds or Glasgow, nor any desire to shine there. The first steps in the ascent to feudal dignity were far more attractive than bourgeois eminence in a provincial city. So Trollope's Mr. Kennedy rejoiced in his new Highland estate of Loughlinter. "He was laird of Linn and laird of Linter, as his people used to say. And yet his father had walked into Glasgow as a little boy—no doubt with the normal half-crown in his breeches pocket" (*Phineas Finn*). So the Laird of Loughlinter married into the peerage, cutting out the impecunious Irish M.P. Both Kennedy and Phineas Finn would have found their matrimonial aspirations regarded as far more audacious in Boston, then or now, than they were in London. The Kennedys thought their investment in landed grandeur paid them well enough. They had little or none of the local patriotism of great American magnates, and this attitude helped to impoverish urban life, outside of London.

[30] By the Act of Union of 1801, 24 peers were elected by the Irish peers to represent them in the new united Parliament. Those Irish peers who

Then, in addition to Irish and Scottish peers, there are the bearers of courtesy titles whose legal position and social rights are in conflict and add to the confusion in the minds of publicists and novelists.[31]

---

did not get elected could sit in the House of Commons (but not for an Irish constituency). The Scottish peers are a less fortunate body. Sixteen of them are elected to the House of Lords, but those who are not elected are ineligible for the House of Commons. This small body is the closest British parallel to the disfranchised inhabitants of the District of Columbia. A Scottish peer who is not a Conservative has a political career barred to him, for his fellows will not and other people cannot elect him to Parliament. It is a special case of the working of the American locality rule. A very promising young Liberal, Auberon Herbert, before the last war had the misfortune to inherit the Scottish barony of Dingwall. That ended his career in the House of Commons and did not give him a place in the House of Lords. So he set investigations on foot and found that he was also Lord Lucas in the English peerage and so entered the upper house. But not many people have more than one peerage in their family.

[31] The rules are little understood in America, even in the shiny-paper weeklies, and are not always understood in England. For barons and viscounts they are simple. Sons and daughters of peers of the two lowest ranks take the family name (which may and often does differ from the name of the family title), preceded by the epithet "Honourable" and the Christian name (Honourable in England is not a political title as in America, Canada, Italy, etc.). The eldest son of an early marquess or duke takes the next highest title possessed by his father *if* it differs from the main title. Younger sons of earls are, like sons and daughters of barons and viscounts, mere Honourables. But *daughter*s of earls, like daughters of marquesses and dukes, are ladies; that is, their Christian and family names are preceded by "Lady" as the sons of marquesses and dukes are "lords"—for example, Lord Peter Wimsey. But all peers, up to and including marquesses, are commonly referred to as "Lord" followed by the title without the Christian name. Dukes, however, are always dukes, never mere lords. (This was not the rule in the early eighteenth century.) Marquesses are frequently Frenchified into "Marquis." None of the titles given to sons and daughters of peers have any but social importance. They are courtesy titles, without legal force. To complicate matters further, the wives of knights (an unhereditary title) and baronets (a hereditary title ranking its owner just below the "nobility") are called "Lady." So Lady Seattle may be the wife of any titled person other than a duke, but including a member of the chief Scotch court, the College of Justice. There are many people in England who would be more ashamed of not knowing these simple rules (apart from the case of the Scotch judges) than of not knowing or, indeed, observing the Ten Commandments.

The House of Lords until this century had very important powers. No bill could become law without its consent, although it was supposed to keep its hands off all financial legislation. But ordinary bills could be amended or rejected as the upper house thought fit. As it was overwhelmingly Conservative, the projects of Liberal governments were the sole victims of this mutilation or assassination. The peers usually showed some tact in opposing the measures of a government fresh from the electorate with a new mandate. But as the first fervour of the electors and elected waned, the peers grew more bold. And the knowledge that many projects were doomed to frustration dampened the zeal of would-be reformers.

Despite a record that is not impressive for judgment or independence, the House of Lords continued to exist as a brake on "too radical" progress until the great Liberal majority of 1906 found itself so constantly thwarted by the peers that the project of "ending or mending" became extremely popular with the rank and file of the party. And when the Liberal budget of 1909, which marked the beginning of a program of social reform paid for by taxation that differentiated between earned and unearned income, was thrown out by the Lords, the cup was full to overflowing. In two elections the Liberals and their Labour and Irish allies got a majority.[32] And the peers paid for having listened to professors and publicists who had forgotten the risks, for an anomalous institution of raising fundamental questions.

It was a body representing, above all, hereditary or acquired wealth that threw out the budget of 1909, which made a beginning with the policy of using the taxing power to make the inequalities of wealth more tolerable, by making the rich pay for some improvements in the economic condition of the poor.

[32] It is usually said that the Liberals owed their majority to Irish and Labour support. But the Conservatives owed their equality with the Liberals to Irish Unionist support. If Irish members are not counted, the Liberals had a small majority, and if they are counted, they had quite a respectable majority.

The action of the House of Lords in throwing out the budget was unprecedented. The complete control of finance by the House of Commons was a basic principle of the unwritten constitution, and its violation resulted in the creation of a written constitution, the "Parliament Act" of 1911.[33] Its violation by the House of Lords brought to a head the problem of the powers of the upper house. Prudent Englishmen like Lord St. Aldwyn deplored the forcing of the issue, but the Scottish Balfour, the German-born-and-educated Milner, the ex-Indian Viceroy Curzon, were ready to "damn the consequences." It was an absurd calculation that the British people would accept the new role of self-constituted guardians of the public weal when the question at issue (as Mr. Lloyd George had planned) was the refusal of the rich to pay taxes to help the poor. "I don't mind its being a rich man's lobby," said a prominent New York Republican when asked to join the Liberty League, "but I do object to its looking like one." The House of Lords was less wise and the result was the passing of the "Veto Bill." On a better-chosen ground the peers might have won, but the identification of constitutional propriety with the interests of the rich was fatal, not only to the new but to the old claims of the House of Lords.

There remains, nevertheless, the political problem of the powers of the upper house. On paper they are formidable. A majority of the peers can, if they will, hold up all ordinary legislation for two years. A strong party majority in the House of Commons can be forced to go through the time- and spirit-wasting process of passing the same bill three times until the House of Lords has exhausted its right of veto. It is true that money bills cannot be held up by the House of Lords at all, and a money bill may be a far more effective instrument of social change (or political robbery, accord-

[33] This constitution is not elaborate, but it defines the distribution of a legislative power which has no legal limits and thus is the basis of executive and judicial power. It is as if the Constitution of the United States was limited to Article I.

ing to taste) than mere alteration of the statute law. But a money bill is what the Speaker chooses to call a money bill and many budgets since the passing of the Parliament Act of 1911 have not been certified as money bills by the Speaker.[34] The House of Lords could delay such bills for two years, which might very easily mean killing the project altogether. For in politics, as in other parts of life, there are many things that must be done quickly or not at all.

What has prevented this issue from becoming acute is the fact that since the end of the war of 1918 there have only been two Parliaments elected which had not Conservative majorities. One of these Parliaments lasted less than a year and the other only two years and a half. In neither had the Labour government of the day an independent majority. The Conservatives have never had to fall back on their control of the House of Lords to delay radical measures. But we may assume that they will do so if they have to. The question then arises: has the Parliament Act made it no longer proper for the King to agree to make as many peers as are necessary to carry a fundamental measure of the government of the day? It can be argued that this drastic remedy, only threatened and never applied, has been made superfluous by the Parliament Act, which now provides a method whereby the resistance of the Lords can be overcome. The proper procedure would be to pass a new statute defining the powers or doing away with the existence of the House of Lords altogether. But that would take between two and

---

[34] One of the most characteristic of English political devices is the conferring of this very important political power on the Speaker. He—and not a court—is to decide, for it is realized that the definition of a "money bill" is a political question, whose decision calls for quite different qualities from those rightly expected of judges. Judges may have them, but not because they are lawyers. Not only was this power given to an official who need not be and very seldom is a lawyer, but when the bill was passed, the Speaker on whom this new power was conferred was a member of the opposition party which had so bitterly fought the reform of the House of Lords. As a Speaker is always re-elected, he constitutes, in fact, a one-man, unpackable Supreme Court. His interpretation of his functions has never been criticized on party grounds.

three years, which might be too long for the radical program to have any chance of success. And in the meantime the electorate might have lost its zeal.[35]

The formal political functions of the Crown and the peerage are less important than their social functions, or so at least it can be argued. And in a country where men are declared artificially unequal by birth, democracy may seem to be, and, in a sense is, a very delicate plant. Because of the survival of the traditional adulation of the monarch and of his family, real merit is neglected and a false sense of values encouraged. Because Clarence Threepwood is Earl of Emsworth he is treated with a deference that he would not otherwise secure, even were he a good deal richer. Even the fact that a "tenth transmitter of a foolish face" is a very rare phenomenon and that a peerage that has had five holders in a row is rare, the fiction that makes of the sons of brewers and the grandsons of bankers the heirs of Norman barons or the bastards of Charles II helps, so it is said, to encourage national snobbery. Probably both charges are true. But a historical phenomenon as deeply rooted as English snobbery is not to be swept away in a night by the abolition of King and peers. Inequality, in endless gradations and variations, is the English religion, and public schools and the monarchy and the peerage are but expressions of a deep-rooted national trait. No doubt if England had had a totally different history, this need not have been true, but for the purposes of a contemporary study, a dislike of equality must be taken for granted.

If it is an unalterable fact, then there is something to be said for the role of the King, and something, though less, to be said for the role of the peerage. The elevation to the top of the social hierarchy

[35] The voter, even in England, is sometimes like the drunk Scotchman who insisted on discussing predestination with the parish minister. In vain the divine tried to put him off, suggesting that it would be better to discuss it when the inquirer was sober. "But when I'm sober I don't give a damn about predestination." On the other hand, predestination, like the issue of bank credit, is a serious subject that needs discussion.

of a man who is neither the richest, the most powerful, the most famous, nor the most talented Englishman has a kind of equalitarian effect. There is or need be in the respect given to the holder of the crown "no damned nonsense of merit about it," as Lord Melbourne is said to have said of the greatest formal honour conferred by the King, the Order of the Garter.

The King is not merely the head of the state but a patron of the arts, of charities, of social activities. His official taste may not be good, but his patronage is, at any rate, a formal acknowledgment of the wider claims of society. And this role of the Crown does hold the country together. We have seen, in Germany, the immense and dangerous possibilities of exploiting the passion of the human race for pageants, for shows, for the intoxicating delights of great public celebrations. We have seen, in France, the dangers that befall a country that has lost the knack of providing great unifying national festivals for its people. And the English King is, quite as much as any Chinese Emperor, the chief priest of national rites. A generation ago the royal share in national rejoicing was more limited. It was circumscribed by the narrow court conception of what was fitting. Had the taboos of Victorian and Edwardian days lasted, the monarchy and possibly the nation would have suffered.

But the reception into the national and ancient code of rites of comparatively new popular ceremonies is one of the proofs of English political genius. Thus in the last century the Derby became a great national festival. On the one hand there is Ascot, with its royal enclosure, to which entry is rigorously guarded; only those with technically unimpeachable characters and backgrounds can hope to enter. On the other hand there is the Derby, which the King also attends and which is not only popular but *free*. If you are content to take your chance in a true democratic fashion and see the greatest of all horse-races from the heath, you pay nothing.[36]

But, after all, the Derby is a horse-race and horse-racing is the

[36] The St. Leger, run at Doncaster in Yorkshire, is even more of a popular festival than the Derby.

"sport of kings." It is therefore more interesting and more important that the Cup Final, the game which decides which of two professional football teams gains the honour of keeping the cup for a year, should have become a great, royal, national, and religious ceremony. The presentation to the King of the twenty-two players, the singing of popular songs by the crowds, more significant, the singing of hymns by the crowd, all make Wembley Stadium, where this great national liturgical act takes place, the English equivalent of the Greek Olympia. And the game thus elevated to the rank of a national institution is very unfashionable; it is definitely plebeian. Whoever advised King George V to adopt it as a royal festival know more about England than many Left-wing thinkers do.[37] Professional football is by far the most important game from the spectator's point of view, but it is only the cream of a very deep milk-jug. Football is *the* national game.[38]

Against this assertion there is the carefully fostered belief that it is cricket that is *the* national game, that it furnishes a code of morals and manners for the nation, that if hunting (on horseback) is the mirror of war, life is the mirror of cricket—at least in England. It is not difficult to see why such illusions are fostered. In cricket, gentlemen (amateurs) play alongside players (professionals).

[37] The problem of all statesmen is the proper use of opiates for the herd. The lower orders were easily cajoled in the days when they had religion, for they were then more or less deterred from excessive indulgence in the pleasures of Bacchus and Venus. If you take away other-worldly prospects, then Bacchus and Venus are too powerful agents and stop work. What solution can be found for this deadlock? Archibald Lyall, who has seen many men and many cities, finds the solution in "sport." " 'Sport' is an obvious opiate for the record-breaker, and even soothes the sympathetic student of the record-breaker's exploits. Therefore the *bourgeoisie* like myself is obviously more comfortable so long as the Royal Family continue to shake hands with football teams. God save the King."—E. S. P. Haynes: *Pages from a Lawyer's Notebooks* (cheap edition), p. 97.

[38] "The immense system of publicity for such arena performances tends to mask the great amount of football which is really enjoyed as an athletic pastime. The Football Association, which is the main organization for association football, has a membership of 40,000 clubs, of which only about 400 are professional." (A. E. Morgan: *The Needs of Youth*, p. 208.)

Traditionally on the village green the squire, the parson, the village blacksmith, and one or two farmers join in a rite which is a bond of union and a social event as well as a game. Men of letters, like Conan Doyle and Barrie, to name only the dead, can make of cricket a backcloth to their literary work. They, too, fit into the pattern. But few Englishmen live in villages, few ever see a squire, and the town parson's chances for cricket are few. Then it is a summer game, and the English summer is often nasty, brutish, and short. Then it is a leisurely game, but not many people have long afternoons free to watch or play a game which takes so long to come to a conclusion—and does not always do that. To think of cricket as the national game is another way of ignoring the urban, industrial, speeded-up life of the majority of the English people.[39]

Over the greater part of England, association football, played by professionals, is the game of the people.[40] In a few towns, mainly in the north, a special professional form of Rugby, "Northern Union," eclipses association football in popular favour among the spectators, but hardly ever among the players. More people may want to see Northern Union but fewer people want to play it, just as few Americans after their college days want to endure the full rigour of the American game. They are willing to die for dear old

[39] In a popular book called *British Sport*, out of 48 pages, exactly 22 lines are devoted to what is incomparably the most popular English game, association football, or, as the vast majority of the inhabitants of this island simply and rightly call it, "football." The author asserts that "Association football at its best is played by the public schools, the universities, and by various amateur clubs, mostly formed from school clubs" (Eric Parker: *British Sport*, p. 38). It is impossible to give any rational, non-English meaning to the use of "at its best" here. It is of course a moral and social judgment. It excludes both the professionals, who play football much better than do the present or past Carthusians, and the overwhelming majority of ordinary schoolboys, who, it is statistically probable, play it as well.

[40] In the capital of the great cricketing county of York, regular spectators at cricket are only an eighth of the number who regularly watch football (including Rugby). The figures for active participants are better, but as much of the cricket is played in the evenings and the season is only from May to the end of July, it cannot compete with football.

Rutgers while students, but as alumni their zeal is vicarious.[41]

The numerous ways of classifying the English people into upper and lower classes extend to sport. For the social historian, one of the momentous days in nineteenth-century history occurred when a boy at Rugby school picked up the ball and ran with it. By now Rugby has conquered nearly all the good schools, although one or two very good schools indeed stick to association or to private versions of their own. So the working and lower-middle classes have their own game, their own heroes, their own great national festivals. The upper and middle classes have their game, their heroes, their annual festival. The popular press gives most of its sporting space to association (after horse-racing); the more expensive press gives most of its space to Rugby (again after horse-racing). One section of the English people does not know or want to know how the other section plays.[42] Rugby is purely amateur and there are fewer polite evasions of the financial consequences of amateur status than in other games. Of course, most association teams are what the sporting journalists used to call "Simon Pure," but the best teams are not. The great English amateur combination, the Corinthians, has now no hope of success in the English Cup, and its Scottish rival, Queen's Park, has little in the Scottish.[43] To get into the last round of the Cup is the legitimate am-

[41] Thus "of the 65 football clubs in York 48 play Association and only 17 Rugby football. The playing membership of the Association clubs is 1,395 and of the Rugby clubs 480" (B. Seebohm Rowntree: *Poverty and Progress, A Second Social Survey of York*, p. 387).

[42] I am told that the spread of football pools, with their appeal to the universal English passion for gambling, has brought together retired colonels and their chauffeurs, each exchanging knowledge of the prospects of Arsenal or Everton. The interest of the gentleman is purely mercenary, but he is at least learning something of one of the most popular activities of his countrymen.

[43] Queen's Park plays regularly against professional teams with a fair degree of success. It owns or did own till very recently the largest football field in the world, Hampden Park at Glasgow. As more and more Scottish schools, "good," "nearly good," and "would-be good," go over to Rugby, it finds it harder to recruit players, but its position is still much better than that of the Corinthians.

bition of every professional football player.[44] For then, though he may not be conscious of it, he is given a chance to do more than play a game; he takes part in a great national festival and bond of union. The presence of the King at the Cup Final dignifies the game; the identification of the King with the Cup Final strengthens the monarchy and makes its basic function of symbolizing national unity, of expressing the Englishness of England, easier.[45]

Forced to face the fact that he does keep his admiration for the institution of royalty just this side idolatry, that if he does not love

[44] The Cup is competed for on a knock-out basis. By lot, teams are chosen to play against one another; the winner has an opportunity to play another team; the loser is out for that year. By this process of elimination, by which a very famous, rich, and skilful team may lose all its chances of the highest distinction (and profits) by one slip, two teams are found that do not necessarily represent the cream of football talent. A system like the American World Series that enables the richest team, the Yankees, to win year after year would not suit a country like England, where the passion for mere games of chance is so deeply rooted. The League Championship, which is a fairer test of skill, confined like the pennant race and the World Series in baseball to the greatest professional teams, has far less interest for the general public, although it has more for the true *aficionados*. In Scotland, conscious of its nationality in a way England is not, the great football event is the international match against England. The difference between the unconscious English nationalism and conscious Scottish nationalism can be easily seen by a spectator of the crowds at Wembley or, better still, at the even larger football ground, Hampden Park in Glasgow, before and after an International. In victory or defeat, English phlegm is in marked contrast to the *præfervidum ingenium Scotorum*. An American baseball fan, once he got used to the immense crowds that attend football matches in Glasgow, would find himself much more at home there than in London.

[45] The solemn English thoughts on the importance of games, which give the intelligentsia a chance to make easy fun, are not always silly in themselves. But they are silly in expression for characteristically English reasons. From conscious or unconscious snobbery, the importance of the amateur is exaggerated and so of the games in which amateurs are not quite ludicrously outclassed by professionals, cricket and Rugby football. So an emotional importance is attached to county championships, university matches, and Rugger Internationals for which there is no adequate justification.

a lord quite as much as he once did, he does not hate him either,[46] the poor Englishman is less ashamed and less conscious of undemocratic behaviour than he ought to be. He does not pursue the ideal of a formal equality without any very precise content. He seeks for more concrete improvements of his own condition, and worries less than any other group of human beings known to me over his relative position. Outside the very narrow circle of his own trade, street, and type, he is the least jealous of human beings. He assumes that inequalities exist all the world over; he is not surprised to learn that there are class distinctions everywhere, only they do not seem to him important because they only affect foreigners. And so he is less shocked to discover that American equality has its limits than might be supposed. He learns this truth where he learns most truths about America, from the movies.

The view of American snobbery given by the movies has, it is to be feared, no educative effect on the English movie-goer. He is puzzled, indeed, by what he sees, but takes it all as American and more or less unintelligible. He fails to see any difference between the social problem presented by a film like *She Married Her Boss* and *Kitty Foyle*. In one, Miss Claudette Colbert finds her love-life made difficult by the aristocratic prejudices of a Philadelphia department-store family. In the other, Miss Ginger Rogers finds her love-life made impossible by another aristocratic Philadelphia family with no such visible means of support, but a startling habit of using dynastic titles. The effort of realizing that there is any real difference between Main Street and Main Line, except money, and that one million dollars does not equal another in Philadelphia, is too much for movie-goers who have no spontaneous understanding of the difference between Rittenhouse Square

[46] The contrast between the English popular picture of the aristocracy as brainless but harmless and the French legend of the heartless and unscrupulous nobleman is worth noting. In France the "wicked marquis" was a powerful myth. In England only baronets, the lowest rank of hereditary titles, are presumed to be wicked. The difference between Count Almaviva and Figaro on one side and Bertie Wooster and Jeeves on the other is worth noting.

and Griscom Street. Like the Prince of Wales (Edward VII), who was told at a Philadelphia ball that a certain attractive young woman was a Biddle and replied: "What is a Biddle?" the pursuit of social distinction in a democracy puzzles him. Titles he knows; money he knows. But social prestige, not in rough proportion to wealth, active economic power, political power, or formal badges of distinction, is too delicate an idea for a rather gross people.[47]

So the picture of America as a free, even free-and-easy democratic society with inequalities of wealth but not of rank, where the story of Cinderella is not mere fairy-tale and where, in the strictest sense of the term, the rank is but the guinea stamp, or dollar sign, is not too clouded over by any shadow of the less romantic and less democratic truth. The English have this moderation in their snobbery; it is exclusive of regard for the snobbery of other people. It is so far equalitarian that an Italian prince and an American millionaire are alike interesting foreigners, but not really upper class, because they are not English. They may be Roman princes or plastics kings, but they are not lords.

So in his dealings with all foreigners, there is a fundamental absence of exportable snobbery that often produces the same results as genuine democratic feeling. Taking all foreigners as much of a muchness in rank, the Englishman is really prepared (as he is not in dealing with his own countrymen) to take people on their own personal merits. As always in social dealings with foreigners, the Englishman is from Missouri; he has got to be shown, but his readiness to be shown is not increased by a realization of the important difference between *Durchlaucht* and *Erlaucht* or between the best society of Boston and Butte.

The proof of the English pudding is in the eating. Not only economically but socially. England has made as much progress as any of the great states—and a small state is able to make more

[47] I have tried to explain what a Philadelphia Assembly was to a young woman who had seen *Kitty Foyle*. "It's like being presented at court. But who are they presented to? The President?" When I explained that they were just presented to the social world of Philadelphia, she gave it up.

progress largely because it escapes the responsibilities of the great states. Notably, the modern English state has won the confidence of the ruled to a degree that has been part of the national salvation. If the English people were more cynical about their government they might be more intelligent but not more wise. Even English hypocrisy, the much decried national habit, has its useful side. It is not only that by hushing up scandals public faith is maintained, but in a society in which the idea of corruption is really novel, really startling in its horror, men refrain from doing certain things because they are not done. No doubt things are made easier for some knaves, but they are also made easier for some weak but not rascally men who can resist temptation more easily if the thought of corruption strikes them with a fearful novelty. In no country in the world is the difference between the public and private reputations of public men greater than in England. In no country in the world are people less prone to mean suspicion or the bitter wisdom that is folly, "there must be something in it for somebody." It is not in England that stories spread of Mr. Churchill going to Egypt to meet Rommel or is it the proof of sophistication to believe that all men are liars. The belief that his rulers were reasonably truthful, brave, and honest was the armour on which the arrows of Dr. Goebbels broke in vain. And that trust, though not fully deserved, was not quite undeserved.

And the softening of English life, the diminution in bitter partisanship, the not quite genuine, yet not quite false good-fellowship of the different classes proved its worth in the great crisis of 1940–1. For many reasons, mainly, I think, the improvement in education, the English had become one of the most polite peoples. The hectoring policeman, the bullying sergeant, were not national heroes any longer. It was just as well. But for the tradition of good manners, of quietness in command, of spontaneous discipline, things might have gone ill in London in the last months of 1940. When so much depended not merely on courage, but on temper and on emotional restraint, the English way, the new English way of doing things, proved its worth. It is a loud voice that can carry above the guns and a rarely peremptory manner that is more terrifying than a bomb.[48]

And as they have come to think of the law as their own creation, the English people have become phenomenally law-abiding, which, too, has its advantages in a besieged country.

One of the oddest changes in the general reputation of the English has been their acquisition of a reputation—a deserved reputation—for being law-abiding. In the eighteenth century the murderous fury of the London mob, culminating in the Gordon Riots,[49] aroused the censorious alarm of statesmen from Paris to Petersburg. Individual crimes of violence were numerous and inadequately repressed. There was no organized police force and the means at the disposal of Sir John Fielding, under George III, were very inferior to those at the disposal of M. de Sartines under Louis XV. The plague of highwaymen was a reflection on the absence of a rural police force like the French and Dutch *maréchaussée*. Not until 1827 did London get a regular police force, and the nineteenth century was well advanced before the system was extended all over the country. And it was some time before the "new detective police" of Scotland Yard lived down the somewhat ambiguous reputation of the Bow Street runners.[50]

[48] I have heard a train conductor ordering passengers on board at Chester, Penna., with more noise and apparent heat than would have been fully justified if the Luftwaffe had just appeared over Camden.

[49] Familiar to readers of *Barnaby Rudge*. These riots were bigger and better London versions of the anti-Catholic riots of the next century that disgraced Boston and Philadelphia.

[50] The early English detective story in the hands of Wilkie Collins had a propaganda value in making the detective an interesting and estimable character, instead of being a shady spy bringing into English life low Continental methods of discovering the guilty. Within less than a generation, English literature had created a new mythology in which the detective played the part usually given in folklore to the brigand. From Robin Hood to Sherlock Holmes is an interesting evolution. Dick Turpin in the middle eighteenth century is the last bandit hero of English popular legend. In the United States, it is only in the last few years that the G-men have made the cops more popular than the robbers. The death of Dillinger in 1934 may have been the watershed.

But the world of Fagin did not die at once. Crimes of violence, culminating in the great garrotting epidemic of the sixties, were frequent and the grim and filthy slums of London and the other great cities did not breed virtue. But in the last forty years improved education, improved standards of living, such harmless alternatives to crime and drunkenness as the bicycle, the cinema, and organized sport have resulted in a striking improvement in almost all crime statistics. In London between 1893 and 1928, murders per million inhabitants fell from 9 to 3; other crimes of violence (excluding rape), manslaughter and wounding, fell from 29 to 8 per million. Rape fell from 48 to 34 per million, although the legal definition of rape was extended. What was true of London was true of the whole country.[51] Improved education was reflected in increases in fraud. Convictions for drunkenness were greatly reduced, but gambling offences went up. One apparently sinister increase is in fact encouraging. The number of cases of cruelty to children went up—but that merely reflected a higher public standard of child welfare since the Children's Act of 1908 made it an offence to keep children in verminous condition. The last World War had hardly any effect on this progress towards a more peaceful, less violent society. The experience of millions of men, scattered all over the world, accustomed for three years or more to violence, had no appreciable effect on the declining appetite of the Englishman for settling his quarrels or improving his economic condition by violence.[52]

[51] In the whole country, burglaries increased while they went down in London. Apart from a general increase, the change was due to advantage being taken of technical advance. Burglars lived in London but operated by motor car in less well protected areas.

[52] This casts some doubt on the popular American pacifist theory that the outburst of American violent crime that followed the enactment of prohibition was due to the corruption of the youth of America by their limited experience of legalized violence in 1918. Sir Edward Troup asserts that the figures show that "The people of London have become much less inclined to acts of personal violence, and with less confidence, that they are on the whole a little more honest; but that the standard of sexual morality is lower" (*London Life and Labour*, Vol. I, p. 392). One odd

English democracy has grave faults. Its aversion to extreme measures may involve a refusal to recognize that nothing less than extreme measures are adequate for extreme evils, or extreme dangers. The often unconscious national pride that accepts an abuse or a failure because it is "English," without even the excuse of an illusion that it has any other merits, keeps old abuses green, from the coldness of English houses to the immunity from criticism of judges, the most pampered of English officials.

In a world where easy optimism is out of place, English optimism is often a national danger.[53] The stranger may well think that life in England is "run under wraps"; in no country are failures let down more easily, or are the victims of their incompetence or misguided ambition less rancorous. And this is, historically, an undemocratic trait. For not only are the English free from the traditional ingratitude of republics; they have a talent for being grateful for mythical services as well as a talent for forgiving only too real faults.

This kindness to the aged and incompetent—indeed, even to the young and incompetent—is notorious in the English theatrical world, where the spectacle of an elderly actress, at best fit to play Juliet's nurse and at worst fit only to play Third Witch, playing Juliet evokes sympathy, not indignation. For the English public is loyal to old stage favourites. Odder still is the extension of this kindness to the field of sport. This may be a by-product of the fact that cricket is a game that persons who are decidedly middle-aged can yet play very well—which may be all that Americans need to know about cricket. But be that as it may, the fact remains. Only

---

effect of the decline in the murder rate is that the number of fictional murders in a regular publishing year exceeds those committed in real life. This is not yet true in the United States despite the growth of the Whodunit industry.

[53] American optimism has, as its counterpart, an equally dramatic pessimism. But the English attitude is credulity about good news and deafness to bad. Perhaps "is" should be "was." Three dreadful years have made the Englishman, if not sceptical, at least hardened to ill tidings, which do not, however, affect his mystical confidence in England's triumph.

in England could the horses which most decidedly let the backers down be tragic or comic heroes like the Tetrarch or Tishy. Only in England could boxers like Billy Wells and Joe Becket be heroes. That American and French boxers found such British opponents easy money merely reflected badly on the kindness and gentlemanliness of the American and French boxers. There is no evidence that the really great boxers produced in Britain in modern times, Messrs. Driscoll, Welsh, and Wilde, were as much national heroes as the gallant but incompetent heavy-weights. Of course such kindness is not good for the arts of acting or boxing. But English kindness is an amiable weakness if, in politics and sport, an expensive one.[54]

A good deal of English life *is*, in fact, a race run under wraps. The full rigour of the game is not expected from politicians or athletes. Yet the extent to which this kindness is carried should not blind us to realities. An unsuccessful general may remain highly popular. The polite fiction that he retired because of ill health may be decorously observed, but he is, in fact, retired. Not soon enough, perhaps, but he is retired. It may be, as has been often suggested, that the doom of the British Empire will come from some incompetent being in office at some critical spot and moment "because it was Buggins' turn," but Buggins' turn does not last for ever. And the generals and admirals and politicians gracefully retired to the House of Lords and dignified unemployment are not as tempted to vain recrimination as in other lands, nor are military campaigns, or even political manœuvres conducted with the same bitter vigilance on the part of colleagues, each of whom, in some countries, has reason to suspect that his most formidable enemy is his rival and not his opponent. In the British services, civil and military, there is a human allowance of ambition, some of it mean enough,

[54] I can well remember an interview I was forced to have in Boston nearly twenty years ago with an indignant fight promoter who had been forced to cancel a big match because a British boxer had refused to come in from Dedham to Boston to fight, because of a bad snowstorm. "And he wants to get a chance at the world title!"

some of it childish enough. But the handful of silver and the ribbon to stick in his coat that the not totally incompetent public servant can count on is a soother of egos and a calmer of passions. It has, with all its manifold drawbacks, saved England from problems like those presented by generals like Leonard Wood or Sarrail.

In all fields of progress the Englishman has much to be proud of, in all fields but one. For the class-divisions in England, exaggerating and overlaying the great economic differences that are common to all Western society, are a great price to pay for national unity, even assuming that they are a necessary part of the price. The English people who have so much in common, so many of whose virtues and most of whose faults are remarkably evenly distributed all over the nation, do not know one another. They are, after the first ice is broken, more at ease with all types of foreigners than with those of their own countrymen whose speech, manner, games, and religion act as barriers. The habit of social suspicion thus inbred accounts for much of the unpopularity of the English abroad, who are often thought to be showing their contempt for foreigners when they are merely concealing doubts about their own social position in the eyes of their own countrymen. It is as a "social" democracy that England is the greatest failure, using "social" in a narrow but not trivial sense. And the belief that somehow *equality* is the clue to Russian success is the most telling point of all those made by the advocates of Russian ways.

And because inequality finds its expression in other ways than material possessions, it makes the problem of English democracy even more urgent. The difficulties of intercourse between various layers of English society are not merely matters of accent. They are matters of posture, of habit, of gesture, of emphasis, of ease or diffidence in speech. The unease may be on either side or on both; the product of Eton and King's, trying to unbend, may be as odd a sight as the product of a council school trying to pass as smart and sophisticated. A Left literary critic expressing his views on "proletcult" or its successors in the manner of the Balliol intellectuals of the twenties is comic, or tragic, or irritating, or futile, according to taste. To be present at a big official party, with opportunities to inspect Cabinet ministers of different social levels, is to be educated in fine shades of class distinction of which accent is only one example and income difference only one cause. A Labour minister may have as much the habit and temper of command as a blue-blooded Conservative, but he will express his habit and temper in a different way. It is true that the differences in the social background of Mr. Roosevelt's Cabinet are less marked than in Mr. Churchill's.[55] But even were they as marked, they would be less a cause of minor friction. For Mr. Roosevelt and all his Cabinet have been accustomed, from very early years, to a society which, despite all efforts of schools, advertising, clubs, and the rest, makes the creation of effective social barriers difficult and their maintenance a perpetually repeated task. American social fences have to be continually repaired; in England they are like wild hedges; they grow if left alone.

Politically, England is a democracy, perhaps the most mature democracy in the world. But democracy is not merely a matter of government, it is an attitude of life. And England will not be a full or anything like a full democracy as long as one of the kindliest and most united peoples in the world are internally divided in a fashion that so impoverishes the national life.

[55] Mr. Churchill's contains more members from the "underprivileged" classes and one or two members from a class lower economically and socially than any represented in Mr. Roosevelt's Cabinet.

The Empire

Her pirate flag it is flying where the East and the West are one.
And her drums when the day is dying, salute the rising sun.[1]

These lines describe one aspect of the British Empire with some felicity. Parts of it have been founded by persons whom it is no gross exaggeration to describe as pirates—as long as we remember that piracy has often been quite a respectable trade. Some parts of the British Empire were acquired to make the slave trade more easy; other parts were acquired to make it more difficult. Missionaries innocently promoted trade, and traders, to their annoyance, were followed by missionaries. Parts of the Empire were acquired in fits of absence of mind; others as a result of presence of mind. Little colonies remain isolated units because Imperial policy changed and the will and resources to develop them were diverted elsewhere or used up at home. Big as the British Empire now is,

[1] I quote (from memory) from the once popular poem of John Jeffrey Roche of Boston. It has not been reprinted since the last war (as far as I know) or even quoted by indignant Congressmen. In the last war the Germans reprinted it and it is possible that a new Flanders Hall edition exists. There are other good polemic lines like:

> *Her robes are of purple and scarlet*
> *And kings have bent their knees*
> *To the gemmed and jewelled harlot*
> *That sitteth by many seas.*

there are quite considerable parts of the world that, for longer or shorter periods, were under English control and from which the English had to be expelled by force of arms. New York, Buenos Aires, Minorca are examples that will jump to everybody's mind and no doubt there are others. Then there are important commercial and strategic positions which England voluntarily abandoned for general and, sometimes generous, political reasons, places like Corfu (so valuable at the moment to the Axis fleets), Java, and Martinique.

Then in the complicated changes and adjustments that marked wars and diplomacy in the bad old days, England, for more or less good reasons, gave up, without undue pressure, quite important places like Dakar, Heligoland, and Havana.

Nevertheless, as a rule when Divine Providence has put a part of the world under English rule, it has usually stayed, often quite willingly, in the state unto which it had pleased God to call it. And contemplating this fact we are inclined to agree with Mark Twain; the English *are* mentioned in the Bible. "And the meek shall inherit the earth."

It is natural that so astonishing a fortune should breed complacency in its beneficiaries and envy and resentment in the spectators of such good fortune. And the envy and resentment have lasted longer than the complacency. For it has to be admitted that interest in the British Empire does not, today, seem to be a very spontaneous attitude in the English people. The intellectuals have long laughed, and rightly laughed, at the naïve gratification at seeing so much of the map painted red which seems to have stirred the simpler emotions of many Victorians, though even they seem to have been often sluggish in their response to the command to think Imperially.[2]

[2] "He doesn't want the money, it is work he wants, though it is beastly work—dull country, dishonest natives, an eternal fidget over fresh water and food. A nation who can produce men of that sort may well be proud. No wonder England has become an Empire." *"Empire!"* (E. M. Forster: *Howards End.*

The refusal to think Imperially was due not merely to national intellectual sloth, but to the extreme difficulty of thinking about so complicated and confused a mass of facts, problems, and possibilities as the British Empire. First of all there was India—but the brightest jewel in the crown, as it was romantically called, was admittedly a thing in itself. It was a problem, a possibility, an achievement so vast that it had to be considered apart from the rest of the Empire, as it is considered in this book. But even so there were many millions of square miles and a hundred million people who "owed allegiance to the British crown." The Empire, even without India, was problem enough. For it was not a unity, geographically or economically or racially or linguistically or culturally or religiously. Millions of white people, most of them, but by no means all, speaking English. Millions of black people, most of them not speaking English, but many of them speaking English better than many of the white people.[3]

Acquired at various times, often as part of complicated transactions that had little to do with the past or future of the colonies acquired, many parts of the Empire have been neglected ever since. Sometimes this neglect was simply a result of a reasonable refusal to interfere (more than bare necessity commanded) with the local traditions and customs. Only thus could the new British subjects be easily reconciled to British rule. So in an age of anti-Papist feeling that made open relaxation of the penal laws against Catholics as difficult, almost, as it would have been in North Carolina, the Church of Rome was allowed to subsist with many of its privileges guaranteed. So, too, with legal institutions. In an age of uncritical adoration of the common law, the old French and Dutch legal systems were allowed to remain in vigour so that, today, you must go to the British Empire to see the law of the old French Kingdom or the old Dutch Republic still in force. Mauritius, Cape

---

[3] I was present at a lunch given at the time of the coronation of King George VI to members of a group of minor colonial legislators. With one exception, all the white members had French as their native tongue, and with no exceptions all the coloured people had English.

Colony, Quebec, Trinidad, St. Lucia, British Honduras, all illustrate this policy. But they also illustrate the difficulty of thinking Imperially, for what have they in common? What does membership of the British Empire mean to the peoples of these colonies and what does "ruling" these colonies mean to the English people? And what have these colonies, with their different histories, languages, and traditions, in common with the colonies, now dominions, that, like the original thirteen colonies, are the result of mass migration of people from the British Isles and which are linguistically, racially, and culturally in the truest sense daughters of England? In the truest sense, but some are more completely children of the British Isles than others. For less than half the population of Canada is of British descent and the single biggest united linguistic, religious, and racial group is that of the French Canadians.[4] More than half of the white population of South Africa is of "Afrikaner" origin—that is, of Dutch and French Huguenot origin—and, again, that majority grows while the British minority relatively shrinks, owing to its lower birth rate. It is, indeed, only in the Pacific Dominions that the white stock is almost purely descended from the British Isles. The small German and smaller French and Italian ingredients do not affect it seriously.[5]

[4] Not only are the French Canadians rapidly becoming the largest group in Canada because of that astonishing fertility of which the Dionne quins are only the most dramatic example, but they are more united than the English-speaking Canadians are. For these are internally divided by religion. The large Irish (and Scottish) Catholic minority may not like the French Canadians very much, but they do not like the Ontario Orangeman either.

[5] There are interesting variations, however. There are far more people of Irish Catholic ancestry in Australia than there are in the British Isles or, for that matter, in the United States, a fact reflected in the personnel of Australian politics, in which men of Irish Catholic origin play a far greater part in high office than they do in the United States. In New Zealand the proportion of Scottish Presbyterian origin is higher than in the British Isles, and the Maori, long thought to be disappearing, are now increasing in numbers a good deal faster than the white population. In the not very long run, European civilization has proved more deadly to Europeans than to the innocent natives whose refusal to reproduce themselves was for so long the subject of kindly concern.

But the Dominions, despite their geographical separateness and their racial university, are profoundly affected by their connection with Britain. That connection is now purely moral. For all purposes the Dominions are independent states. They can make peace or war; they have complete economic autonomy; they can exclude British immigrants as if they were so many Chinese attempting to enter California. There is, for example, no Imperial equivalent to the American law which forces the businessmen of Hawaii or Puerto Rico to send their cargoes by expensive American ships to American ports, rather than making the best bargain they can and using more efficient (that is, cheaper)[6] Dutch or Japanese or British shipping facilities. A British subject born in the British Isles has no rights, as such, in the other Dominions. The English recognize obligations to the other members of the British Commonwealth, but reciprocity is not so generous.

When the victory of the French fleet and of the joint Franco-American army had decided at Yorktown that the Declaration of Independence was not to be one of the many proclamations of ideal principles of which history (especially German history) is so full, the lesson learned by the English governing classes was not what it is commonly believed to have been. They did not decide that they had made a mistake in repressing local liberties in the thirteen colonies; they decided that it was the laxity of Imperial control that had led to the American Revolution. Not only was it the case that in colonies like Connecticut and Rhode Island, Imperial control did not extend even to the naming of governors by the King, but in no colony was there as much control of local political and economic life as there is in modern Puerto Rico. The remaining colonies, Canada (the modern provinces of Quebec and Ontario), New Brunswick, Nova Scotia, and the other lesser remnants of the

[6] It is perhaps worth recalling that, in common English speech, the word "efficient" means adequate service at a competitive price. It does not mean adequate service at a price fixed, in effect, by congressional legislation. In England, "rugged individualism" is not interpreted as involving an exclusion of non-voters from competition.

Empire were, therefore, more effectively controlled from London than any of the original thirteen colonies had been. It was an experiment in concentration of power that failed. And the real claim to political wisdom of the rulers of England is that when it had failed, they noticed the fact and retraced their steps.

By the middle of the nineteenth century the colonies whose population was predominantly of European origin were increasingly freed from Imperial control. They were allowed to dispose of the public lands as they thought fit (Disraeli saw the importance of this concession and disapproved of it). They were allowed to impose any tariffs they liked and to build up, by that expensive method, infant industries that drove out many competing English firms from the colonial markets. They were allowed to exclude English immigrants and, in all economic questions, were completely autonomous by 1914. In the war of 1914 they came of age. They made great sacrifices; they suffered great losses. They entered the League of Nations as individual units, and by 1931 their constitutional evolution was complete. "Dominion status" was equivalent to independence; there was no power of an independent state which could not be exercised by a dominion. At the Ottawa Conference of 1932 England was forced (or the MacDonald-Baldwin government thought she was forced) to enter in the new bad way of tariff exclusiveness, to imitate the United States and other monopolizers of their natural resources. The decision was a bad one for the world; no worse but no better than the Smoot-Hawley tariff of the year before. But, be that as it may, the elements of an Imperial economic unity were created. It should be stressed, however, that the Dominions were not dragged by the mother country into this thoughtless course. She was dragged by them. They got at least as much as they gave; and an old-fashioned mercantilist statesman like the elder Pitt or Alexander Hamilton might well have wondered at the meaning now given to "Imperial." It most certainly did not mean rule.

The nature of dominion status was made plain by the outbreak of war in 1939. The British Dominions made up their own minds

As Washington said, influence is not government, and it was not even influence that bound London and Ottawa and Canberra and Pretoria together; it was sentiment. And sentiment, it has been found in the British Empire, will bear very heavy strains, but not light ones. Australians and Canadians will die for the Empire, but will not adjust their tariff or immigration policies for the Empire. They will insist on complete political independence, internal and external, but they will not put themselves to the strain, in peace-time, of using that independence and thus incurring responsibilities as well as exercising rights. But this criticism of the peace-time British Empire only makes it evident how absurd it was to represent it as a mere cover under which cunning English statesmen could deceive the American people, to picture dominion status as being merely a device to hide a conspiracy to undo the Declaration of Independence. From that danger of stifling the "Spirit of '76," a vigilant handful of senators saved the United States. They are not slow to claim credit for their work. But as far as their apprehensions were based on a belief that dominion statesmen were or are mere stooges for astute imperialist rulers in London, they were baseless. And it is time the news got around.

If the old sense of "empire" has gone as far as the Dominions are concerned,[10] it still survives in the rest of the territories attached to the British Crown. Nigeria, Jamaica, Aden, British Guiana—these are Imperial possessions in the old sense, and some Dominions, like Australia, have their own minor empires, like Papua. But in the non-dominion Empire, although legally all power is in the hands of the sovereign Parliament in London, there are varying degrees of self-government, ranging from powers equivalent, roughly, to those of an American state, through territorial status, down to complete control by English officials sent out from London and carrying out policies determined on in London. Over part of this Empire, including the most valuable colonies in Africa,

---

[10] An attempt has been made to get England and the Dominions called "the British Commonwealth of Nations," but the phrase does not come trippingly off the tongue. It exists in print but not in speech.

international treaties prohibit preferential tariffs, and in the rest of the Empire in the recent but now dead free-trade era the absence of tariff barriers made the complaints of the "have-not" powers that they could not get access to the raw materials of the Empire as baseless as most German and Italian propaganda is. But there were to England advantages in controlling these areas, all the same, even before London imposed a tariff policy on the colonies. Service in the colonies offered a career, not unprofitable, interesting, and with some prestige value, to young men, all fairly able, some more than that, and, by physique and temperament, ill suited to sedentary lives at home as bankers or bond salesmen. The Empire was, so the joke ran, the place "where the Blues governed the Blacks." [11] These colonial service officers were men of honesty; they often (as in Kenya) made themselves almost as unpopular by fighting the white settlers as the missionaries did. But they were exclusively British, and many a German or Italian had a genuine grievance when he saw jobs that he could fill, automatically reserved for the arrogant Britons. Whether the natives lost much by being deprived of the privilege of being ruled by the type of young German or Italian who worried about not having a colonial career is rather more doubtful. Poles and Abyssinians might answer the question, too hastily, too dogmatically, but not necessarily wrongly. The colonial service had and has grave faults. Although it has recruited abler men than it did twenty years ago,[12] it is not unified in its outlook and it can hardly be said to have a colonial policy of its own. It suffers from the colour prejudice of all English-speaking peoples and thus makes enemies where Dutch, or Belgian, or French methods make friends. But it is not the colonial service,

[11] "Blues" are people who have made major teams at Oxford or Cambridge. The dark and light blue emblems of these ancient universities have some, if not all, of the prestige of a "letter" gained at a great American university.

[12] Partly because it now gets men who would, a generation ago, have chosen the Indian Civil Service.

but the whole problem of colonial control that is at issue. Is England delaying or preventing completely the natural and healthy development of the colonies assembled, rather fortuitously, under her rule?

That England is preventing changes may be admitted at once. In Africa, for example, she is, with varying degrees of energy, fostering small-scale production in West Africa by a native peasantry, providing the necessary political framework for a white plantation economy in the Kenya Highlands; refusing to merge the economic, political, and financial systems of Kenya and Tanganyika, or of Northern and Southern Rhodesia. She created probably quite unnecessarily complicated property rights in favour of a class of native landlords in Uganda who might have vanished in the great crisis of African society, and she has cut off the Gambia from its natural hinterland, French Senegal.[13]

Obviously, over a great area of Africa, English power has given different but powerful directions to native society, as well as in some areas introducing a white population and so a colour problem. She has supported the power of great Moslem chiefs in Nigeria and of a Christian aristocracy in Uganda. Like all the European nations, her gifts to Africa have been of a very mixed character. If she was one of the great promoters of the slave trade in the eighteenth century, she was its chief enemy in the nineteenth, spending energy and money in pursuing American slavers in the Atlantic and Arab slavers in the Red Sea. The long devastation of Africa by the slave trade is a sin in which all the Western nations share about equally; their share in the war against the slave trade is less uniformly distributed. The introduction of European commerce, the improvement of transport, the forced or voluntary migration of peoples, have spread disease as well as knowledge of modern techniques. It is possible that, but for European intrusion,

[13] It may be forgotten that had the Gambia been ceded to France (as has more than once been projected), the situation of the United Nations, vis-à-vis Dakar, would have been even less satisfactory.

the tsetse fly would not have spread so far and fast as it did; it is certain that native society, left to itself, would not have had the technical knowledge to fight the plague. Entomology and all the related sciences of tropical medicine are not techniques that a poor, backward, uneducated society masters easily or at all. A withdrawal of Imperial control at this moment would simply be to make the worst of both worlds, to leave all the sorrows of Africa that white men have caused (along with those bred by native crimes and follies) in easy possession. Europe would have no power to make reparation. And Liberia is not an encouraging sample of what Africa can do for herself, even with the kind of approach to modern ideas and techniques that the educated Afro-American ruling class of Liberia has.

Africa, it must be remembered, is poor. Tropical disease, bad feeding habits, insufficient food, the most meagre capital equipment, little natural wealth that does not require great capital investment to develop, an insufficient population which, whatever may have been the case four hundred years ago, is today in general of poor physique and stagnant in a native culture very inadequate for the needs of the modern world. These are the basic facts of the African problem. They are not to be solved by merely repeating either "imperialism" or "anti-imperialism."

Nor is there any likelihood that if one imperial power, England, withdrew from the race, all the other runners would withdraw too. The choice is not between a symbolical, morally gratifying, expensive washing the hands of sin and a continuation of imperial exploitation without scruple and with immense immediate profits to whet the appetite. It is between a less and more intelligent and honest imperial policy and possibly between enlightened and honest imperial administration and an international administration.

English colonial administration has grown more intelligent and, with one important exception, more honest in the past generation. Some of the controversies over native land tenure and over forced labour have arisen because the public conscience has become more sensitive.[14] In West Africa and the West Indies more is being done to diminish the gap between rulers and ruled and education is beginning to produce a class of coloured officials who are more and more competent to lead their fellows into the full technical and political life of the modern world. We are not likely to see, after this war, a recrudescence of the political and economic illusions that led to the last desperate attempt to create a white ruling class of primary producers in Kenya at a moment when the tide of world economy was beginning to run so strongly against primary producers whose position was so much older and stronger than that of the Kenya colonists. As progress is made in the techniques of tropical agriculture and medicine, as the motor truck and the aeroplane provide an answer to transport problems hitherto insoluble except at impossible expense, the economic possibilities of the great tropical areas improve. And, as far as political barriers permit, the shift in the methods of basic food production help Africa against Iowa. It is quicker and better to produce fats directly in the form of vegetable oils from tropical nuts than to go through the more elaborate process of raising corn to feed pigs (hogs) to make lard.

But it will not be enough for the prosperity of the tropics, under English or any other rule, that they can produce more and cheaper than they could a generation ago. For unless this production raises the standard of life in the colonies, it is a gain in which the people most concerned, the natives, have no interest. And that means that the tropical farmer must be paid more in manufactured goods, in services, in capital investment. If the ground nuts of West Africa cannot be sold in the United States because of their competitive effect on the products of Iowa or Nebraska, the tropical farmer cannot buy American goods unless, in turn, somebody else is buying his. It is this circle that is the only justification for the imposition of preferential tariffs on the British colonial empire. Under a

[14] It might be more exact to say that that portion of the public which is "Empire-conscious" at all, is now more likely to be critical of imperialism than it was a generation ago, but it is not improbable that a smaller proportion of the total population cares for the Empire one way or the other.

pure free-trade regime these colonies could buy in the cheapest market but not sell in the dearest. In other words, free trade here guaranteed open access to American business in Africa, but gave no guarantee that those who sold would also buy. If Nigeria could sell to Britain and, with the proceeds of the sales, buy from the United States or any other equally high-tariff country, all was well. But the power of Britain to buy from Nigeria was affected by the increasing impediments to international trade and by the shrinking share of Britain in that trade. It was necessary for Nigeria to keep her customers solvent and, on paper, there was something to be said for "Imperial free trade." But the British colonies had no real power of bargaining. They were too small, too scattered, too poor, and, politically, too weak. There was no danger that in trade negotiations the fully self-governing Dominions would make bad bargains in their dealings with the mother country. There was no danger that India would either. The "Government of India" represented too great a vested interest for the imposition of one-sided bad bargains. But the smaller colonies might and did, in some cases, suffer from their political inferiority. The Malay states, with their basic product of rubber, could have made far better bargains with the United States and, still more, with Japan than they were allowed to make. It was discovered (as those familiar with tariff-making practice as apart from tariff-making theory knew would be so) that, once you start juggling with tariffs, you breed with tropical speed vested interests of all kinds. Smoots and Hawleys spring out of the ground; lobbies appear and even a political system which (unlike the American) is well designed to minimize the effect of local pressure groups finds itself unable to resist the manifold pressures to which it is subjected.

And the whole trading world which had an interest in the stability and peace of the British Empire when that Empire was open to the free competition of all had less of an interest in its survival when it was, in varying degrees, excluded from Imperial trade. It was not the retention by England of the old German colonies, very minor assets on either side of the Imperial ledger, that was the real economic grievance of Germany, but the world-wide movement towards exclusive protectionism, of which the creation of British Imperial tariffs was one of the later examples.

But the change in tariff policy has had marked effects on the distribution of British exports. The Empire takes a higher proportion of a total which is less important to the economic life of England than it was.[15] And, of course, movements in the direction of self-sufficiency limit the market open to the colonies. The highly subsidized beet sugar is not only a charge on the English taxpayer, but an economic handicap imposed on the West Indies and other sugar colonies. Every subsidy paid to keep home agriculture afloat is a corresponding charge on the economic progress of other parts of the Empire; the English population cannot eat twice as much wheat to provide a market for Alberta and for Norfolk. And even if it could, its fundamental power of paying for the double meal is not increased.

It is not a mere paradox to say that the more Imperial British economic policy has become, the less easy Imperial economic relations have become. Whether there was any choice open to England in the great economic crisis of 1929–33 may be doubtful. But with each interference in what used to be called the course of "normal" trade, the political problems of a central economic policy have become greater. The Dominions might be better off for a completely free entry into the home market on equal terms than they are with a preferential entry into a restricted market. And England might be better off with easier entry into Dominion and non-Imperial markets than with the chance to fight business wars

[15] "There has also been a relative change in the destination of our exports. Whereas in 1913 we exported 37 per cent (by value) of our merchandise to British countries, in 1937 we exported 48 per cent; even in 1929 before the adoption of a protectionist policy it was already 44 per cent."—M. Compton and E. H. Bott: *British Industry, Its Changing Structure in Peace and War*, p. 154.

with political weapons. But that is water over the dam. England is committed to some form of control, by tariffs, by quotas, by currency adjustments. And the temptation to make these adjustments without sufficient regard to the interests of the weak, inside or outside England, is great.

The internationalization of the Empire would not be a solution unless the markets (for example, England, the United States, Germany, etc.) were themselves under the international authority. Complete free trade with no power of negotiation imposed by international fiat on so large an area of the world would be a colossal example of the difference between sauce for the goose and sauce for the gander. For if the orthodox free-trader will still assert (with a good deal of force) that, even so, the tropical lands would benefit by free trade, the spectacle of the white world imposing this blessing on the black world but austerely refusing to share in its benefits would be a comic or irritating spectacle according to the taste of the spectator.

It is doubtful if overseas investment of the old type will ever be resumed on a great scale. The chief exporter of capital, England, has had to liquidate nearly all her resources of this kind and it will be difficult to restore the assets that have gone to buying aeroplanes in the United States, raw materials in Latin America, all the costs of making modern war which must be borne by countries which have not the German resource of organized plunder to eke out the deficiencies of their own home territory. Nor even if private investment does play its old part does it follow that the investor is under any temptation to invest in the British Empire or in the poorest parts of it. They are poor because they have a poor capital equipment; they have a small capital equipment because they are poor and capital sunk in developing their resources gets comparatively small and slow returns. Most of Africa is no more attractive to the private investor than the Tennessee Valley was. Where there were great resources worth exploiting, they were exploited. In the course of that exploitation, the level of life of the natives in regions like the Katanga copper field has been greatly raised.[16] Only a government with other than strictly actuarial ideas of return would invest money, men, and national interest in most of Africa or the other tropical colonies of England. The indirect returns may justify the investment, but they are only paid to the whole community. Can this possibly irrational view that England does gain by the extension of her territory be acquired by a new international authority? Will "Europe" stand the costs of empire if the gains are so generalized that no one country can see where its own share comes from—and maybe rightly, since, for some countries, there may be no direct share?

There has been no precedent for the mobilization of the resources of a group of nations to administer, objectively and disinterestedly, a great undeveloped territory. The one botched experiment of the Congo Free State proves nothing one way or the other.[17] The mandate system set up at Versailles, despite its deficiences, proved that standards could be imposed or, at any rate, suggested. Abuses in Southwest Africa and in the French Cameroons were exposed, and the exposure, no doubt, had some effect on the conduct of the officials and governments concerned. Perhaps the fact that Tanganyika was under mandate had some effect in making it easier for the British government not to unite Kenya and Tanganyika. General acceptance of minimum standards of administration by all the colonial powers is an easier and a more practicable solution than the transfer of power to any world

[16] Labour conditions among the native workers of the Rand are the exclusive business of the South African Government, which is fully independent.

[17] No change in standards of government has been more dramatic than that which turned the odious tyranny of King Leopold's Congo into the well-administered Belgian Congo. Some of this improvement was due to a diminution of the temptations of the wild rubber trade, due to the great Dutch and English investment in the cultivated rubber industry of Malaya and the East Indies. But more was due to the working of the public conscience in Belgium, expressed in effective democratic institutions. No international assembly, yet created, is as effective an agent of control as a free parliament.

authority which has not far more power in other fields than the League of Nations had.

But uniform standards of administration are not all. What of uniformity of policy? That, too, might be achieved if uniformity of policy could first of all be agreed on. But it is not yet agreed that there is only one good colonial policy. For example, tenderness, perhaps excessive tenderness, for the existing economic system in West Africa has prevented as rapid an increase in production as Dutch or French methods would have given. A choice has been made against which much can be said—and for which much can be said. Some anthropologists, fearful of the damage done by the destruction of the social basis of native society, tend almost to regard as ideal Portuguese methods, which leave the native almost entirely alone, when it is not to the manifest interest of the white rulers to interfere with him. Left to himself, not given the strong economic stimulus of European tastes and needs, the African may seem idle—or wise. It is probable that only by forced labour and a most rigorous system of health policy could the French Cameroons have been raised to their present level of hygienic and economic progress. Is forced progress real progress? The same question is in dispute all over British Africa. A simple answer is easily given only by those who think there are simple, right answers to all political questions. A generation ago the simple answer would have been based on an uncritical belief in "progress"; today it would be based on an uncritical belief in "liberty."

But the problems of the Empire are problems of England, too. For the willingness of the average Englishman to think about "his" Empire is a basic presupposition of Imperial policy. Otherwise there is no possibility of an Imperial policy based on the choice of the English people, there is simply a policy hammered out by conflict and compromise between missionaries, businessmen, officials, soldiers, between people with all kinds of axes to grind, from the saving of souls to the making of money. The inertia with which the average Englishman regards his Empire has its good side. It keeps him from being too touchy or arrogant when he contemplates what he "owns" and the envy with which he is regarded. His Imperial zeal is tepid. For one thing, the connection between Imperial and English power and prosperity is less close than is often thought. What the English businessman and the English working man in the nineteenth century wanted was an extension, over as much of the world as possible, of reasonable opportunities for trade, investment, missionary effort, free institutions. He was ready to provide these blessings when the natives were slow or incompetent to supply a demand felt by the English, but not necessarily by the Chinese or Turks or Zulus. From trading settlements like Shanghai or Durban or Cape Coast Castle or Singapore, the threads of English interests spread all over the globe. Sometimes they needed the protection of the Imperial authority to save them from being broken (they were delicate); sometimes they only required special privileges like those wrung from China; sometimes the minimum facilities were provided by other civilizing powers. New York and Batavia were great trading centres where business could be done on almost British lines.

The flag had, at times, to follow trade, but there was nothing narrowly parochial about the Englishman in his great century. He was willing to make money without worrying too much about the colour of the flag or of the people concerned. Consider how much effort was wasted trying to divert British emigration from its natural outlet, the United States! Sentimental thinkers might regret that Liverpool and Glasgow took as much interest in the port of Buenos Aires as in the port of Montreal. But in that great age of true internationalists nobody cared very much about such points. The deplorable lack of fine feelings in Manchester cotton merchants irritated people like Tennyson, but the modern world, where the breed is scarcer, does not seem to be notably improved.

An orderly, well-conducted, bourgeois world in which industry and good conduct were properly rewarded was the old English ideal, and while it was no doubt preferable that as much of this world as possible should be under British rule, any reasonably modern government would do. It was certainly a question not worth fighting over. So compromises were made; no great international wars were fought, and to the surprise of more profound thinkers, when the first great war came, it came not over the mineral resources of Morocco, but over the old-fashioned question of the coexistence of the Habsburg Empire and the Serbian nation. And the second had no more rational—that is, simple economic causes—than the first. British businessmen were often rather stupid, but they were not stupid enough, in 1914 or in 1939, to think that a war was a really businesslike way of dealing with competitors who were also customers.

Apart from a small "Empire-conscious" minority, the English people had vague and mixed views about all parts of the outside world, inside or outside the Empire. To a large section of the population of Glasgow, the most important town outside Glasgow was Paterson, New Jersey. To a smaller and more prosperous section it was Rangoon. To others it was Montreal or New York. But the Imperial aspect of Poona or Pretoria did not make either of them half as well known to the Glasgow textile workers as Paterson. Even the obviously profit-making parts of the Empire were so because of investments which were not necessarily much more profitable because the money had been sunk under the shadow of the Union Jack.[18]

[18] Probably the most unpopular aspect of British Imperial policy in American eyes in the period after the last war was the Stevenson rubber scheme. This sellers' cartel put up the price of rubber for a time by the now standard methods of restriction of output. But the high price thus made possible was charged equally to all customers. It was in vain to plead being a British subject to the sellers. The scheme may, for a short time, have been profitable to a large number of other nationals (especially Dutch nationals) who also had holdings in rubber companies. The other restriction schemes that have been adopted work the same way. "A disproportionate advantage is secured by countries having colonial investments—not necessarily colonial possessions in the political sense. . . . It is as an investor that Great Britain finds her chief interest in the restriction of rubber, tin, copper, tea and so on" (H. V. Hodson in *The Empire in the World*, p. 205). As England liquidates her foreign investments under the

Such a frame of mind was not conducive to an acute sense of political responsibility. A Glasgow businessman whose son found an agreeable opening in Burma, thanks to the special connection between Glasgow and Burma that arose from the role of Glasgow businessmen in developing the Burma oil fields, did not necessarily feel any more interest in Burma as a community than a Liverpool businessman did in the Argentine Republic where his son had a promising opening made for him. That English rule in Burma made that country safe not only for Scotsmen, but for the even more unpopular Indians was not a truth much pondered on in Glasgow, where, had the question been raised, the solution suggested might have been a joint Scotch-Burmese campaign against the Indians, for the technique of anti-Semitism can be used in countries where there are no Jews, as the Japanese have shown in Siam, Indo-China, and Burma.

If this picture of the Englishman, or even of the Scotsman, as lukewarm in his Imperial enthusiasm is less formidable than that of a nation of land-grabbers, it, of course, raises a fresh question. Is there much justification for the rule of so indifferent a master over so great a part of the world? It is possible that England is

---

pressure of war, her interests change no matter what happens to the political ownership of the territories. And should she never go back to overseas investment on the old scale, the problem of providing the capital equipment, the skilled direction, the diversion of effort from home to foreign fields, remains. The rubber industry in Malaya and the Dutch Indies was not created either by nature or by the natives. And starting a rubber industry is no easy job, as Mr. Ford and Mr. Firestone have found in Brazil and Liberia. The English and Dutch creators of the East Indian rubber industry, who made millions of rubber trees grow where none grew before, deserved some reward. They may have been overpaid, but if they were, they were not the only examples of that fault in the modern world. As far as the English debarred from social equality the basic labour force, the Chinese, and left the political system of Malaya almost untouched, they showed no more responsibility for the duties of a community's leaders than is displayed in many a New England industrial city where the business rulers would almost as soon admit a Jew or a Canuck or a Bohunk to the country club as the English in Singapore would admit a Chinese. Both should have had the good sense and good humour of the Dutch.

land-poor, and even had she devoted all her energies to the Empire, the task of giving first-class government to so many scattered and varied territories may have been beyond her. The two model colonial powers, Holland and Belgium, gained from the comparative simplicity of their Imperial problems and from the fact that neither was a great European power, with the distractions and conflicting duties of that status. Sweden might have taken over bits of the British Empire to the advantage of everybody, but the small powers only held their imperial assets with ease because the greatest sea and imperial power was satiated. The basic power that preserved the Dutch and Belgian as well as the British Empires needed all sorts of bases, coaling stations, supplies of fresh water. Many small British colonies represent totally vanished needs like those that led to the occupation of St. Helena or decaying industries like the logwood trade in British Honduras, or the prizes of forgotten wars like minor West Indian islands. They were not so much assets as relics, as trophies.

The British public knew nothing of them and left—and leaves —their rule to officials who have other things to do that may seem and may be more important than the welfare of a few decaying settlements on the edge of Africa or lost in the Caribbean. A more acute Imperial sense, not a complete indifference to the idea of Imperial duty, is the remedy here.

In another department of Imperial policy it is unlikely that England will ever again play her role of an exporter of men and women, a role whose most important result was the foundation of the United States. There is (or was) in the United States a good deal of loose talk about the need for exporting millions to fill up the wide-open spaces of Canada that have for so long obstinately remained open and unfilled.[19] But the days when

[19] I have been asked in the United States why the English did not have a higher birth rate in order to have surplus children to send to Canada to prevent Ontario from becoming French. It was not clear to me why the English-speaking population of Ontario should not take the necessary steps. At any rate, this attempt to call in the Old World to redress the balance of the New is doomed to failure.

England was over-populated are past. The population is soon going to fall and there is going to be a shortage of just those elements which make the best emigrants, healthy young men and women of the type that is now not being born in sufficient numbers to keep up the population. To avoid a catastrophic fall in wealth-producing power will be difficult; and few in England take the ultra-Imperial view that it is no loss what the Empire gains. Unless the prospects of life in the Dominions are much better than they have been for ten years past, there will be no pressure on the young people of England to emigrate.[20]

But the view that the Empire cannot expect a tide of emigration, and the view that the Empire matters less economically and psychologically than orators assert, make it more difficult than ever for the average American to understand how it is that so many people live (and live moderately well) and play so great a world-wide role on an island not as big as New York and New England put together. There is to hand an easy but wrong answer: the wealth and power of England are purely a result of her Imperial possessions, and should her hold on the Empire weaken, she would sink rapidly into a decay not much less complete than that of tidewater Virginia a century ago. From that error it is an easy step to another: that it is for the Empire that the average Englishman is fighting, that to keep control of Hong Kong and Nigeria he resisted the *Blitz* and is fighting on all seas and in the air and on land half-way round the world. But this is an illusion; it is not for the Empire but for England that he is fighting; the Empire means far less to him, spiritually and materially, than the small though rich island where by far the greater part of the English-speaking population of the Empire lives and means to continue living. The American error arises naturally from applying to English history the rules of American history, but an error, however excusable, is still an error.

American economic history since the first settlements until our

[20] In the ten years before the outbreak of war in 1939, the standard of living in England rose relatively faster than in the Dominions.

own time has been based on the exploitation of great and untouched natural resources. Immense deposits of iron ore, of coal, of oil, of natural gas, vast areas of fertile soil, all repaid capital investment and ruthless industry. Until the present century it was not necessary to take thought for the morrow. As long as there were great areas of virgin soil or of uncut timber to repay the speculator and the settler, it was possible to neglect the eroded lands of tidewater Virginia, the cut-over forest areas of Michigan. American economy was less development than mining.[21]

It is, therefore, difficult for Americans to understand how a small, densely populated though fertile island can feed and house its people, much less be rich and powerful. That the main capital of a country, within very wide limits, is the skill, industry, character, and view of life of its inhabitants is a truth easily neglected. That political and educational methods, traditions of certain skills, inherited capital assets and prestige may all be more important than mere undeveloped natural resources is difficult to believe, although in New England the United States has an example of this truth even more striking than that furnished by Old England.[22]

[21] The lesson that the United States may be living beyond her means is the main theme of the new edition of Professor J. Russell Smith's admirable descriptive geography, *North America*. And between this edition of 1940 and that of 1925 the added emphasis on the need for national economy is the main difference. Between 1920 and 1930 the area of forest in the United States increased for the first time since the white man came. But this was less due to national husbanding of resources than to the growth of timber on abandoned land and to a less intensive development of agricultural resources.

[22] It is probable that if Chinese or Japanese had settled New Zealand, it would be more populous and have a greater gross economic equipment than it has at present. It would also have a much lower level of economic life per head of population than it has at present. The Maori natives, left to themselves, would not have reproduced either the English or the Chinese economy in New Zealand. Their kin, the Malagasies, have notably failed to develop the vast island of Madagascar. It may be argued that both the Maoris and the Malagasies have a happier life than Chinese, English, or Americans. Against this it may be pointed out that the French have had great difficulty in inducing the inhabitants of Madagascar to stay alive

So the American man in the street is inclined to regard the indisputable fact that the small island of Britain is rich, powerful, and populous as mysterious, unnatural, unjust, and probably due to some confidence trick. He is prone to believe, therefore, that it is simply explained by Imperial exploitation. Even if this explanation were adequate, it would leave unanswered the question of why this exploitation was done by the British to the exclusion of other peoples. "Nice work if you can get it." Why did the British get it? Why did the Dutch get it? But England and the Netherlands were rich countries by the standards of their age long before they had empires. Why was Spain not enriched by her vast Empire to the same degree? It is like asking why the Sioux did not develop the Mesabi range, or the Congo Negroes the Katanga copper field. Did it make no difference to Minnesota that it was settled by Scandinavians and not by migrants from the worked-out tobacco and cotton lands of the South? Would the Portuguese have developed the Katanga field as the English and Belgians have done? To state these questions is to answer them. It is not, indeed, to answer a large number of other questions; the physical beauty of the Maoris or the Malagasies is not less than that of the English or French because their economic efficiency is less. The Castilian, the Southerner, the Portuguese have many points of superiority over the Norwegian, the Yankee, and the Englishman. But they are all inferior at laying up treasure on earth. This may be to their credit, but it is a fact to be noted when we are considering the question of how England became and has remained rich. Like Plunkitt of Tammany Hall, she "seen her opportunities and [she] took 'em." And when the high visibility of those

---

and it is only in recent years that the Maori population of New Zealand is beginning to increase. If the present differential birth rate between whites and Maoris continues, New Zealand will become Maori again. But a New Zealand inhabited by Anglicized Maoris, like a Madagascar inhabited by Frenchified Malagasies, casts little light on what these islands would have been like if they had been left to their own devices, which included, in the case of New Zealand, cannibalism, and in the case of Madagascar the wasteful exploitation of the subject tribes by the ruling class of Hovas.

opportunities is considered, that she was able to take them is not due merely to her seeing them, but to having what it took to seize time by the forelock.

England had what it took. Most of the things that she had were due to no moral or intellectual superiority, but to luck. But this is common to other peoples, too. Twenty-five years ago the western prairies of Canada were all set to become the bread-basket of Europe. Western Ontario was a wilderness of lakes and scrub. The future of Canada lay in the prairie provinces. It has not turned out that way. It is not the fault of the prairie provinces that the world's bread-basket has got smaller, not larger. It is not the moral superiority of the few inhabitants of western Ontario that led to the discovery of gold, nickel, chrome. The political and technological changes that withered the high hopes of Winnipeg and Regina (as of Bismarck and Walla Walla) made Cobalt and other mining towns of basic importance to the solvency of Canada. And the basic advantages of the English position were not, primarily, of a different order from the gold that made San Francisco or the oil that made Tulsa.[23]

But although the economic and emotional interest of the English people in the Empire—and in the outer world—is exaggerated

[23] There is another reason, I am convinced, for the bewilderment of the average American in face of British prosperity. The United States has been a high-protectionist country for eighty years. The United Kingdom has become a protectionist country only in this generation. (The general tariff is only ten years old.) The basic arguments for free trade are simple and not much distorted by popular presentation. They are consistent with the other political and economic presuppositions of a capitalist free-enterprise economy. The good arguments for protection are complicated; they are inconsistent with a good deal of the presuppositions of a free-enterprise economy. The simple arguments for free trade are good as far as they go. The simple arguments for protection are bad. A slogan like "Protection means dear food" is intellectually respectable in a way that a slogan like "Make the foreigner pay" is not. Politicians, journalists, voters, all like simple slogans, simple arguments. In a free-trade country these arguments and slogans will be inadequate, but not in themselves false. In a protectionist country they will be both inadequate and false. This will be reflected in other areas of economic controversy than that of tariff policy.

by friends and enemies alike, it is genuine.[24] The Englishman is ready to welcome in a kindly if not profoundly interested way the loyalty of the other members of the Imperial family to the centre of the Empire. When the West or East Indies produce a great cricketer like Constantine or Ranjitsinhji, he feels a kind of paternal pride. If he knew anything of a great physicist like Lord Rutherford and knew that he was a New Zealander by origin, he would take the same mild paternal pride. That so many millions of people in all parts of the world should look on England as "home" is a story that gratifies his pride, although, of course, he thinks it quite natural, for, after all, England *is* home. It is true that he often annoys the zealous loyalist from the Dominions by his ironical treatment of Imperial symbols that are fighting words in Toronto or Dunedin, but are not exempt from irreverent treatment in London. He maddens Canadians by failing to distinguish them sharply enough from Americans, and Australians by assuming that they are mostly descended (and very romantic he finds it) from convicts. His profound indifference to any standards of snobbery but his own makes him thoughtless in his attitude to the pride of men who went to Upper Canada College or Paramatta. One may be the Canadian and the

[24] Between "1913 and 1938 average import prices fell by 6 per cent, whereas average export prices rose by 35 per cent, a tendency which . . . released income for expenditure on domestic demands and thus facilitated the transfer of resources from export to home production." A result was that the proportion of British industrial output sold abroad "fell from more than a third in 1912 to 27 per cent in 1935, and 15 per cent in 1938. . . . The volume of world trade rose by 30 per cent between 1913 and 1929 . . . and it moved to within four points of the 1929 level in 1937." (*The Economist*, September 5, 1942.) England was turning her activities inwards, a great material and spiritual revolution that has not yet had time to produce its full effect on the Englishman's attitude to the world. He is still more conscious of the unity of the world than his new economic interests encourage him to be. There is a welcome time-lag. No doubt a drastic contraction of the area of the Empire would accelerate the trend of public opinion towards a European isolationism. Whether any great power is psychologically prepared to take the place of England is, I suppose one must say, an open question.

other the Australian Eton, but for the Englishman the adjective cancels out the noun. He even forgets, from time to time, that the word "colonial" is now almost as much a gaffe as "Yankee" addressed to a scion of the first families of Virginia.[25]

If he displays complete ignorance of the internal politics and progress of the Dominions, the fault is not altogether his. By a disastrous convention, the English press seems to have agreed to treat Dominion politics with a reverence and tact even exceeding their tactical treatment of American politics. One body of patriotic and competent statesmen launch violent attacks on another body of equally patriotic and competent statesmen and one becomes the Administration and the other the Opposition and the English reader is left just as baffled as Little Wilhelmine. That all is for the baffling best in the Dominions is a comforting thought, but not one that rouses much spontaneous interest.[26]

The present war, the memory of the dark hour when only the Dominions stood in arms with England in face of the powers of darkness, has made the bond closer even than it was in the last war. That the Empire means something more than a formal relationship is proved by the rush of Canadians and Australians and

[25] That now traditional home of strip-tease in London, the Windmill, in its fine old Victorian way, prides itself on the public spirit with which it provides entertainment for its "colonial" patrons. News of the Statute of Westminster has not yet crossed Shaftesbury Avenue.

[26] Australia escapes, to some extent, from this numbing convention of excessively good manners. It is possible to conceal the fact that Australian politics differ in many ways from English, but not to hide the fact that Australian notions of legitimate conduct on the cricket field differ quite a lot from those of the mother country. The great body-line bowling controversy made Australia alive to Englishmen. That the Australians thought that the cricketers from England played too rough was a source of general satisfaction. For the Australian soldier, universally admired as a fighting man, had created a tradition of robust fun that is one of the English legends. And he is the hero or victim of innumerable jokes. The best is, I think, the story of the Cockney soldier who was told by a gushing chaplain that the Australians had captured Bethlehem on Christmas Eve. "I'll bet the Shepherds watched their flocks that night," was the uncovenanted-for reply. It is legends like this that make the Imperial relation a live one. There are, alas, no stories about the Canadians.

New Zealanders to fight in a quarrel that was, indeed, theirs, but which they only saw to be theirs because it was England's. And what was true of the Dominions was true also of most of the colonies. Indeed, the loyalty of some of those neglected children ought to have shamed the preoccupied parent. Some colonies have no doubt different destinies. Only very old-fashioned or naïve imperialists of the school of Lord Croft can imagine the people of Cyprus have a duty of "loyalty" to England, instead of to the Hellenic nation, now as much as in the brightest hours of Greek history the civilized world's creditor. And to very few Englishmen is the Empire as important as England is. For to the Englishman there will always be an England, while there may, in time, be no British Empire. In time, but not probably in our time, for it is a mistake for a ruler, however old and weary, to abdicate before his heir is ready and competent. The inheritor of the British Empire is not in sight. It takes more than blueprints and manifestoes to create or hold an empire. In the great days of English Empire-building, Latin tags were on the lips of the builders: and looking over the world, the Englishman, then and now, might quote:

> . . . *multosque per annos*
> *Errabant, acti fatis, maria omnia circum.*
> *Tantæ molis erat Romanam condere gentem.*

The British Empire was not built in a day or without effort. Nor will it fall in a day, to be succeeded with ease and grace by an organization that needs little more than ink, paper, and colour-process printing to get into working order.

India

"TO THE REFLECTIVE MIND, pondering on the general course of history, the British connexion with India cannot but appear one of the most astonishing things in the record—more astonishing than the conquests of Alexander, which carried Greek culture, for a time, into India, and even diffused its influence in Turkestan and China; more astonishing than the expansion of Rome, which carried the arms, the empire and the law of Rome as far as the upper waters of the Euphrates and Tigris; more astonishing than the Crusades, which carried the Frankish Knights of the Western Mediterranean into Syria and Palestine. A little island in the bleak North Sea; a vast sub-continent under a fiery sun, thousands of miles away; and the two conjoined together by the process of history. . . . The conjunction began in trade, as a business proposition, nearly three and a half centuries ago. Trade in its turn begot government, some two centuries ago, after the battle of Plassey, in 1757. A century ago, when English became the language of education (after Lord William Bentinck had stated, in 1835, that 'the great object of the British Government ought to be the promotion of European literature and science among the natives of India'), trade and government, the two previous links, began to pass into a contact of culture which made a firmer and far subtler link. In this new but now century-old process of culture contact, the old culture of India has drawn on the culture of the West; it has absorbed Western ideas of nationalism and constitutionalism; it has begun to fuse into a new amalgam with Western culture—an amalgam which has still to settle the nature of its own further development and (more important still) the nature of the contribution which it can make to the general progress of man."[1]

Professor Barker very rightly uses the word "astonishing" to describe the connection between India and Britain. Were it not impudent to describe the present political situation of a fourth or fifth of the human race so flippantly, one would be tempted to put "absurd" in the place of "astonishing." The relationship between the English people and the Indians is unnatural, outrageous, and makes it uncontestable that there is something very unusual, very out of the common, about one of the two peoples concerned. To deny this is to deny that there are any political norms, that any political relation is more odd than any other. That view *may* be defended, but it is a poor basis for warm interest in changing the political status of India. Those who do wish to change the political status do so on the assumption that there are more or less normal political arrangements, that the present arrangements in India are abnormal and should be replaced as soon as is prudently possible, or simply at once, by more normal institutions. These institutions will be Indian; the connection with Britain will be broken; that connection is so unnatural that other problems of "normal," "good," or "modern" government are unimportant. The abnormality is admitted by the British as well as by the Indians. But there is no such concurrence as to the origin of the abnormality. One view is very flattering to the British. This view maintains that British rule in India, the maintenance of this outrageous breach in political rationality, is the result of British craft, brutality, strength, ruthlessness, and political talent for tyranny. This is a tribute one nation seldom pays another. *Non Angli sed diaboli* is almost as flattering as *non Angli sed angeli*. If

[1] Ernest Barker: *Ideas and Ideals of the British Empire,* pp. 113–14.

the English are really political devils, with all the maleficent strength of their diabolic brethren, their role in the world is and must be of the greatest interest and promise. But this view which makes the English the sole or even the main authors of their connection with India is far too flattering and would not be accepted after a moment's reflection by such successful defiers of the diabolic power as the Americans or Irish, or such current competitors as the Germans or Japanese.

The unnatural connection between England and India is the result of some abnormality in India, not in England. Only such an abnormality could account for the rule of a population nearly ten times as great, half the world away, by the English, or rather by a small part of the English. For to the English state, India, though important, has never been nearly as important as the politics of the near-by European states. French or German threats to British immunity from invasion have been far more dominant themes of British policy than anything that occurs in India. And as for the Englishman in the street, vague gratification about the "brightest jewel in the crown" and a general indifference to Indian problems have been the main features of his attitude to India for a century past. That indifference, that refusal to take thought on Indian matters, no doubt prove that rule of India by so mentally lazy a democracy as England is outrageous. But this indifference does make it still more strange that England should rule India, if conquering India and ruling it were, in fact, a full-time job. If it had been a full-time job, if the whole strength and attention of the English state had been needed for the acquisition and maintenance of the English "Indian Empire," then it would not have been founded nor, if by accident it had been, would it have lasted for over one hundred and fifty years.

The first abnormality in the Indian situation is the ambiguity of the word "India." By it do we mean something like "France" or something like "Europe"? Both views can be justified, up to a point, though it is less misleading to think of India as being equivalent to Europe than to think of it as being equivalent to

France or England or even pre-Bismarckian Germany. In many ways India is less united than Europe was before the rise of nationalism. There are many more varied languages—but there are more effective common tongues than Europe has had since the decline of Latin. India, indeed, has the good fortune to have an equivalent of Latin, a tongue common to all the educated classes of India, and that tongue is English. Owing to its eclectic character, Hinduism is more a source of religious unity than Christianity has been in Europe since the Reformation, but on the other hand, there is no equivalent in Europe to the focus of disunion presented by the great Moslem minority outside the Hindu community, or by the caste system inside it. India is more of a natural geographic unit than Europe is, but no more than the Iberian Peninsula, North America, the delta of the Rhine, all areas provided with irrational but important boundaries like those between Spain and Portugal, the United States and Canada, Holland and Belgium. India had some kind of political unity in the past; so had Argentina and Uruguay, to name a pair of kindred but separate states; so had Holland and Belgium, so had central Europe under the Holy Roman Empire. These past memories do not prevent real national feeling dividing what geopolitics, even race, language, and religion, seem to have united. The present unity of what we call India is a British creation; materially, since the provision of a basic authority over all the territory between the Himalayas and Ceylon has been the work of the English; psychologically, since dislike of English rule has been a great if inadequate unifying force. It is, perhaps, thanks to this unconscious nation-building talent of the English that there is a chance of one or two nationalities taking control in India, instead of a dozen or so, that there is some ground for hope that the history of a free India will be more like that of the United States or China than that of Europe or of South America.

But it should not be forgotten that the creation of a national feeling has its dangers. It may be a force making for unity inside a given political unit, but it may be a force making for irreparable disunion. It is too often forgotten that the *religion* of nationalism is new, a Western invention, perhaps the most deadly invention the world has ever known. Old-fashioned patriotism was attachment to a particular area, or loyalty to a particular dynasty or political organization, or to a religion, or was simply dislike of "foreigners," including the people in the next village. States could exist which defied all modern nationalist dogmas, which were not united in race, language, religion, or even political structure. As long as the Hungarian Kingdom was content to carry on its business in Latin and to allow for anomalies like the semi-independence of Croatia, it was reasonably united. But as soon as the Magyars insisted on making their exotic language compulsory and insisted on making Magyars out of all the subjects of the crown of St. Stephen, they created new nationalities as fast as they strengthened their own. Slovaks, Croats, Rumanians, all imitated their masters. Nor was this the only example. As Renan pointed out to David Strauss, the moment the Germans in central Europe began to become mad with racial pride, to be conscious of themselves as a divinely selected people, not merely as the chief people of the racial mosaic of central Europe, the other peoples reacted. Czechs, Italians, Poles were all educated in nationalism by the German example. It is very doubtful if Belgium or Switzerland could have been founded any time after 1870. The belief that only united national states had any right to exist was too strong. Yet, from any but the nationalist point of view, Belgium and Switzerland are more civilized, more useful, more promising states than some purely national agglomerations that could be named.

Nationalism is new in India; it is new in Europe, too. But it is a creed or disease with powers of growth that recall Iowa corn rather than English oak. Because there was no Moslem national feeling a generation ago, or ten years ago, is no guarantee that there is no such nationality well on the way to mature life now. The Poles for long refused to admit that there was a genuine Lithuanian national feeling because there wasn't in the time of

Pan Tadeusz or Pilsudski's youth. The Poles were wrong. The nationalist force of disunion can grow very rapidly inside a hitherto united political area, especially if one nationalist movement provokes a reaction. Ireland is a fine example. The more the dominant Irish party insisted on its Gaelic and Catholic and archaic character, the more the Ulster Protestants insisted that they were not Gaels, not Catholics, not corporative peasants. Belfast is less Irish today than it was in 1798; Dublin is more. We have no present means of knowing what will happen in India once the artificial steel frame of British rule is withdrawn. But the modern history of Europe does not suggest that unity over so great an area will be easy to attain or maintain or that, once the idea of an Indian nation has taken root in the minds of the majority, they can prevent the idea of Indian nations taking root in the minds of the minorities. If that time comes, the Moslem leaders of the Congress party may come to seem as unnatural as the Ulster Protestant founders of the United Irishmen seem in modern Belfast.

When, therefore, liberals in Washington or London talk simply of giving "freedom to India" they may be guilty, in some cases, of over-simplifying a complicated situation. For they may not have asked themselves what they mean by "India" or by "freedom." By India, they mean the political unit constructed by English rule. As far as they assume that there was something inevitable in that unity, they are assuming something that requires a great deal of proof. For there is nothing in the political demarcation of the rest of the world to suggest that united national states are formed inside every apparently appropriate geographical area, whether that area be the Danube Valley, so long united by the Habsburg dynasty, or the Indian peninsula, so recently united by the English. And when they talk of "freedom," they do not mean freedom in the political sense, freedom in the economic sense; they mean freedom in the nationalist sense, which is simply freedom from the rule of a foreign nation. That freedom not only need have no connection with freedom in the sense that Jefferson or John Stuart Mill or Lincoln meant freedom; it may be incompatible with the other freedoms. The other freedoms may all be sacrificed to national self-sufficiency, economic, cultural, military. It is rather odd that critics who have been lamenting (often very uncritically) the so-called Balkanization of Europe which is alleged to have been brought about by the Treaty of Versailles should take so lightly the risk of a Balkanization of India, that liberals who are highly critical, even today, of the national resentments of European peoples, who believe or profess to believe that nationalism is not enough there, that the Dutch or the Norwegians will only fight for national independence if they are promised a New Deal as well, take it for granted that all that is necessary to make formidable belligerents of the peoples of India is just that national independence which, in Europe, is thought to be out-moded.

And this acceptance of the nationalist claim in India is not often accompanied by an explanation of two interesting phenomena of the recent Japanese triumphs in Asia. The Japanese have been most successful in Siam, which is entirely independent, and in French Indo-China, where the old type of imperialism is most firmly entrenched, where native nationalist aspirations are most ruthlessly repressed. In these two countries we have no mere case of passive acquiescence in Japanese conquest, but of important and effective help being given. Against the simple view that British rule in Asia is condemned by the failure of the defence of Burma and Malaya, I should like to set the simple view that it is condemned because it was too liberal. The example of Siam shows that "free" Asiatic nations may take the Japanese side out of fear, greed, or genuine admiration for the most successful example of what Asiatics can do with freedom. The example of Indo-China shows that a European imperialist power, even at the lowest point in its history and prestige, can both repress native discontent by the guillotine and do a profitable deal with the victorious Japanese. There are lessons in the recent history of southeast Asia, but they are not all lessons of one kind. The view that what was wrong with the British in Malaya and Burma was weak, liberal sentimentality has the same *prima facie* plausibility as has the opposite view, that they were not liberal enough. Neither view is more than a sophomoric debating point, but one is no more sophomoric than the other.

There is a real problem concealed under the ambiguous word "India" and a real problem concealed under the word "freedom." This second statement is not so evidently true as the first, for it may be that the whole meaning of "freedom" in "freedom for India" will be exhausted when its primary meaning, the cessation of all political connection with Britain, is achieved. We know no more, on this view, of what "India" will do with "freedom" than we know what Poland or Lithuania or Greece will do with their freedom when it is restored. In advocating freedom for India, we are, then, advocating a political status as a good thing in itself without any views as to its consequences in other political goods, for the "life, liberty, and the pursuit of happiness" of the eighteenth century has been reduced to one aim, independence.

This view is not foolish, but it is not, in the ordinary sense of the term, "progressive." It makes the attainment of national independence the *summum bonum* of political science, which is a retreat from the more complicated ideas of national good held over most of the civilized world in the late nineteenth century and generally paid lip service in discussions of the future of old, highly self-conscious and successful nationalities in Europe.

The American and English friends of Indian freedom who hold this view are, in doing so, showing themselves more realist, more trustworthy observers of contemporary political realities than they usually are. For it is a fact that nationalism is as strong as ever, probably stronger, that attempts to provide substitutes for it in the form of international political or religious creeds have miserably failed. And there is no reason why India (whether that be a unity or a plurality) should differ from Europe or America, or why Indians should not be allowed their own way even to the point of folly, as much as the inhabitants of Haiti are (with liberal approval), or the inhabitants of the Danube Valley (with the fairly general disapproval of the defenders of Haiti). For as Bernard Shaw pointed out long ago, in the most valuable of his political tracts,[2] until the national question is settled, the other questions that perplex a nation cannot even be tackled; all the solutions provided by the foreign country are sterile, however well intentioned. There remains the problem of whether there is a "national question," and that is a problem easily solved. When, in fact, a large number of people in any geographical area assert that there is and do not limit their expression of this conviction to words, there is one. The political customer is always right and the Indian political customers have given the temporary British masters of the land notice to quit. The Indians who know what they are doing and are prepared for all the consequences of such a change are, of course, a minority. So were the Americans who got rid of George III.

So much may be taken for granted. There is in England a general indifference to India, combined, in the case of the man in the street, with a natural if unfortunate impatience with arguments and conduct of the type associated with Mr. Gandhi, who is, indeed, a profoundly un-English or un-American figure. And, at a more sophisticated level, there is a scepticism about the whole process of imperialism, a realization of its necessary impermanence and superficial character, and a readiness, based on ignorance as much as on informed judgment, to write off British rule in India as discreditable, uninteresting, or obsolete, or all three. That refusal to take any interest in the successes of their fellow countrymen in India which Macaulay lamented a century ago has certainly not been weakened in the last twenty years. The tradition that makes the returned Anglo-Indian the most formidable of all bores, so that words like "Poona" or "pukka" are sure of a laugh, like "Rotary" or "D.A.R." in America, is too strong for the case for British rule in India to be given a ready hearing in Britain. But it is impossible to keep the English mind, when

[2] The Preface of *John Bull's Other Island.*

it *does* reflect on India, from wondering how, if the Indian problem is as simple as it seems in, say, Berkeley, California, the Anglo-Indian problem ever arose at all. The Englishman is ready to get out, but not to get out and pretend that all basic Indian problems were created by his arrival and will be solved by his departure. Indian problems are manifestly so real, so complicated, and on such a scale that even the most self-satisfied Englishman, even that inverted type of Englishman who carries the basic national complacency to its logical extreme and sees in his countrymen the most important root of evil, cannot quite accept the magnificent historical role attributed to him by his Indian critics and their friends.

He may be indifferent about the whole business; he may await the results of English withdrawal with ironical scepticism or genuine hope; but he cannot pretend to think that more than a rudimentary beginning of the solution of India's troubles will have been achieved when the last British soldier and official leaves. But if he knows India, if he has served there, he may have deeper feelings, and feelings less like those with which he is credited in Indian nationalist demonology. He may have passed the most active years of his life in India. He may have been the second or third generation of his family to do so. And with his acute appreciation of the reality and complexity of Indian problems, there goes a natural anxiety. It is a fact, however deplorable, that modern India, politically speaking, is a British creation. A mere political structure may not be as important as politicians think it is, but it is important nevertheless. And the English official in India or retired from India has in his mind the nightmare possibility of violent and endemic disorder. It was this general disorder that made British rule in India possible and, for a time, even welcome. Once British rule is ended, how can we be sure that India will not undergo the experience of China, of many years of internal and external war? That the Anglo-Indian civil servant should fear this is not unnatural; that he should wish his fears to prove groundless is far more common than may be credited by people who know the Indian civil servant as a comic figure or as a stock figure out of Kipling.

In the last generation the English official in India has had to adjust himself to a new and difficult world. In the old days he had as his equals and superiors his own people, men who spoke his own language in every sense of the term. He had, too, an unshaken belief in the intrinsic worth of what he was doing. That British rule in India was good for India was the belief not merely of uncritical bureaucrats, but of men of the talents of Macaulay, John Stuart Mill, and John Morley. This belief was part of the general confidence of the Western world in progress, in the adoption by the whole world of liberal ideas in economics, in politics, and in religion. The English in India, in some cases, developed a genuine interest in the culture of the country, but they did not, any more than Greeks or Romans or Americans, doubt that where they and the Indians differed, they were right. Taos is very interesting and worth preservation, but not at the cost of barring the way to the Santa Fe Railroad. So with many aspects of Indian life. Some were not even picturesque; they were simply wrong. The English officials who decided to outrage Indian opinion by making the burning alive of widows a crime knew that they were taking a political risk. Some were against taking the risk, but none of them thought that there was much to be said for this solution of the problem of what to do with widows. So suttee was forbidden. Indian opinion has come round to the point of view of the English officials and the tiny body of Europeanized Brahmin reformers, but the action of the English in interfering with Indian domestic law was, from the nationalist point of view, wrong. And it may well be that, in fact, this foreign intrusion, though it may have accelerated the ending of suttee (assuming that there would have been a spontaneous Indian criticism of it, without European contacts), did in fact prevent the growth of a genuine native criticism of some of the less attractive features of Hindu family law. Left to themselves, the Indian reformers might have had an easier time in converting their fellow countrymen to a more humane viewpoint, without the clouding of the issue by the natural nationalist resentment of foreign intervention. But a century ago the English rulers of India had no doubts. They knew what was right and good for India as they knew what was right and good for England.[3]

They saw the Indians, with a good deal of arrogance, as the heathen in his darkness, which they proposed to enlighten. And, pending the enlightenment, they proposed to keep the heathen from doing things which the light vouchsafed to Englishmen, the light of gospel truth, showed to be wrong. They would not actually prohibit idolatry, but they would prohibit such by-products of it as suttee and thuggee. Such a faith was as necessary to make the English Empire in India possible as was mere physical energy and martial skill. The latter could have produced a series of raids and fortunes, but not that upturning of the Indian soil by English ideas which was deliberately undertaken by the conquerors. They risked the upturning because of their profound faith that they were right.

And where the old confident, evangelical view that salvation was not too generously awarded, even to professed Christians, was absent, there remained a great deal of the confident conviction of the moral and intellectual superiority of Christian morals and Christian doctrine (however broadly conceived).[4]

[3] On the other side must be set the fact that a considerable number of Indian widows did, in fact, escape a horrible death. The same problem arises in the United States. It is obviously better that Southern opinion should condemn lynching than that it should be suppressed by federal intervention. But although this general principle is accepted, the conviction with which it is held is weakened with each individual lynching which a federal law might have prevented.

[4] And not only Christian. That representative English Broad Churchman Charles Kingsley welcomed the attempt to reform Hinduism made by the Bramo Somaj and defended its founders against the criticism of more orthodox churchmen. "I trust that no bigotry here will interfere with men who, if they are not at the point to which St. Paul and St. John attained, are trying honestly to reach that to which Abraham, David, and the Jewish prophets rose: a respectable height I should have thought" (*Charles Kingsley: His Letters and Memories of His Life*, Vol. II, p. 318).

With the decline in the missionary fervour of the English, with the decline in the confidence in the superiority of Western ways, and with a corresponding scepticism of the results of their adoption in India, the English official in India, like the Englishman at home, was left face to face with the rising, hopeful, believing force of nationalism, the most powerful political force in the modern world. He had anticipated the growth in India of Western political ideas. That the Indians should begin to demand "liberty," a free press, representative institutions, complete equality before the law, even independence, had been anticipated with more or less approval or resignation. But Macaulay and Mill and Morley and the early official sponsors of the Indian National Congress had not anticipated that these demands for liberty might be unaccompanied by any corresponding willingness to take over the related institutions and ideas of Western culture. That the impact of English rule should break through the cake of custom of Hindu society was anticipated and welcomed. So Nehru is a legitimate if formidable end product of English rule. Macaulay would recognize in him a natural result of his educational reforms, Morley of his administrative reforms, Mill of his own political principles. But what would any of these believers in progress, in industrialism, in rationalism make of a Gandhi? What would they make of the exaltation of the Hindu past, of the ingenious manipulation of Hindu history, of the contempt for Western views of life displayed by the Mahatma and his followers? What would they make of the role of a saint in the modern world? They did not like the rule of saints or near saints in England or anywhere else. This phenomenon, the domination of Indian life by a saint, is proof of how thin European culture is in India. The Indians may be quite right, but it is ignoring an important aspect of Indian life to disregard the fact that Gandhi's role in India shows how unlike our Western world India is, and how rash it is to use simple Western political language and analogies in Indian matters. It is only by ignoring the side of Mr. Gandhi which is most important to him and to his followers that we can treat him as just another politician. And this is to display a racial arrogance as deep as any shown by an English soldier or official. Unless Gandhi means what we mean, he must be wrong, but he is a great man and therefore cannot mean what he says!

Some of the difficulties which the Englishman (and the American) feels in understanding, or praising, or abusing Mr. Gandhi arise from the tacit acceptance of the convention that religious ideas are unimportant or identical. Mr. Gandhi is a religious man; so is Mr. Henry Wallace; so is Chiang Kai-shek; so is Lord Halifax. "Mahatma" means no more than "Reverend." It is true that Mr. Gandhi's insistence on spinning cloth, slowly and inefficiently by hand, is odd. Why not take the goods that the gods of machinery provide? But Mr. Wallace practises with the boomerang. Mr. Bernard Shaw is a vegetarian. Mr. De Valera is a teetotaler. There is little readiness to ask the question: "What is Mr. Gandhi's religion?" Is it the same as Mr. Wallace's, or General Chiang Kai-shek's or Dr. Salazar's or Dr. Buchman's or the Pope's? Is his insistence on spinning cotton thread a mere personal allergy to machine-spun thread, or is it something fundamental? These questions are not asked, so Mr. Gandhi is insulted by having his most important ideas taken as irrelevant, the principles which are his springs of action treated as trivial details. A man who wishes to lead his people backward in time, who wishes to undo progress not merely because it is British, but because it is a blind alley, in Chungking or Chicago as much as in Bolton or Bombay, is given the reverent admiration of believers in the Five-Year Plan and the technological revolution. When Mr. Gandhi proposes to deal with the Japanese as he proposed to deal with the British, his admirers were startled much more than they should have been. His behaviour is all of a piece. Being no fool, the Mahatma does not believe that India, the Congress party that is to say, recruited as it is from the races which by British policy have not in modern times been given the chance to become or remain martial races,[5]

---

[5] I have no views on the justice or injustice of the British claim that the martial races of India as raw materials for an army are superior to the mass

could organize effective resistance to the armies and fleets of the only Oriental people to take over the military and other techniques of the West on their own terms and at their own time. If "India" has to fight for her freedom in the crude Western sense of the term, she is not well prepared to do so; if she were, she could have thrown out the British long ago.[6] But if passive resistance works, it is a perfect solution for the problem that faces the Indian nationalist. Indeed, it is the only solution. For a truth that was hidden in 1939 is as clear as noon in 1942. Only a nation with first-class industrial equipment can resist a nation with first-class industrial equipment—and the will to use it as an instrument of war. India is not such a nation and, if Mr. Gandhi is to have his way, will be even less such a nation after independence than before. So it matters little whether the reasoning takes this form. Only great industrial nations can win or keep freedom by fighting; India is not such a nation; India must win and keep freedom by other means. Or this freedom can be won and kept by non-military methods; India can win freedom by non-violent methods; India does not need modern industry to gain or keep freedom. The result is that the sacred leader of the Indian nationalists is an enemy of progress as the Western world understands progress. The Western world may be wrong about progress, but if so, a conviction of sin ought to have more results than an approval of Mr. Gandhi.

Of course, the sympathizers with Mr. Gandhi do not believe

---

of Hindu peasants. Such a judgment is not necessarily true because it is stated by British officials or false because it offends a certain naïve egalitarianism among chronically anti-militarist elements on the Left. But it is not improbable that it would be an economy of time and resources to start training a shock division with Pomeranian rather than Neapolitan recruits. The same may be true in India—or Spain.

[6] According to a good authority, a high Washington official has recently asserted that if the Indians were free they would make a Japanese invasion impossible. "They could defeat the Japs if they only combined to throw rocks at them." I first heard this theory in another form from an Anglo-Indian official. "If they would all spit at us at the same time, they could drown us." The Indians did not drown the English.

that he is right about progress. He is merely a tool whereby the Indian masses can be roused to action against the enemy of progress, the British government. Once that obstacle is removed, Gandhi's hobbies and fads will be gently put aside. The realists will come out on top. So shrewd, realist businessmen and publicists argued in the early days of the Russian Revolution and especially in the early days of the New Economic Policy. A man like Lenin couldn't *really* want to abolish capitalism. If he did, the real bosses of the machine knew better and the old man would be gently edged out.

That Mr. Gandhi will be put on one side in an independent India I can well imagine. That realists will come out on top I can well believe. But that any of us knows who those realists will be or can identify them at this moment, I do not believe. That they will be parliamentary orators or "democratic" politicians seems to me most unlikely. The rulers of the world at present are a miscellaneous enough lot. So were their immediate predecessors. Herr Hitler, we all know, is an unsuccessful artist and moderately competent house-painter. Signor Mussolini was a Socialist journalist. General Chiang Kai-shek is a professional soldier. Mr. Stalin is a spoiled priest turned professional revolutionary. Mr. Churchill has been everything but a lawyer; and being a lawyer is one of the most unimportant parts of Mr. Roosevelt's equipment. So such eminent pleaders as Mr. Gandhi and Mr. Nehru will be pioneers if they make the grade and, alone of all their lawyer tribe, ride the revolutionary storm in which such acute and eloquent lawyers as M. Blum and M. Kerensky so speedily sank.

The problem of the "freedom" of "India" is not merely the problem of the freeing of India from British control. It is not even the much more difficult problem of securing India from foreign (but non-British) control, or from native (but undemocratic) control. For India is part of the world, and the role of India has implications for other peoples than the Indians and other causes than that of Indian independence. It was the outbreak of the World War that halted the progress (such as it was) of the Indian reforms. The Congress party governments in the Indian provinces resigned after the outbreak of war (in 1939). Their basic grievance was serious and genuine. The English government used its control of the "Indian" executive to involve India in war with Germany, instead of leaving the choice to the Indian people or, at any rate, to the Indian legislature. The Congress party asserted that India had as much right to choose whether she would enter the war or not as the Dominions like Canada, Australia, New Zealand, South Africa, which were not bound by the English government's action. To assume Indian belligerency was to deny the Indian claim to nationhood and to belie English promises of dominion status. Stated in these terms, there is no answer to the claim. But the terms do not exhaust all the relevant facts. It may be that a fuller consideration leads to the same result, but a fuller consideration is called for. In the British Dominions which chose to declare war, responsibilities of defence and of military organization were entirely met by local means. How adequately they were met is another matter. The governments of these Dominions (except in the case of South Africa) were really representative of their peoples, as far as ordinary democratic standards of representation go. No such government or method of representation existed in India or could be improvised overnight. It would not have been so difficult to have some consultation of the Indian population as it would have been to have had a consultation of the (coloured) majority of the South African population, but it would have been difficult.

But it is probable that among the motives that led the English government to involve India in the war without any consultation of the Indian people (even within the framework of existing political institutions) was a doubt of what the decision would be. For there was no very apparent reason why, if asked, the Indian people or any Indian representative body should have agreed to enter the war on the side of Britain against Nazi Germany. That the attack on Poland was the beginning of a world war, that the British people were determined to see it through at whatever cost, that the interests of all the free (or would-be free) nations were involved in active resistance to Nazism, seems evident now. But it was not evident in Washington or Moscow in 1939, so why should it have been evident in Delhi? And if the promise of dominion status is presumed to have been sufficient inducement, why did the attainment of dominion status not induce Eire to join the anti-German alliance? [7]

The consequences of Indian neutrality would have been immediately serious and, in the not very long run, disastrous. That neutrality would have made the English position in the Near East very difficult and thus opened an easy way to Nazi seizure of Iraq's oil. And, as far as China is concerned, the decisive point would have been the loss of the Burma Road *at once,* and the loss, in the not *very* long run, of the substitutes for the Burma Road. For there is no convincing evidence adduced that an entirely independent Burma would have done anything more than was

[7] If it be replied that the partition of Ireland is the cause of Ireland's refusal to join the United Nations or even to permit active sympathy with the other traditional oppressed Catholic nation, Poland, it should be remembered that Mr. De Valera has made it plain that were the unity of Ireland under his government effected tomorrow, Ireland would still be neutral. That neutrality already inflicts great handicaps on the United Nations. It endangers the lives of American soldiers and makes victory more difficult and more remote. But such representatives of Irish opinion as Mr. De Valera and Cardinal McRory have made it plain that no consideration of the general issues involved in the cause of the United Nations will have any effect on Irish policy. If they had their way, there would be no British and no American soldiers or sailors in any part of Ireland, even though this exclusion would still further embarrass the United Nations and probably cost the lives of a great many American soldiers of Irish origin. Is there any evidence that Indian feeling for the United States is likely to be stronger than that of the Irish? Or that in the mass of the Indian people the wrongs of China would have seemed to justify entry into a remote war when the wrongs of Poland leave the Irish frozen (as far as their leaders represent them)?

done by Siam.[8] That the Burmese sense of duty to their Chinese and Indian neighbours is so great that they would take the risk of resisting a Japanese invasion is a view which it is possible to assert, but not with any great intrinsic power of convincing anybody who has realized the fact that the essence of modern nationalism is that a nation has no duty to anything but itself. And if it be answered that the leaders of India or Burma would have seen that the spread of Japanese power was a menace to their future, why should they not have been tempted to imitate the English or American statesmen who thought that Hitler would stop eating when he had been given enough food, or that the sight of Japanese rule spreading over eastern Asia would stimulate the anti-Japanese feelings of the Indians or Burmese as the victories of Hitler were to "make fascism more repulsive to the American people." That the rulers of India would have felt deep sympathy with the Chinese can well be believed (the same belief is not so easy in

[8] The general question reappeared in a fairly simple form when the temporary closing of the Burma Road was decided on in 1940. The decision was made because English power in eastern Asia in 1940 was even weaker than it proved to be in 1942. As soon as that power had been strengthened (very inadequately as the event proved), the Burma Road was reopened. But the decisions were not made by the Burmese government. And the decision to reopen the Burma Road was as much an outrage on the independence of Burma as the decision to involve India in war with Germany was an outrage on the independence of India. It may have been necessary for the independence of *China,* but that was no more the business of the Burmese than the freedom of Europe is, apparently, of the Irish. And if it be said that a neutral Burma could have insisted on her right as a neutral to ship munitions to China, the answer is to be seen in the fate of neutrals all over the world who had not the power to defend the rights they might have insisted on. The blockade of Burma would have been primarily a naval affair. No navy can be improvised, the Chinese have no navy, and the British Navy *ex hypothesi* has been excluded from these waters (and, anyway, what duties has England to China, on the pure nationalist theory?). If it be further argued that Burma should and would have fought for her rights as a neutral, it can be answered that, practically, it doesn't matter and that, in any case, the old view that a neutral has a duty to insist on her rights has become obsolete. At least it is very hard to hold it after the series of neutrality acts passed by the United States between 1937 and 1939 inclusive.

the case of Burma). But in this grim modern world no song evokes less applause than "I can't give you anything but love."

And, at the risk of being tedious, it must be repeated that the most famous, most representative, and most powerful Indian leader does not merely believe in non-violent resistance, but believes that Chinese lack of faith in the power of non-resistance is due to their not having reached the moral level of Mr. Gandhi's followers. If you believe that Mr. Gandhi is right in this, you can not only solve the problem of getting the English out of India without letting the Japanese in; you can solve the problem of getting the Japanese out of China and the Philippines, too. All that has to be done is to convert the Chinese and the Filipinos, which is a legitimate missionary activity.

There is no certainty that, had the English rulers of India referred the question of Indian belligerency to the existing Indian legislature or to the Congress party, neutrality would not have been the preferred policy. Citizens of the United Nations who believe that national autonomy is the only or the basic issue of this war, and who extend this view all over the world (even to Europe), and who believe that the old maxim "Let justice be done though the heavens fall" is a political and moral imperative and are really prepared to have the heavens fall on *them,* are entitled to condemn English policy at once and without conditions. Other persons may condemn it, but only after thought and after weighing the issues, which are not simple. And they are not simple because issues in this war (or other wars) seldom are simple, if by "simple" we mean that they can be stated, at once, without qualifications and without reflection.

Considerations like these are in the minds of a great many honest Englishmen who have had little reason in recent years to believe that revolutions can be made with rose-water, that "democracy" is bound to win, or that force, in internal or external argument, is no remedy. They fear that a sudden change in the system of government, the throwing away by the leaders of the Congress of the support given to political authority, to *civilian* authority in India, by the prestige of British power, may be a great mistake. They understand, intellectually if not emotionally, the passion that drives the Congress leaders and rank and file to risk the dangers, which, nevertheless, are not merely English inventions. And they are a little irritated by the assumption that their attitude merely is stupid, selfish, or fantastic. They may worry, genuinely, about the risk about to be run by so great a portion of the human race, without having any faith that the risk can be avoided. For they know that peoples insist on making their own mistakes and that only a profound conviction on the part of the tutelary power that it knows the answer can nerve it to impose on a great mass of human beings the kind of discipline a parent imposes on a child it sees playing on the edge of a precipice.

That the arguments, the fears of the foreign ruler should make little or no appeal to the ruled is inevitable. The leaders of the nationalist party may be conscious of the political incompetence that, in the past, made their nation's conquest possible or easy. As far as they are conscious of this fact, they may see their own role as that of redeemers of the national reputation. There lies upon them, as on Conrad's Lord Jim, the heavy burden of national redemption.[9] So they welcome the opportunity of showing that, at last, the lesson has been learned and that an appeal to the past experience of the people is irrelevant and insulting. But a commoner attitude is that of stout denial. The national weaknesses are denied, or explained away as signs of a higher spiritual character. The conquest is accounted for either by making the conquerors something like gods—if wicked gods—or in terms of the treason or folly of individuals; if Dermot McMurrough had had a more respectable private life, there would have been no English

9 I am informed by one of the few Englishmen who know anything of Poland that the need to redeem the political futility of the old Polish Republic was one of the dominant themes of Polish thought in the nineteenth century. The same theme ought to have been dominant in Irish nationalist thought, but I have never noticed its presence in any serious quantity.

conquest of Ireland.[10] Such explanations do not tell us very much. They do not, for example, account for the different histories of Scotland and Ireland. Scotland has had as fine a collection of traitors of high rank as any country can boast. But Scotland, fortunately, had her Celtic polity destroyed in time to become an independent state, not merely a nation. This explanation is, of course, most offensive to the romantic side of the Irish nationalist movement which uses "Celtic" as a term of unqualified praise instead of one of condemnation in the political sphere.

So in India the fiction of a heroic, politically successful past is cherished although India, for three hundred years at least, has been the victim of a series of foreign invaders whose success has shown some disastrous weakness on the political side of Hindu society. The more naïve Indian nationalist, in his happy indifference to the political facts of life, to the truth that political failures are as common as successes and are great disasters, does not worry lest the past should repeat itself, for he sees that past through a golden haze. The realist is determined that the lesson of the past *shall* be learned. So if he is a Bengali, he trains himself to accept and practise those military virtues to which he attributes, rightly, the success of the English, the Sikhs, the Mahrattas, the Pathans. He takes to rather brutal sport with a religious zeal that astonishes the disillusioned Briton, and whether it is a matter of playing football in bare feet or assassinating a magistrate, determines to show—and does show—that mere want of courage is not inherent in his people.

The majority of that minority of the English people that has any views on India is perplexed and anxious, but resigned to seeing the Indian people go their own way. But it is still further perplexed by its inability to make up its mind on the question: is there an Indian people or several? For it is one thing to let

---

[10] One traitor may not be enough.

> Let Erin remember the days of old
> When her faithless sons betrayed her.

people do what they like with their own lives and happiness, and another to let them do what they like with other people's. If an independent India has to face disorder, or a temporary lowering of the standard of public services and economic efficiency, it gets an immediate return in self-esteem and a possible future return in the revolutionary changes made more easy by the withdrawal of the hand of the foreign ruler. But if there are large sections that do not share the emotional life of the majority, they get less than no dividends from the triumph of the majority, and one of the revolutionary possibilities opened to the majority by the withdrawal of the foreign power may be just the oppression of the minority. This argument for British hesitation about turning over complete power at once to an "Indian government" is stated in two parts. One of these seems to me to have next to no value, to be a legal argument, ignoring that what is going on in India is some kind of revolution and that all the English can do is to try to limit the destructive side of the revolution. When delay in transferring power to an Indian government is made dependent on the consent of the Indian "states," this truth is being ignored to a point that weakens the whole English case.

Nearly a century ago Disraeli, who gained clarity of vision from his alien origin, defined the Irish problem neatly when he described that distressful country as suffering from "a thwarted revolution." The power of England prevented the natural solution of the Irish social problem, a peasant revolt and a liquidation of the landlord system. In fact it did not prevent it for long; the Irish made themselves enough of a nuisance to be allowed to carry out the revolution and overthrow alien feudalism. But the revolution was delayed and made more difficult by English power (although it should be noted that it was made possible by English openness to argument, once English respect had been gained by Irish rebellion, assassination, and miscellaneous outrage).

India has been thwarted in her revolutionary movements by British power, although had Indian tenacity and revolutionary efficiency been a tenth as great as Irish, English rule would not

have lasted a year. Be that as it is, the solution of the Indian community problem, by compromise after the test of war or endemic
disorder, by the complete triumph of one side over the other, or
by the destruction of the political unity of the Indian peninsula,
has been prevented.

An even more striking example is the survival of the present
set of Indian principalities. Not the survival of Indian principalities. Rule by a hereditary prince is not only the commonest form
of government all over the world, it is the only indigenous form
of Indian government. The maharajáh and the villages, these are
indubitably native political relations. That they would inevitably
have disappeared with the progress of humanity towards representative democracy was a belief that observers who were not con-
genitally credulous might have held in 1914, but which it is very
hard to hold today. But for British intervention, armed intervention, there might have been more great principalities, not fewer.
There might still have been a Peshwa of the Mahrattas and a
King of Oudh. The Sikh army might be lording it over the Moslem
majority of the Punjab, or a new Moslem dynasty might be ruling
most of India from Delhi. There might have been an Indian Ibn
Saud or Riza Shah, instead of an Indian Kemal Ataturk or a Sun
Yat-sen. What it is impossible to believe is that the pattern of
principalities, ranging from fairly large kingdoms like Hyderabad
and Mysore to mere country estates, would have been preserved
by anything but British power freezing the Indian territorial set-
tlement according to the pattern of the middle of the nineteenth
century. The history of Germany would have been very different
had Napoleon and Bismarck never existed, but the imperial
knights and the minuscule principalities set up as sovereign by
the Treaty of Westphalia would not have survived. British rule
in India has maintained an Indian Treaty of Westphalia. Some
Indian states may be better governed (for example, Travancore)
than the provinces under British or Congress rule. The state system may give a chance for fruitful experiment. Rule by maharajah
and dewan may be more in keeping with the Indian tradition

than Western importations like parliaments and parties. And the converse of the German parallel is worth noting. India has been prevented from liquidating her obsolete princelings, but she has also been prevented from paying the price of that liquidation, which, judging from German precedent, might have been very high in blood, wealth, and internal freedom. But no people or peoples like having themselves saved from making expensive alterations to their political dwelling-place. And no British argument can be more irritating than that which stresses the rights of "the princes," all the princes, as an obstacle to Indian unity. It might turn out in fact that some princes were representatives of natural, historically valid units. But many would vanish the moment British protection of the *status quo* is withdrawn. For the states are in part a British creation. Some of the dynasties are old, have deep historical, social, and religious roots, but others are purely artificial creations. The Sikh religion and the Sikh army organization were at least as deeply rooted institutions as the dynasty of Patiala and much more deeply rooted than the dynasty of Kashmir. That the Sikh religious-military state disappeared and Patiala and Kashmir survived was due to British policy and to nothing else. The survival of these political units may have been a reasonable price to pay for ending internal war, but why should the peoples of India not be allowed to pay the price that the Germans paid between the time of Napoleon and Hitler, the Chinese from 1912 to this day, the United States between 1861 and 1865? Only an unconditional pacifist could immediately provide an answer to this question.[11]

It should be noted, too, that some of the arguments used to defend British rule lose whatever validity they have when applied to the states. For British power, which freezes this state structure, is not used to impose British standards of government on the

[11] Many Americans and Englishmen who favour Indian nationalism are unconditional pacifists, but that merely shows confusion of thought or a simple optimistic readiness to take the risk of civil war that is emotionally quite compatible with "Anglo-Saxon" pacifism.

princes. Some of them may provide better government than any provided in British India. Many provide worse, but unless it is *much* worse, British power is not used to reform abuses that British power makes possible. Even if no British-protected state has seen such exploitation and disorder as have, for long periods, been rampant in some Chinese provinces, that is not a very glowing testimonial to a foreign government which, to justify its affront to natural human sentiment, must have very marked superiority in the practical sphere over the potential native government which it prevents from springing into existence. There is, of course, no guarantee that all princely governments would be swept away; some might survive; some, if their rulers had luck and talent, might even increase their territories and power.[12] What is certain is that the whole state structure would be profoundly altered were British protection withdrawn.

To underwrite a political system as has been done in India requires for its justification very strong faith in the value of the system, and not only are the states the most vulnerable part of the system of British India, but they are the part which British opinion is least prepared to defend with vigour or rigour. The British public may be a little puzzled as to why the Congress party does not test its strength in some of the greater states, but it is, unconsciously, relieved that its own legal duty to the princes is not subjected to this strain.[13]

[12] The Indians with most experience of political responsibility and administrative techniques are the prime ministers of the great native states. They belong more to the city-manager class than to the mayor (or boss) class and may be lacking in political appeal. But Dr. Dykstra is not necessarily a less valuable public servant than Mayor La Guardia, not to speak of Governor Talmadge.

[13] Where there is complete confidence in the rightness of the political system that is to be underwritten, it is possible to accept cheerfully very onerous duties of protection. Thus the *New Republic* (August 10, 1942) accepts with apparent enthusiasm the duty of repressing communal disorder by the use of an Anglo-American bombing force (or by the loan of such a bombing force to an Indian [for instance, Congress] government; the obscurity of the style makes it difficult to decide which is the true

Another British argument has more relevance than the treaty rights of the princes. It is an important and immediately relevant fact that, while all the Congress, Moslem League, Hindu Mahasabha agitation has been going on, over a million Indians have enlisted in the (British-controlled) Indian army. This phenomenon is sometimes adduced to prove that India is "loyal," or contented, or willing to postpone independence until the war is over. An appeal at a different level is made when the soldiers of the Indian army are represented as being volunteers won over to military action by their enthusiasm for the cause of the United Nations in general, or of China. There is no evidence so far produced that shows these enlistments to be proof of Indian loyalty either to the British connection or to the United Nations, or to China, or, for that matter, to "India." Soldiering is a hereditary and highly regarded occupation in many Indian races or communities. The war and the great expansion of the Indian army

---

interpretation). "War is impossible between any two groups if one side possesses many bombing planes and the other side possesses few or none. If India were to be given immediate independence, subject only to her accepting an Anglo-American army to fight off Japan and prevent *civil disorder* until the warring minorities can be reconciled, the problem would not be difficult. It would only be necessary to keep all military aircraft in the hands of the Anglo-American force. The British strategists who believe otherwise are thinking in the terms of twenty years ago." Whether the Indian minorities will prefer being bombed even by American planes to being beaten up by Congress-controlled police is open to question. The British use of planes to repress disorder on the northwest frontier was vigorously criticized by humane people, both in England and in the United States. To underwrite Congress rule by bomber is to show deep confidence in the Congress solution. There is a sense in which there is far more chance of the minorities seeing the Congress light if Congress has bombers instead of lathis or rifles. But if there is a real minority problem (which is an open question), few in Britain have this faith in adequate amount to volunteer to support Mr. Gandhi's authority by flying planes for him. No doubt rulers of great empires in the course of repenting and expiating their sins should be made of sterner stuff, but it might be hard to get Englishmen enough to impose a democratic majority solution on India by this method as it was to get enough Americans to impose a democratic (i.e., majority) solution on the state of Mississippi in the 1870's.

have offered new opportunities to these communities to enter an honourable and profitable profession. British practice, which has recruited troops from Moslems, or Hindu heretics like the Sikhs, or foreigners like the Gurkhas, has secured, more or less deliberately, that a high share of the income to be got from soldiering goes and has gone to these minorities, just as British educational and civil-service policy has, in effect, secured that a high proportion of the best civil jobs have gone to the Hindus. But although there is a sense in which the willingness to fight for a cause shows that cause to be truly national,[14] the willingness of the Indian martial races to fight in British-controlled units does not prove that they are animated by what in the West is called nationalist feeling or even patriotic feeling. But it is a modern illusion that people will only fight for "causes"; most wars have not been about causes, and most soldiers in history have fought for all sorts of reasons, few of which could be given an attractive ideological character. What the Indian enlistments prove is that the classes and races who produce most Indian soldiers do not feel, as the orthodox Congressmen feel, that British rule is the great overriding Indian grievance. For by enlisting in the British-controlled army they are undertaking not merely to defend India by the best method open to them, but to take part in a World War which may involve, and has involved, fighting in Malaya, in Egypt, in Abyssinia. The Indian troops who stormed Keren may have thought that they were fighting for India by acquiring military glory and military experience. Just as many Jews argue that unless Jewish

[14] Lenin said that the Russian Army in 1917 voted for peace "with its feet"—by deserting. The Russian armies are now voting for the Soviet regime by fighting. But in each case the numbers involved and the terms of service offered made the decision to desert or to fight a true people's plebiscite. The Indian army, even now, is only a drop in the Indian bucket, and the conditions of service are relatively so good that no moral choice is involved in enlistment. In 1914 the proportion of Irish soldiers in the British Army was far higher than the population of Ireland justified. But the annual enlistment of Irish youths in the British Army did not prove loyalty, only poverty and a national fondness for the career of arms.

troops, organized as such, fight successfully in this war on the side of the United Nations, the Jewish case, however good on paper, will not appeal to the nations who have actually fought against the Axis by other means than verbal or spiritual weapons, so some Indians by enlisting in the Indian army may wish to put Indian claims on the map. This, after all, was the calculation of the most worldly-wise democratic leader of the nineteenth century, Cavour, when he sent Sardinian troops to fight in Crimea in a war that was no business of theirs, merely to get Italy a *locus standi* at the inevitable peace congress. It is possible that such has been the calculation of some thousands out of the million-odd volunteers who have enlisted in India. But that it has been the calculation of only a small minority, and probably a calculation confined to the officers, I find it hard not to believe. That these enlistments should go on proves that the power of Congress among the martial races is limited, just as the failure of Sinn Fein and orthodox Irish nationalism to prevent enlistments in the British Army before 1914 proved that the hold of the nationalist tradition on the types that provided recruits for the British Army was not absolute. In India, as in Ireland, enlistment in the British Army is a tradition. It appeals to races which love fighting and who, from long experience, believe that England wins her wars and keeps faith in the matter of pay and pensions.[15]

[15] There is, of course, a large enlistment of Irishmen from neutral Eire in the British Army in this war. Many of these do, in fact, think they are fighting in a good cause, some, no doubt, foresee that a permanently neutral Ireland runs the risk of seeming a highly uninteresting country to the peoples of the United Nations when victory comes. But most of the Irishmen in the British Army enlist, as their fathers did before them, because soldiering seems to them a good way of life. The habit of enlisting in the British Navy was so deep-rooted in parts of Cork and Kerry that the zealous patriots who now see the bright side of a possible Nazi victory had to murder a few people to discourage it. But that does not prove that "Rebel Cork" has become "loyal." It merely shows that the modern liberal view, in which a man only takes part in a war after a spiritual crisis recalling the conversion of St. Augustine or of Cardinal Newman is not universally accepted in backward countries like Ireland and the Punjab. Mr. De Valera does his best to hide these distressing enlistments and

The Congress apologists make a good point when they attribute these enlistments to the attractions of five dollars a month and rations. But if this is a point against British complacency, it is not really a bull point for the future of India. For the future of democracy in a country where hundreds of thousands of mercenary soldiers can be raised by a foreign, unpopular, and retreating power is not obviously bright. Their Chinese friends could tell the Congress leaders something of the problem of the mercenary soldier in a great unwieldy state system undergoing a profound revolution. Why should we expect the Indian army to obey the Indian politicians once the habit of obedience to British authority is broken? Why should the Gurkhas (who are not even British subjects) not enter Japanese service as, for a century past, they have entered British service? We are accustomed (when we do not think realistically) to consider an army serving no ideal but

achievements from the Irish people, but even he may be suspected of only moderate indignation at the unneutral conduct of Captain Fogarty Fegan, V.C., General Sir Richard O'Connor, Grattan-Esmonde, V.C., and other Irish violators of neutrality. And it may be more than suspected that the typical Irishmen (which Mr. De Valera is not) behaves, when he hears such news (which the censorship cannot wholly hide from him), as the father of James J. Corbett did. That eminently respectable Irish-American was most anxious that his good-looking son should have a dignified business career. He secured for him a promising job in the Nevada Bank in San Francisco, but, to his horror, his son persisted in consorting with prize-fighters. He who could have been a Flood, or a Fair, or a Phelan, one of the great Irish magnates of California. But "Gentleman Jim" insisted on going his own way. His family kept the matter dark and so, when it could no longer be hidden that young Mr. Corbett was challenging John L. Sullivan, the most famous Irish-American (with the possible exception of General Philip Sheridan), it was assumed that shame mantled the elder Corbett's brow. So it might have done if Jim had lost, but he won. And when the news came through, Corbett *père* uttered the classic comment: "To hell with the Nevada Bank." Which thing is an allegory; many good supporters of Mr. De Valera and of Mr. Gandhi must have behaved like Mr. Corbett at the news of the Irish and Indian triumphs in this war. There can be no doubt about the Irish and, if Mr. Gandhi has no supporter of the Corbett school, the prospects of Congress remaining in control of India are even poorer than I suspect they are anyway.

its own or its leader's ambitions or greed as a past phenomenon. But we have seen over twenty years of Chinese *condottiere* wars; we have seen Franco's Moors in Spain; we have seen the French Foreign Legion in the last two years follow its officers into the camps of Pétain or de Gaulle. We have the American purchase of Darlan. The problem of the soldier is not solved in India, and although the British have done nothing to make it easier of solution (except by cutting down in normal times the number of mercenaries and accustoming them to pay instead of plunder), they have not invented it. The most valuable British asset, control of the army, is also the British asset of which the Congress has most need and which, with all the will in the world, may be the hardest to transfer. For the Indian army has now its own prestige, its own veterans, and its new class of Indian officers. Why should an Indian leader who has won the confidence of his men in Abyssinia or Egypt take orders from a semi-pacifist party? Wardha and Keren are two achievements of the Indian peoples, but in what higher synthesis are they to be united?

What is a Congress government to say to an Indian army that takes the line of the plundering soldier in Georgia who retorted to Sherman's sermon with "You can't expect all the cardinal virtues for thirteen dollars a month." The Union armies had their own national as well as professional *ethos,* which in the nature of things cannot be present in the "Indian army" of the King-Emperor.[16] And if there has been no mere pronunciamento, on Spanish or Chinese lines, in modern Indian history, one reason has been that the decisive military power has been reserved to the British by their control over the white garrisons. These troops were not mere mercenaries, but persons bound together by common national traditions and put at the service of the civilian governors of

[16] At the best, Congress will be lucky if it gets off with a war bonus payable, almost entirely, to those sections of the Indian population least emotionally attached to Congress. The Grand Army of the Republic was nuisance enough between 1870 and 1910, but think of American history in that period with the whole Union having to pay pensions to the Confederate Veterans alone—under pain of a new civil war!

India, who were their own countrymen.[17] But once that security against the application of military power to the solution of political problems is abandoned with the British connection, the problem of the minorities becomes of great material importance. The old British argument that the Moslems would exterminate the Hindus, if it was ever seriously advanced, was stupid. But civil war, even without extermination, can result in disunion, and even if the unity of the country is formally preserved it can be dearly bought in resentment and bitterness that breed repression and, in turn, more bitterness, as any Southerner knows. Even if the fears for the loyalty of the Indian army turn out to be groundless, the minority problem will still remain. In a homogeneous state the minority may not need *any* guarantees, for the homogeneity of the state guarantees that the minority will not always be the same. In a state divided in religion, but closely united in other ways, there will be friction as there was in Holland or in Germany, but the things that unite carry the things that divide, although there is usually a tacit agreement to let certain sleeping dogs lie, no matter how good the paper case for prodding them may be. Such is the political custom in Switzerland and Canada. And however serious the minority problems in Canada and Switzerland, they are not as serious as those in India. A little reflection on the Indian minority problem is, therefore, not just a British device to delay action in India, but a necessary preliminary to thought about Indian freedom.

Nothing can seem more just and reasonable—at first sight—than the application to India of the simple principle of majority rule. This seems true even in the United States, whose Constitution greatly limits the area in which majority rule, as such, is freely applied, and, of course, even more true in a country like England, whose political system makes no paper provisions for the protection of minorities at all and which strives, by its electoral and par-

[17] The only mutiny in India in modern times was that of some Irish troops protesting against the Black and Tan atrocities.

liamentary arrangements, to make certain that there will be a majority with political omnipotence to take over the government. The parties represented by the Congress are, so the argument runs, the majority of the Indian people. To deny them the right to rule their country because of the real or alleged fears of the minority or minorities, the Moslems, Christians, the depressed classes, or any other group, is undemocratic. This argument is sound (a) if there is no ambiguity in the use of the words "India" and "Indian peoples"—which is not self-evidently true. But even if it were true, the acceptance of the principle that a majority has all the rights that it thinks it needs to have, and that a minority cannot be wronged if the conditions of which it complains are expressions of the "will of the people," would have odd consequences. It would lead to the conclusion that the American Negroes can have no substantial grievances in any state where discrimination has the support of the majority, so that political injustice to the American Negro is confined to the one state in which he has a majority or to the ten states in which he is customarily denied a vote.[18]

Whether the Indian Moslems are a minority as cut off from the rest of the Indian population as some of their leaders say may be doubted. Islam is not in itself exclusive. But it is not enough to point to China as a country with no Moslem problem. Not only has China had Moslem trouble in the not very remote past, but the Chinese Moslems are a drop in the bucket; the Indian Moslems are a fourth of the contents of the bucket. The Chinese Moslems

[18] The attitude of a caste-conscious majority is neatly expressed by a citizen of Georgia writing apropos of the incident in which Mrs. Roland Hayes was made to realize that she belonged to an outcaste group. "The segregation of the coloured race isn't the question in this case at all. I am not trying to set myself up to judge whether that is right or wrong. All I know is that there is accepted segregation, and when the Hayes woman refused to abide by the rules governing her race she was entirely to blame for the consequences" (*Time*, August 17, 1942). The author of this letter is exempted by the blanket authorization of majority opinion from having any opinion on the justice of the case. The majority is the keeper of the conscience of its members—who are defined by colour.

are culturally assimilated to the rest of China. The Indian Moslems are not so assimilated, for the question is not the tolerance of Islam but the compatibility of two groups of citizens, one belonging to the most equalitarian and the other to the least equalitarian religion in the world. Both religions have their rituals, but unfortunately these rituals clash. The relation of the two religions in the past has been highly belligerent, and if there have been times of mutual tolerance, those times were pre-nationalist. The fact that Hindus accepted Akbar has not much more importance today than that they accepted the English. The Hindus have grown up. Nationalism has invaded the peninsula and nationalism, alas, cannot be kept from growing in various directions, often to the annoyance of the original inventors. It was one thing for Moslems and Hindus to combine against the English, but the moment the English seemed likely to go, it was natural for the Moslems to begin to think of what their future would be in a Hindu-dominated society, a prospect that they have not had to fear for many centuries. The more Indian nationalism has become national—that is, has gone about creating a national myth—the more natural it is that the great section of the Indian population which cannot be expected to share Mahatma Gandhi's religious and political views (and they are not to be separated) should begin to think of its own traditions, which are, in fact, traditions of conquest in India and of the world community of Islam outside India. The same split has occurred in other nationalist movements, once they have got to the tradition-making stage. And the charge that the English have encouraged this division, even if true, does not take us very far, for no government that has been so feeble in its public-relations policy as the English government in India has been could do much in that direction if Indian history had not provided the raw materials. And one of the problems of Indian life that the English did not introduce was the creed of Islam or the profound differences between the Hindu and Moslem views of social life.

That Britain has failed to unify India in the deep national

sense must be admitted, even though speculation as to the degree to which British rule has helped or hindered the evolution of India to that national unity is barren. A foreign government, of men or of angels, cannot be a creator of that kind of unity; its very existence is a check on its growth; its very merits (if it has any) work against that identification of good government with national independence that is the basic principle of the modern national state. Indeed, there is only one way in which a foreign government of the type set up by the British in India *can* breed national unity. A government sufficiently oppressive, sufficiently indifferent to the feelings and sentiments of its subjects, sufficiently identified with all that is of ill repute in the eyes of the masses, can be a very effective maker of unity. So the English government in Ireland unified the Catholic Irish; so the Russian and Prussian governments unified the Poles; so the "Reconstruction" governments in the Southern states after the Civil War unified the white population, creating that minor unified nationality known as "the Solid South," a minor nationality of which the local Democratic Party is only one expression. At times, Britain has almost managed to unite India by brutality. The Amritsar massacre, whose victims were Hindus, and the repression of the Moplah rebellion, whose victims were Moslems, helped to unite India twenty-odd years ago, and more rigour of this kind might have done for India what the Germans have done for Poland: unite Poles and Jews in a common hatred and misery that weakens their mutual dislike. But British rule has not been rigorous enough for that. Both Hindus and Moslems dislike it, but not warmly enough to dissipate their distrust of each other.

Yet it is not enough to suggest that Indian divisions are real, that there is no simple solution to her problems, and that these problems do not all have one cause. To say this is merely to assert that India is part of this unsatisfactory world. It is not to justify the past or present of British rule. Nor is it my purpose to attempt any such tremendous task. But if it is taken for granted that British rule in India has been an unmixed evil, to be ended at once, on any terms, there is danger not so much of hurting the feelings of the English people (which is not very easy to do), but of implanting in their minds doubts of the political realism of their American friends. And these doubts will spread to other areas of Anglo-American relations than the Indian problem. For the English have learned in a muddled way that in politics the golden rule is that there is no golden rule and that there may be no good solution of a problem, simply a bad and a less bad one. When Mr. David Lawrence asks if British rule in India has been entirely unselfish,[19] he displays that confusion between public and private morality on which Hitler has played so successfully. It may be the duty of the Christian to act unselfishly (by which, I presume, Mr. Lawrence means that no self-regarding motives are to be given weight), but it is not the duty of a state or of its rulers so to do. And if they pretend that they do so act, nobody begins to believe them. But a state acting in its own best interests may also be acting in the interests of other states or peoples. The British rulers of India might, in pursuing a policy of *enlightened* self-interest, incidentally be benefiting India. One argument used in the past to persuade the English rich to allow the power of the state to be used to improve the living-conditions of the poor was that it was impossible to guarantee that a typhoid epidemic would respect income levels once it broke out. The improvement in the water supply that followed the acceptance of this truth should not be imputed to the rich for righteousness, but it was imputed to the poor for health all the same. Enlightened self-interest is the best we can expect from states and rulers and it is wise to begin by accepting the fact that perfect truth and perfect unselfishness are not to be expected in rulers, or necessarily to be welcomed if by accident they appear. A man may save his soul if he loses his bodily well-being; a nation has but one life here below. Persons whose consciences are too tender to accept these conditions of political life should keep out of politics, national and international.

[19] *United States News,* August 7, 1942.

The English feel that they are entitled to have their rule in India judged not by Utopian standards, but by reasonable standards of what can be expected of weak, selfish, fallible humans put in an unprecedented situation. For the situation was unprecedented, at any rate in modern times. Absolute power over a vast territory and a dense and very foreign population came to a community that had the normal human disposition to abuse its power. That power was often abused, but less often than might have been expected. Only the Roman Republic has had to stand such a test, and it failed to meet it. Not till Rome had become a despotic monarchy did the Roman Empire become more than an organized plunderbund. (An organized plunderbund, it should not be forgotten, is better than an unorganized one, which may be the only alternative. Tammany Hall is better than an anarchy of district bosses.)

There are many black episodes in English relations with India. But there is one bright one: the refusal of the English people to exploit the full financial possibilities of their Indian conquests. This truth is concealed from many critics by one very obvious fact: India is very poor. The sight of Indian poverty, its scale, its dramatic contrast with the official splendour of the Viceroy, of the princes, of the great cotton millionaires, all of them, in one sense, the result of British rule, strikes and shocks every humane visitor. He does not always ask himself whether he is being shocked by the inequalities of Indian life or by its poverty. He can more easily think of a remedy for the inequality than for the poverty. The abolition of British rule might end the excessive wealth of the princes. It might, though this is less certain, lead to a reduction in the level of official emolument and, though this is still less likely, it might weaken the position of the great cotton millionaires who support the Congress party. A great peasant upheaval might destroy the money-lenders, without causing such an interference with the machinery of economic life as to reduce the total wealth of the country. British rule is foreign rule and foreign rule is either ruthless, tyrannical, and exploitative, or it is timid.

Whatever be the truth about the past, in the present British rule is timid. So it is likely that an orderly native government would do for all India what Congress and other native governments did in the provinces just before the war: use their taxing power to reduce economic inequality, as they used their political power to carry out experiments noble in purpose like prohibition. The British rulers of India, in the last century as in this, were forced by the nature of the problems facing them to go in for a good deal of state socialism like owning the railways and for a good many internal improvements like the great irrigation works. But not only had India not the Chinese tradition of great public works as part of its own political order of priorities; the English rulers were hostile to state action in India as they were at home. To make a rough but not unjust comparison, they were forced from the position of an old *laisser-faire* Democrat to the position of Mr. Hoover. But they stopped a long way short of the activities of the New Deal. And perhaps India needed a new deal. What India got was a thrifty, cheap, and almost too cautious government which spent less of its money and man-power on war and preparations for war than any comparable body of people in the world enjoyed.[20] Perhaps what India needed was a series of five-year plans;

[20] "Thus manual labour as a whole may not be getting a large enough share of the national dividend and too much may be going to the administrative direction (e.g., directors, managing agents, etc.), or to the providers of capital (moneylenders, bankers, or shareholders and debenture holders), or in taxes to cover the costs of administration and defence. Or again, Indian producers may be getting too low a price for the goods which they export in relation to the price which they have to pay for imports. These are at least arguable points. *But* no relative change of this kind could have a major effect on the Indian situation, and it is safe to say that for any appreciable advance in the standard of living of the Indian masses there is only one method, and that is to increase the productivity of their labour. If the whole of the profits of 'big business' in industry (taking the average profits for the last ten years of the registered companies engaged in cotton mills, jute mills, tea-planting, coal-mining, and the manufacture of iron and steel, sugar, cement, and paper) were divided equally among the whole of the Indian people, that would only give them an extra 3 annas per head per year (about 3½ d. [or 7 cents]). If the whole of the peace-

it did not get them any more than England got them. But it should be remembered that there was behind Stalin a strong Russian tradition of governmental enterprise of this kind; there was Peter the Great; there was Nicholas I; there were Witte and Stolypin. England believed in capitalist free enterprise at home—and in India. And one result is that Indian debt is comparatively low, English mortgages on Indian resources small—and, possibly as a consequence, Indian economic life backward.

Another important English influence on Indian economic life was, like the limited public-works policy, negative in character. With the adoption of free trade in England, it became an article of public political faith that economic life at home, and in the territories under English control, was to be governed by a rigorous rule of the survival of the fittest. Under that competition, the native Indian textile industries died, as the English hand-loom weavers were ruined or the domestic industries of Vermont or Tennessee wilted under the competition of Lowell and Lawrence. That the old village industry could have survived in India is highly unlikely, for an India so technically backward would have been an easy victim to aggression, even if we assume that an independent India or Indias would have survived in the nineteenth century when, for the first time in history, there was a decided technological superiority on the side of the West. The only Oriental nation that remained master of its internal and external policy in the nineteenth century was Japan; and she did so by adopting the relevant Western techniques. She gave up her own domestic industry for the politically indispensable weapons

time cost of the army and the whole net annual charge of the Indian national debt were remitted and a corresponding sum divided among the people equally, that would only give them about 1¼ rupees (about 1s. 10½d. [or 50 cents]) per head per annum. If the value of all India's exports (taking the figures for the last year before the war) were increased by 25 per cent and there were no corresponding rise in the cost of India's imports, the net benefit to the Indian people would only amount to 1 rupee (1s. 6d. [or 36 cents]) per head per annum."—George Schuster and Guy Wint: *India and Democracy*, p. 260.

of modern military and industrial equipment. Mr. Gandhi, who does not believe in progress, is entitled to lament the coming of modern industry, but critics of English rule in India who share his views ought to be philosophical about the delivery of towns like Manchester (that in New as well as that in Old England) from the corruption wrought by the dark satanic mills where so much cotton and money was once made, as it is now being made in Bombay and Osaka.[21]

But it is argued, or, at any rate, stated, that it was a criminally selfish act on the part of the English to prevent Indian industry from flourishing under high protective tariffs. The picture of an India able to impose what tariffs she liked on the industrial products of the Western powers is interesting but not convincing. The Western powers prevented China from imposing protective tariffs and the belief that India would have been better able to resist this imposition than China is highly improbable. The best that the friends of Chinese political autonomy could secure for her was the "open door"—that is, an equal chance for the United States to sell in the unprotected Chinese market. It was not fear of *Chinese* tariffs that made the acquisition of the Philippines attractive to so many Americans around 1900, but the fear that,

[21] "In the five years up to 1914 India imported as an annual average from the United Kingdom goods worth £61 millions and exported to the United Kingdom goods worth £37½ millions, i.e., a favourable U.K. balance of £23½ millions. In the last full year before the present war, 1938–39, the position had been completely reversed. Indian imports from the United Kingdom were £34.8 millions and her exports to the U.K. £43½ millions, i.e. a favourable *Indian* balance of £8½ millions. In the pre-1914 period India took 63 per cent of her imports from the U.K. and sent to the U.K. 25 per cent of her exports. In 1938–39 imports from the U.K. were no more than 30½ per cent of India's imports while the proportion of India's exports which went to the U.K. had risen to 34½ per cent. The transformation indicated in these figures is a still more striking testimony to British policy when the story underlying it is examined. The fall in British exports has, as is well known, brought widespread misery and disaster to Lancashire. Yet this has been accepted as a necessary result of the principle of allowing India fiscal autonomy."—Schuster and Wint, *op. cit.*, p. 313.

without control of one of the gateways into China, there would be no chance of competition at all. From this scramble for concessions and exclusive privileges India was saved by British control.[22]

The Indian peasant was also saved from having to pay the cost of Indian industrialization. The American farmer, by voting Republican, gave more or less conscious consent to this sacrifice. But how was the Indian peasant of 1870 to be consulted? The historical alternative was not between an independent, strong, united India doing what she liked and, if she liked, accelerating the process that has created the great textile fortunes and textile slums of Bombay, but between an India with a tariff imposed by England and an India with free trade imposed by England. For the sake of English politics, English honour, and English economic health, it is surely a matter for rejoicing that free trade was imposed. How could any representative government, open to domestic pressure blocs, have avoided manipulating the tariff to suit English vested interests—or favoured Indian interests? The history of the French Empire and of tariff-making in the United States provides an answer. Fortunately for India (comparatively fortunately, that is; there is no absolute good fortune in this world), England followed a policy of enlightened self-interest as the Dutch

[22] Of course in a study of American imperialism it would be wrong to omit the illusions as to the commercial possibilities of the Philippines *if* once they were forcibly incorporated into the American tariff system. "No one in this Colony [Hong Kong] believes for a moment that American goods could be successfully imported into the Philippines if any form of the open door policy was adopted by the Islands. To England and Germany would fall 75% of the trade" (U.S. Consul-General Wildman to John Hay, January 6, 1899. Tyler Dennett: *John Hay*, p. 287). Fortunately for the United States and the Philippines, the mercantilist delusions of Lodge, Beveridge, and others proved nonsensical and the temptation to betray its founding principles was withdrawn from the American people. In the great formative period of the British Empire in the nineteenth century, British public opinion was, fortunately, hard-boiled. Businesses that couldn't pay their way without tariff protection were not worth saving, whether they were English or Indian.

came to do. The "open door" was maintained in India for all the world to enter.

In the last twenty years, indeed, things have changed. Free trade is no longer an English religion and with the decline in the English will to impose its wishes on India and the English conviction that she knows what is good for India, Indian tariffs have risen steadily, to the disadvantage of Lancashire and not *necessarily* to the advantage of India, if by India we mean the peoples of India. The Lancashire cotton-spinners talked and sometimes talk still with that naïve identification of their interests with the public good which is the mark of tariff-mongers in the days of Cordell Hull, as of Grover Cleveland or Adam Smith, but their laments have not been listened to. That India is a poor country and that some of its poverty is due to British timidity and incompetence is true. But that it is poorer than its neighbour, China, or that it would have been less poor if the industrial revolution had been kept out of India by force (although force, in the modern world, is a function of industrialization), or that cheap cotton goods made in Lancashire or Japan, rather than dearer cotton goods made in Bombay, are or were an outrage on the rights and interests of India —these are assertions to be proved, not axioms to be simply stated.

But when all this is said and done, it merely means that not the worst has been made of a very bad and almost impossible job. Some of the English virtues acquired in the nineteenth century, like financial probity, administrative competence, and industry, were, possibly, too dearly bought. A more amiable, less orderly government might have suited India better. The change from adventurers of genius who really assimilated some of the spirit of India to religious, upright, stiff, and alien bureaucrats was not an unmitigated gain. Warren Hastings, like Boss Croker, knew some things about human nature that were concealed from reformed English civil servants and from American municipal reformers. It was particularly unfortunate that in a country where caste in one form was the great local curse, caste in a new form should have been introduced. The public-school stiffness, the too easy division of the world into gentlemen and others, helped to breed ill manners in the ruling race. The terror of bad form, of letting down the side, made for a social exclusiveness that Indian society made too easy and, in some ways, too justifiable. Since, until modern times, there could be no social meetings between the English males and respectable Indian women, English women in India helped to increase social tension. The general European, American, and Indian complaint about English bad manners could not be disregarded even if it were inherently improbable that it was justified, which it certainly is not. A few cheerful knaves might have leavened the lump of righteous and self-righteous Englishry. Even the fact that a high proportion of the great civil servants were Irish did not do the good that might have been hoped for. For they did not display any more social plasticity than the English; and they brought to the problem of Indian government the national talent for intellectual as apart from the snobbish brutality which was the English rock of offence. An Irishman saying (or obviously thinking): "You're a damned fool" was really no improvement on an Englishman thinking: "You're an outsider." [23]

The Scotch were free from some of the English and Irish vices. They had more tolerance for merely metaphysical argument, more patience, readiness to do the job, no matter how much they disliked the personal relations involved in doing it. But their very

[23] In some ways the Irish agents of English rule in India were less well qualified to deal with Indian nationalists than were the English themselves. Some of the most vigorous and rigorous officials in India were Irish Catholic nationalists—at home. The original "Bengal Tiger" was not that eminently capable Scot Sir John Anderson, but Lord MacDonnell, and the most outspoken embodiment in recent times of the old view that the Indians ought to be ruled for their own good was Sir Michael O'Dwyer. Here the difference in national tradition made the Irish officials unsympathetic to nationalist movements conducted on non-aggressive lines. The countrymen of Wolfe Tone and Patrick Pearse are not temperamentally disposed to admiration for the methods of Messrs. Gandhi and Nehru. It is possible that Sir Michael O'Dwyer had more understanding of the type of Indian nationalist who finally shot him than of the type that argued with him.

habit of metaphysical thought did not lead them to take seriously enough the metaphysics of Indian politics. Mr. Gandhi is not the type to impress a countryman of Adam Smith as a thinker, and he is not the type to appeal to the administrator either, however much he may appeal to the moralist.

And the British peoples share in the "Anglo-Saxon" colour-prejudice which, whether it be a new phenomenon or not, and whether it be increasing or diminishing, is still a mighty force weakening the political and moral power of all the English-speaking peoples, especially in Asia, where resentment of this bias is most forcibly expressed by the coloured people which has most successfully mastered the secret of white superiority, the gun, the plane, the warship. However much the Chinese may hate or the Indians may fear the Japanese, there must be few Asiatics who have not been tempted, in the last year, to think of Pearl Harbor and Singapore with just a little gratification. Such gratification is, of course, a luxury which neither Indians nor Chinese can afford, but people sometimes indulge in feelings that are beyond their means.

Behind all the failures and limited successes of English rule in India lay the fact that it was foreign. Had the English settled in the country, made themselves a new ruling caste, played the part of the Manchus in China, many good things they did would have lasted longer and taken deeper root in Indian life. Foreign rule could not be a permanent cure for the varied ills of Indian society that alone made foreign rule possible. But that the English solution was worse than any alternative solution, or that there was any alternative solution for "India," is not certain, perhaps not even probable. It is likely that long before the second centenary of Plassey (1957) the Empire founded by that battle will have gone the way of other empires. In Chinese terms, the mandate of heaven has been withdrawn, and not the least proof of that withdrawal is English scepticism about their Imperial mission. How much trace those generations of alien rule will leave, none can predict. The use of the English language, of English political methods and vocabulary, of English administrative practices may linger for a generation or two, but the greatest English legacy to India, the political unity of the peninsula, is what is most in doubt. For the English in refusing to impose their own way of life on India in any but superficial forms confessed the impotence which was inherent in their position. It was Indian weakness, not English strength, that made English paramountcy possible. But from that weakness could not come the strength to make of India that spiritual unit which real national freedom calls for. That unity has only been bought in other countries at a great price. India has, thanks to her colonial position, been reduced to having her Gettysburg Address without having a Gettysburg, but whether government of the people, by the people, for the people can be got as easily and cheaply as optimists in India, America, and England think remains to be seen. If she passes on to national independence and democratic government without paying the heavy price exacted of other comparable regions, India will be as lucky in the future as she has been unlucky in the past.

The English at War

"THE METEOR FLAG OF ENGLAND shall yet terrific burn." Thomas Campbell had no ironic intention when he wrote the line.[1] But the Englishman may be forgiven if he stresses the "yet" in a "jam tomorrow" spirit, for not only has hope been long deferred in most British wars; it has become a national habit to assume that it will be so and, in a sense, should be so. No people is less surprised by reverses or less easily cast down by them. When a war has been a series of brilliant successes, the public has forgotten it. Thus the great Duke of Marlborough has never had the popular fame of the Duke of Wellington, who is pictured as performing the simple role of putting a number of English infantry regiments on a hill and letting the French exhaust themselves trying to persuade them that all was lost. But in the army and outside it, much less successful generals have been much

---

[1] Campbell was a Scotch radical poet. His other chief contributions to English popular literature were a poem commemorating the least glorious of Nelson's victories, "The Battle of the Baltic," and "Hohenlinden," which recounts the triumph of a French army over England's ally, Austria. The only other military poems commonly known are "The Charge of the Light Brigade," of which the best known line is "Someone had blundered," and "The Battle of Blenheim," a sceptical assessment of the importance of the most brilliant of English victories. A thousand people know these not uncritically patriotic verses for one who knows Thomas Hardy's "Albuera."

more popular. The army, that is, has never been taken with sufficient seriousness. Its moral rather than its intellectual qualities have been stressed, and victories won with the odds on the side of the victors, the object of good generalship, are less popular than victories won against the odds. Getting there "fustest with the mostest" may be a motto worthy of American or other foreign generals, but in the confused image of war that does duty for history in the English mind, it is not how the deeds that won the Empire were done.

Of course, this attitude reflects the unconscious arrogance of a country that could afford a good deal of military inefficiency because it was an island—and a safely guarded island. *"L'Angleterre est une île,"* said Michelet. That was the keystone of English policy, and again and again there has been struck a note of exultation:

> *Oh Thou, that dear and happy isle,*
> *The garden of the world erewhile,*
> *Thou Paradise of the four seas,*
> *Which Heaven planted us to please,*
> *But, to exclude the world, did guard*
> *With watery if not flaming sword.*

Such a garden island could afford to rejoice that

> *the gardener has the soldier's place.*

Because she was an island, England escaped that militarization that overtook Europe in the late sixteenth and early seventeenth centuries. She escaped the identification of the gentry with an officer class and, no doubt, paid a price for that escape in an insufficiently professional attitude in those members of the ruling class who did become, for longer or for shorter periods, officers in the little army that adequately served the purposes of the great sea-power.

The contrast between England and the Continental nations became more striking with the transformation wrought by the

French Revolution. On one side of the Channel, the nation in arms; on the other, a rather random handful of the gentry controlling a small army of poor men, enlisted for simple material motives, living apart from the nation in the new barracks, serving for twenty-one years, often thousands of miles away from home. Such an army was not part of the nation as the French Army was, still less the armature of the whole state as the Prussian Army was. The rising middle class might not have a single soldier in its acquaintanceship; the rank and file were too poor, the officers too exclusive, to have anything in common with the merchants of Manchester or Birmingham. The world of Kipling's *Soldiers Three* was as much a novelty to the English middle class as to the American.

Wars took place, but off stage. There were victories and defeats, Tel-el-Kebir and Maiwand, from which bronzed commissionaires and slightly crippled doctors like John Watson returned to the full civilian life of Victorian London. There were reforms in the army; the old long-service army gave place to a more modern professional army, imitating in an English half-hearted way the Prussian helmet and the Prussian staff. But the army was still a minor and slightly un-English institution. At the time when its literary apotheosis was complete, came the humiliations of the South African War. And when the next test came, the old professional army, almost bled to death in the first months of the war, was merged, swamped in the first great national army, millions strong, that was needed to destroy German power. For the first time the average Englishman of all classes knew the army at first hand, not as a subject for standard pride or standard jokes, but as an institution whose strength and weakness was a matter of life and death for the individual and the nation. Into the army were sucked some of the most critical minds in England, to whom almost everything in the army was equally new and equally odd. As the bloody battles succeeded one another, with no visible result, the stereotype of battles in which the incompetence of the leaders was too much for the courage of the led, was stamped on the public mind. The P.B.I. (the "poor bloody infantry") were the victims, less of war than of the War Office. The island was no longer a privileged place:

> *What luckless apple did we taste,*
> *To make us mortal, and Thee waste?*

When peace came, the first desire of the millions of citizen soldiers was to get back to civil life as fast as they could. Attempts to build up a soldiers' vote, or a soldiers' block, failed. The English veteran of three or four years' service, ranging from France to the Caucasus, had no desire to be reminded of his past ordeal. The British legion, as a lobby or as an institution, quickly sank into comparative obscurity. Once a year, on Armistice Day, its members paraded in shabby civilian clothes, with their medals on their chests, unimpressive figures trudging through the November mists to the local war memorial. How unlike the organized glorifications of their achievements that marked such German veterans' organizations as the Stahlhelm! How unlike the saturnalia of an American Legion convention turning Cleveland into Paris for a week! Never was English life so civilian in tone as when most vigorous male adults had been soldiers.[2]

It was the epoch when the Oxford Union voted not to "fight for its King and Country," a resolution immediately and widely misunderstood, but which did represent a natural reaction against "mere" patriotism, and a very English but dangerous belief that what was out of date in Oxford must be out of date everywhere. But for once Oxford abandoned a lost cause long before it was

---

[2] In the late summer of 1936 I was in Chattanooga. I was awakened in the morning by the noise of what I took for a machine-gun. It was, in fact, the exhaust of a Ford that had been made to imitate the sound of a machine-gun by some Legionnaires who had arrived to take part in the State Convention of the American Legion. This trick had the population, white and coloured, rolling in the aisles. I told this story a week or so later to one of the wisest of Americans. I said to him that I didn't think there was a place in Europe where that would seem funny. He replied that he didn't think there was a place in America, even his own state of Kansas, where it wouldn't.

lost and the English intellectual assumed too easily that all colonels were Blimps or even that Blimp was always wrong.

The return to the old professional army system broke the brief contact between the soldier and the public. Less than ever was soldiering a career that could appeal to the intelligent young man who had no emotional bias towards it—and to admit such an emotional bias was to write yourself down a gangster, a sadist, or a fool. The old view of the honour of the profession of arms seemed dead.[3]

It was inevitable, then, that only the most conservative minds were attracted to the army. Prospects in it were not bright. Had the last war not been fought to end war? Endless peace-time preparation for a most unlikely eventuality, a spell of service in the tropics, made only mildly interesting by a feeble Burmese rebellion, retiral on not very handsome pensions in early middle age—these were the prospects offered to the would-be officer.[4] There might, indeed, have been no officers at all, but for the survival in many otherwise cultivated breasts of the old bias in favour of the soldier's career being possibly the most brilliant of all. And in addition to those who took Dr. Johnson's view of the matter, there were enough families where the army was a tradition, as the pulpit had been among the New England Brahmins, or where the social prestige of the officer counted to tip the scale against the

[3] In the great debate raised by the calculated indiscretion of Sir Frederick Maurice in the last war, some good Liberals who sympathized with General Maurice's hostility to Mr. Lloyd George were yet scandalized by his admitted pride in his profession. How you got soldiers at all, or what kind you got if the profession was merely odious, was a question not asked often enough.

[4] The American situation was not quite the same. There were fewer officers to be provided out of a much larger population. And the pay and prospects of the American officer were much better than those of the English officer. Nominations to West Point were valuable parts of congressional patronage. Nominations to Sandhurst or even to Woolwich (where cadets are prepared for the artillery and engineers), even had they been in parliamentary hands, would not necessarily have been much sought after, at any rate by very able boys who could have won Oxford or Cambridge scholarships.

English equivalents of selling bonds or insurance or entering a good law firm.

It would have been idle to expect of officers so recruited a ready welcome for all modern ideas. If they had been open to all the winds of current doctrine, they would have been at least as tempted to leave the army altogether as to try to modernize it or themselves. When the intellectuals did turn to military matters, it was to quote Clemenceau to the effect that war was too serious a matter to leave to soldiers—and then to leave it to soldiers.

Interest in military matters was confined to the reduction of military science to staying on the defensive and on winning wars without very much blood and tears. But, until the Spanish Civil War, there was no real interest on the Left at all. War was a sin to most of the leaders of the Labour Party who had been pacifists in the last war.[5] The Spanish War did open the eyes of many of the Left to the sad truth enunciated by Mr. Dooley. You can refuse to love a man or to lend him money, but if he wants a fight you have got to oblige him. Yet, contemplating the Spanish War, not enough attention was paid to the fact that the Fascists won it and never, except for a brief moment, looked like losing it. And if that victory was due to German and Italian aid, that showed how formidable international Fascism was. Yet the Labour Party took no critical interest in British armament policy and, on the very eve of the war, when Hitler and English public opinion had at last forced some semblance of realism on the Chamberlain government, the party that had been most vociferously in favour of standing up to Hitler voted against conscription. It was against their principles; so were war, disease, poverty, rain on May Day, and many other disagreeable aspects of this vale of tears. There

[5] One of the two Labour governments showed its fine confusion of mind by stopping the grants to cadet corps in the secondary schools, but continuing grants to the Officers Training Corps in the public schools. The children of the workers would be saved from the sinful contacts which were not denied the sons of the boss class. It is difficult to believe that people who thought like this took the dangers of war or Fascism at all seriously.

were exceptions; some Labour leaders joined the Territorial Army, the suddenly expanded National Guard. Some (off the record) deplored the lack of realism that was being shown, but if the British Army in 1939 was not notably well prepared for the ordeal of 1940, the best that can be said for the official Opposition is that they had done nothing to make it fit or unfit.

The record of the Conservative (or National) government is, of course, worse. They were the government; they were paid to see that no harm befell the Commonwealth, and the Conservatives were the traditionally patriotic, not to say jingo, party. Yet in 1939 England was less well prepared on land than she had been in 1914.

There is a special as well as a general reason why Britain was less well prepared for war in 1939 than in 1914. In the critical period before the war of 1914 England had a Liberal government. And the old Liberal Party was far better equipped to prepare for war than either a Conservative or Labour government could be. The Liberals were by tradition anti-militarist, sceptical of the beneficent effects of war and of the worth of military glory. For two generations, at least, the assets of military glory had been taken over by the Tories. The last attempt by a Liberal to cash in on the political profits of a belligerent foreign policy had been made by Palmerston. And Palmerston's success had been purely personal; by a noisy "Liberal" foreign policy, by ostentatious atten-tion to armaments, he had been able to follow out a profoundly conservative policy at home. The Liberals learned their lesson. They benefited by public reaction against expensive and unsuc-cessful imperialism in Afghanistan and South Africa. They made a mess of it when they attempted, in a half-hearted way in the Sudan, to rescue General Gordon, with due attention to Liberal principles in finance and Liberal principles in matters like the slave trade. They were the party of "peace, retrenchment, and reform."

But although they were the party of peace, they realized that it took only one to make a quarrel; no number of pious resolutions could guarantee peace. So there was nothing illiberal in making preparations for war while hoping and expecting to avoid war. But they were also the party of retrenchment. And waste was rampant in the military establishments—waste of a kind which the Liberals were well equipped to spot. For the "pride, pomp and circumstance of glorious war" made little appeal and the fine feathers and social graces of the army were among the most obvious forms of conspicuous waste. Then the beneficiaries of this waste were nearly all stout Tories to whom the army was something not to be administered in any narrow functional sense, but something as wrapped up in sacred ritual as cricket or the hunting field. So it was easy for a Liberal government to lay radical and sacrilegious hands on these parts of the military establishment most treasured by the Tories and least relevant to military efficiency. And such economies could be accompanied by reform since reform, again, took the form of stressing the professional as against the ornamental and conservative side of the army. So the great reforming ministers were Radicals like Cardwell and Campbell-Bannerman and Haldane. They undertook to provide and did provide a cheaper, more efficient, less conservative army. In doing this they made many deeper but few new enemies and they alienated no friends. To carry out valuable reforms entirely at the expense of the vested interests of the rival party is a dream of every politician. Of course, it required more than a steady indifference to the lamentations of the foe. There must be a positive content to the reform as well. But two great Liberal War Ministers, Cardwell and Haldane, were first-class administrators who thought the problems of military administration worthy of the full exercise of their energies. And the Liberal prime ministers who chose and supported them thought the War Office a worth-while job.[6]

[6] An example of the attitude of the academic Liberal to army reform is given in the letter which Jowett, Master of Balliol, wrote to the young Lord Lansdowne when he became Under Secretary for War in the great Gladstone ministry in 1872. There is no interest in military efficiency as

The navy was less of a mere vested interest, its reform more divorced from party and social politics, but the Liberal government in 1914 had shown full appreciation of the importance of naval efficiency, not only by its readiness to spend money, but by the appointment to the Admiralty of one of the two rising hopes of the party, Mr. Churchill.

Alas, the parties which alternated in power after 1922 were not run by realist Liberals, but by two different kinds of sentimentalists. The Conservative war ministers never got down to thinking out the problem of what preparation for war meant, in either the diplomatic or the military field. The old ways were good enough for them. A Conservative government tackling the cavalry stranglehold on the army should be like a Conservative government making the public schools really public, an anti-Conservative government.

But there were other than narrow party reasons why England was ill prepared for war in 1939, reasons, indeed, that make it almost creditable that she was so ill prepared. For the change in the character of modern war made it impossible for a democracy to prepare adequately in a time of formal peace. In 1914 the Queen of Battles was the machine-gun and, to a lesser extent, the quick-firing field-gun, both defensive weapons. So the initial weakness of the Allies could be prevented from being fatal to them. The tactics imposed on both sides by the nature of the weapons available helped, in the long run, the side that had unmobilized resources. But in this war the decisive weapons, the tank and the

---

such; there is evident a desire to find some good reason why a reasonable young man should be zealous for army reform. "I sometimes think of the Army Reorganization Bill as a great measure of education. The army is one of the two great public schools of England. This is not a point of view that can be stated prominently. Yet to those who reflect that in the next thirty years we shall probably spend on the two services a sum equal to the National Debt, and as we hope without even engaging in war, it may be a consolation to remember that our military arrangements have improved the national character and physique of the people."—Abbott and Campbell: *Life and Letters of Benjamin Jowett*, Vol. II, p. 45.

aeroplane, helped the offensive. The victorious onslaught of the superior army paid its old dividends in accumulating strength on one side and debility on the other. It is obvious now (though it was not obvious in 1940) that the hopes of a second Battle of the Marne entertained by many people [7] up till the fall of Paris were illusions, based on inadequate knowledge of the nature of modern war. The success with which the Germans drove to the Volga and the Caucasus shows what little chance the French had of resisting the power of the German armed might. Our admiration for what the Russians have done is proof enough of how we have accepted the fact of the overmastering power of a well-equipped modern army on the offensive against an inferior foe. Napoleon could not have won in 1940.

But the preparation of this German might had involved so profound a distortion of "normal" German life that only a country in which the difference between war and peace was purely formal could have endured the strain. Freedom of all kinds had to be suppressed to make the arming of Germany practicable. All doubts as to the necessity of the war plan had to be suppressed; all means of judging had to be removed; enemies had to be provided, Jews, then Czechs, then Poles, then English. The immense diversion of economic resources had to be kept from producing its natural result, an increased demand for consumers' goods. Germany conquered unemployment by abolishing the normal reasons for employment. It was a solution—of a kind.

There was current in pre-1939 Germany, a story that perfectly described the situation. A worker in a Berlin baby-carriage factory was about to become a father. He took away, bit by bit, all the parts necessary to build a baby-carriage. He tried to do so, but, as he lamented to his wife, "No matter what I do, it always turns out to be a machine-gun." Which is a parable. Whatever a free society did in the way of rearmament, it could not prevent its rearming creating a demand for baby-carriages, cars, refrigerators, silk stock-

[7] Including myself.

ings. And such a demand diminished the resources available for rearmament. Silk on a girl's legs cannot also go into parachutes or barrage balloons.

Only an authoritarian government can refuse to let the workers spend their wages, can depress the standard of living, can give cannon instead of butter. A free government can only do this in presence of imminent and immediate danger. That there was such danger was obvious to those who can face unpleasant truths, but they are always a minority. Could a free government prevent the power against whose plans it was belatedly preparing from confusing the public mind by encouraging organizations like The Link or publications like those issued by Flanders Hall? Only when the danger was so obvious that all but the most pertinacious optimists or partisans were silent could a free government at last begin to do, with general assent, what the authoritarian governments do by mere decree and by the manufacture of public opinion. And by that time it was too late. The totalitarian power had gained a great start; it is that start in the race which is belatedly perceived and which at last breaks down the natural reluctance of the citizen of the free state to sacrifice some of his freedom. And it is doubtful if anything but actual war, or even actual imminent danger, a Dunkirk or a Pearl Harbor, really shakes the mass of men out of their complacency.

The Conservative government in England was faced with the dilemma of admitting openly that German rearmament was a grave and increasing danger to England and demanding full powers to deal with it and, at the same time, preserving normal diplomatic relations, playing the comedy of being just big boys together. A very strong, far-sighted, daring ruler or rulers might have taken the risk. But the English people had not elected MacDonalds or Baldwins for their energy or daring. They were no Dantons awaiting the chance to show boldness; no Pitts confident that they could save the country and that no one else could. So we had chaotic policies like the Anglo-German naval treaty that had any value only if German good faith could be counted on and an attempt, at the same time in a sheepish and inadequate way, to make the R.A.F. the equal of the Luftwaffe. The public could see the inconsistency and was deaf to the timid suggestions that the situation, though well in hand, was serious all the same.

It is true that the English government before 1939 made all the extra mistakes possible, down to the nonsensical promise of "peace in our time," accompanied by more armaments, but although no government could have done much worse, no democratic government of the usual type, in which the customer—that is, the voter—is always right, could have done much better.

Leaders whose more or less avowed principle is that they know no more than the average man or that, if they do, they must not act on this knowledge are not confined to England. So Mr. Churchill was kept out of office, and in the United States the vigilance of the President in naval and diplomatic matters was taken as a hobby of an otherwise sagacious executive, when it was not taken as the hallucination of a man who had not the profound knowledge of the outside world that inspired Senator Borah. As far as their political systems are truly representative, England did not deserve to have Mr. Churchill in reserve, any more than the United States deserved to have Mr. Roosevelt in office. That they had them all the same suggests that the old proverb: "God looks after fools, drunkards, and the United States," ought to have added to it "and England." France, which had neither a Churchill nor a Roosevelt, had to fall back on superannuated soldiers and political admirals, neither of them worthy rulers of the country of the Revolution or of 1914. Lincolns and Clemenceaus are more indispensable instruments of democratic victory than Grants or Fochs—which is only perceived when a country has to fall back on Grant or on very inferior versions of Foch.

The English Army in 1939 was too small, too ill provided with modern weapons, too much impressed with the lessons and the personalities of the last war to play anything like the role it had played in 1914. The war was even less like what had been foreseen than it had been in 1914; the bad diplomatic preparation made the British share of the military effort more inadequate to the needs of the alliance. Instead of a retreat from Mons, the Marne, the Aisne, Ypres, there was disaster and the abandonment of the Continent.

Menaced with invasion, forced to fight with inadequate forces far from its bases and to fight alone, it was no wonder that the British military record was poor. Military thought had not been encouraged during the long armistice years, and an army needs constant stimulus to thought.[8] Nor was this initial defect easily remedied. Germany had gained a good deal of technical knowledge, cheaply, in the Spanish War; every victorious campaign taught her more. But the English Army was always labouring behindhand with no time to seek perfect or even adequate solutions. Where the barest minimum of equipment was scarce, fine improvements in design were easily neglected. Where the nearest approach to modern equipment that was available had to be sent on a voyage of 14,000 miles, a voyage taking months to make, it was natural not to wait on perfection.[9]

And for modern war of armoured divisions striking like thunderbolts over great stretches of country, no country could be a poorer training ground than the crowded island. The nearest approach to an open manœuvre area such as the Germans have and the Russians have and the Americans have is Salisbury Plain, which a good-going Panzer division could cross in an hour. There is no English equivalent of Pomeranian heaths or Louisiana

[8] "The army ages men sooner than the law and philosophy; it exposes them more freely to germs which undermine and destroy, and it shelters them more completely from thought, which stimulates and preserves. A lawyer must keep his law highly polished and up-to-date or he hears of it within a fortnight, a general never realizes he is out of training and behind the times until disaster is accomplished."—H. G. Wells: *Bealby*.

[9] The boldness of the decision to send the most modern weapons to Egypt and to take the offensive there can be more easily understood if for London in 1940 Washington in 1862 (or 1864) is read and the constant fear of a raid on the capital which cramped the freedom of both McClellan and Grant is remembered. Lincoln was less bold than Churchill or the population of Washington less phlegmatic than the Londoners.

swamps, where mimic war can be practised with some reasonably close approximation to the real thing.

So, for two years, the British Army had to fight battles at the end of one of the longest communication lines in history, or to train in a crowded island where real battle conditions were almost impossible. The army so constituted had to find its officers from a mass of not highly military young men whose very virtues were not always assets. Quite often the new junior officers were much cleverer than their professional chiefs; even more often they thought they were; it took time and the stern test of war to find leaders. Thus, but for the Burma campaign, General Alexander might not have been given a chance to show those talents of leadership, of making bricks without straw, which he later used to more obvious advantage in Egypt. But however useful a lost campaign may be for testing men and leaders, it is not stimulating to the outside observer. The American newspapermen had a very different estimate of McClellan from that of his soldiers, and Lincoln had to pay a great deal of attention to newspapermen in an election year. Churchill had not the same temptation and Alexander and Montgomery were given their chance.

That they succeeded is a matter for general gratification, but it must have been a matter of surprise for many Americans who took too seriously the ingrained English habit of not expecting much (in words) of the army. What they expect in their hearts is a final victory when more brilliant and professional armies have got tired and see by the rules of the game, as Ludendorff did in 1918 and Pétain in 1940, that all is lost. It is then that the English soldier gets his unprofessional revenge. And then that he and the English people reap the harvest of their generosity. Because they are kind, not to say generous to unfortunate generals, the survivors in the elimination contest do not suffer from delusions of grandeur, nor do the unsuccessful feel that since they have failed, there is no hope that any other leaders or methods can succeed. The most successful English generals have had stern critics, some of them not even young, in their own armies. As readers of Thackeray may remember, good Tories backed Webb against Marl-borough and in Wellington's army smart young Whig subalterns were ready with socially superior sneers at the ease with which Wellington was outmanœuvred by Masséna or Marmont and cynical at the luck which persistently followed that pushing general who would not be admitted to Holland House.

It has been no bad thing for the British Army that, even in its own eyes, it has no unchequered record of success. Other armies have taken a grim pride in gallant but unsuccessful actions. The Continental Army was not ashamed of Brandywine or the Army of the Potomac of Fredericksburg. Virginia has not forgotten Pickett's unavailing charge, or Georgia the last campaign of Hood. But no army has made such a cult of the gallant and often foolish last stand as the English. No other country has a nursery rhyme which tells how the "grand old Duke of York" marched his men up and marched them down and marched them back again. And that very English figure was a more popular commander-in-chief than Wellington and occupies a pillar in London almost as high as Nelson's, while Wellington is commemorated by Achilles posing awkwardly, in the nude, like the advertisement of a physical-culture school.

The British Army is a very English institution, even to letting the chief credit for its not infrequent victories go to the Scotch and the Irish and the Australians and other peoples with more taste for martial glory than the nation of shopkeepers, the most soldierly of unmilitary peoples.

The English are a nation of players of team games and makers of engines and runners of races. So the success of the R.A.F. has nothing surprising in it. The countrymen of Watt and Parsons and Rolls [10] were not at a loss, mechanically, nor were the countrymen of the great sailors or the great aviators of the last war un-

---

[10] Watt was Scotch, but his workmen were English as was his practical business partner, Matthew Bolton. Parsons, the inventor of the marine turbine, was Irish. Both he and Rolls (one of the two makers of the Rolls-Royce and a pioneer airman) were the sons of peers.

worthy of their predecessors. It is unnecessary to insist that the R.A.F. was a good thing; even those who have not watched their arabesques in the air over London in September 1940 realize that in the fate of the handful of fighter pilots who then defeated the invading aerial army lay the immediate destiny of the world. It was a Thermopylæ that succeeded. And the new Spartans were largely the products of the new secondary schools that had conformed, from necessity, largely to Athenian standards.

There is one permanent exception to English irony, resignation, indifference, or whatever you like to call it. Ships and the sea, above all the Royal Navy, are exempted from this complacency. In the last war, as in this, it was naval disasters or failures that astounded and angered the man in the street—and almost everybody lives in this street. It is not merely that Britain is an island, that the sea is all around and near at hand, that no one lives more than thirty or forty miles from tidal water or that there are few fields that have never seen a sea-gull. It may be because these are basic facts that the devotion to the Royal Navy is so deep and wide, but that devotion is now a thing in itself.

The military tradition is one of victory, but of victory by muddling through, of success won mainly by toughness, of not knowing when you are beaten and of applying horse sense. English war on land is (in the national tradition) an extension of sport, last-minute victories won by gentlemen over players. Some of the most popular English soldiers have been not notably successful, but unsuccessful admirals do not become heroes, if only because the Englishman never remembers that there have been any. His picture of naval war in the past is a picture of endless victories, won often against formal odds, but won by skill, by energy, by initiative. The typical English land victory, as seen through the eyes of the man in the street, is won by standing an attack until the attackers get tired of it. Such was the great symbolical victory of the last war, First Ypres. Such was Waterloo. Such was not Trafalgar or the Nile or the Baltic. It is not Wellington waiting till the French had got tired of attacking—and until Blücher turned up—

but Nelson who is the national hero. Nelson finding excuses for not receiving orders that might have kept him from attacking, Nelson breaking through French and Spanish fleets like a modern Panzer division, as Rodney and Hawke had done before him, Nelson winning with sailors and ships at the highest degree of technical efficiency. The British Army traditionally has got along by taking it, the Royal Navy by dishing it out.[11]

It is because the Englishman has thought himself immune from invasion at home that he has been able to afford the luxury of his Imperial commitments over all the seven seas. It was because the Royal Navy saved England from the militarization imposed on all other European countries that capital and energy, human and material, could be sent off to points as remote as Hong Kong or Aden. It was this political freedom of action that gave what truth there was to the old claim that English naval supremacy maintained order on the oceans, put down piracy in the China Sea or slave-trading in the Persian Gulf. But such police work did not call for the great battle fleets that cruised in the Mediterranean or the North Sea. Much smaller fleets would have kept Malayan seas safe for commerce, or protected missionaries in the Solomons. But it was because the home of the merchants—and the missionaries—was saved from exterior political pressure by the great fleets at home that much smaller investments of the power paid such handsome dividends to British and all other business civilizations in the last century. A serious threat to naval supremacy at home weakened English power to the ends of the earth; the rise of a first-class naval power in the Pacific presented a problem that could only be solved if there was no threat to British security in

[11] That British ships were often less well designed than French or Dutch; that not all aggressive actions succeeded; that not all British admirals were aggressive; all this is true; but that these truths are forgotten is more important. The reaction of the average Englishman to such an abnormal phenomenon as a foreign admiral behaving like an English admiral is to commiserate, unconsciously, with the Bailli de Suffren or Admiral von Hipper for being reduced to serving in the French or German navies, like great violinists having to lead inferior orchestras.

Europe. A Berlin-Tokio Axis was in the nature of things; a power seeking to establish a new empire in Asia was, in fact, dependent on the appearance of another would-be world empire-builder in Europe. This is the basic explanation of the fall of Singapore and of Burma.

But, of course, there are other reasons, too. Nearly every technical improvement in shipping methods, or in the character of modern war, has told against English sea-power, has made its traditional task more difficult. The change-over from coal to oil has made the fleet dependent on a foreign source of power; the coming of the submarine and the aeroplane has made the command of the surface of the sea less decisive. The decline in international trade, a decline that has affected England more than any other country, the growth of subsidized mercantile marines, has reduced the English share of world shipping, the great pool on which the navy draws for men, for ships, for technical resources of all kinds. At the same time defeat on land has made the long coastline from Narvik to Biarritz one great base from which the Germans, with perfected weapons, can carry on a more deadly war than they did even at the height of their naval power in the last war. The carrier plane, the submarine, the shore-based bomber have all diminished the effect of sea-power; the loss of Crete and the siege of Malta are proof enough of that. It could be said, it has been said, that the role of sea-power is now of little importance, that the blockade matters less, that the heirs of Blake and Nelson are defenders of an effete tradition. It may be so, and yet, just as Napoleon thought himself forced to march east and south when he had failed at Trafalgar, so Hitler thinks himself forced to march on Moscow and Cairo and, possibly, on Madrid as the master of the land mass squirms in the slowly tightening coils. For if sea-power is not what it was, the absence of sea-power is as great a handicap as ever. Europe, west of Russia, is almost an island. It has lived by ships, by rivers, by canals all terminating in ports. The great railway nodal point, Chicago or Kansas City, is rare in Europe. It is to the ports that the arteries of Europe run.

And there European economic life clots as the British blockade forbids the free circulation of the blood that is the life of armies as of peoples.

In their attitude to other navies and other maritime peoples, the English are, if not arrogant, at least paternal. Only fleets that have fought great actions against the Royal Navy really count. Great admirals like Santa Cruz and Duquesne or Farragut are forgotten because they did not win or lose a battle against a British fleet. De Ruyter, Van Tromp, Tourville, Hipper, Suffren, these are great names: as Villeneuve, Grasse, De Winter, von Spee are honoured names. They all played in the World Series that is always won, in the last game, by the same team. But some clubs give the Yankees a better run for their money than others. So, at various times, great men or great fleets have given the Royal Navy a great deal of trouble. But as, it is believed, the navies of the world wear three lines on their collars in innocent commemoration of Nelson's three great victories and a black scarf to mourn his death, all sailors acknowledge (or should acknowledge) the pre-eminence of the navy whose power has not been really shaken in the three centuries in which primacy on land has passed from Spain to France and then to Germany.

But the prestige, the pride, the unshaken fame of the navy is extended to all seafarers, to all aspects of sea life. Far more real than his alleged love of the land is the Englishman's love of the sea or, at any rate, his reverence for the sea. That, and not the narrow acres of the little island, is the field he harvests or wishes to harvest. "A ship is a floating prison," said Dr. Johnson, but its servitudes and its grandeurs have won many generations of the countrymen of Collingwood and Dr. Johnson. There are few villages in England, even the inland villages, where a link with the oceans is unknown. Sailors come from Wharefdale as well as the coastal ports; and men who have made fortunes, or simply livings, in all regions of the world can be found in the most rural and untroubled spots. But sailors who follow the sea because their fathers did before them are common enough, especially in the great naval ports, and going down to the sea in ships is still a normal avocation, with its own risks and perils. More than any of the other great nations, though not more than the Greeks or Norwegians or Dutch, the English have the sense of the sea in them, the tradition of the sea not far below the surface, the acceptance of the demands of the sea as a kind of second nature. How well and how properly did Joseph Conrad protest in the last war against the simple, ill-mannered surprise of a politician who had noted that the sailors of the merchant navy showed an automatic discipline that a mere factory could not expect of its workers! The traditions of the Royal Navy affect the merchant navy, and the existence of a great sea-faring population keeps the Royal Navy from being too narrow a caste. Both have made great sacrifices in this war as in all wars. Their losses have fallen on the same social groups and both can say with equal truth:

La mer fidèle y dort sur mes tombeaux.

The English and the Outside World

"THEY ORDER, SAID I, this matter better in France." "Niggers begin at Calais." In these two characteristic English phrases two very different attitudes to the outside world are summed up. But the point to note is that the attitude of Laurence Sterne is today more common than the attitude of the Pukka Sahib looking down on all "natives." [1]

The days of mere complacent indifference and contempt are over. But although the English may be and are friendly on the whole to foreigners, they seldom pay them the compliment of objective and cool appraisal. They tend on one hand to regard them candidates for the rank of Englishman, they assume that, once the

[1] An example of this change is the practical disappearance from English speech of those derogatory names for other nations that are still so common in America. There are no English equivalents for "Limey," "Mick," "Wop," "Bohunk." The word "Yankee," even when applied to a Georgian, is meant to be friendly and complimentary. Even the old term "frog" or "froggie" has disappeared from use. It is odd that the only distinguished Englishman who continues to exemplify the old brutal tradition by his insistence on using the word "nigger" for Negro is Mr. Hilaire Belloc.

facts are made plain, the foreigner will see the necessary superiority of English ways and strive earnestly to master the art of being as English in thought or habit as is possible. Of course he cannot succeed completely, but the efforts which it is assumed he is making are very much to his credit. On the other hand, there is a smaller band of super-Sternites who feel that most matters are ordered better in France, the U.S.A., the U.S.S.R., Ruritania, or Utopia or whatever the pet country may be. And this type is, if anything, more English than the other. The merely complacent and stupidly superior type exists, especially in the class of not very important official or businessman who has lived protected by the official prestige of his colour in Africa or Asia, but his antics, at home, wakes surprise, amusement, or indignation, seldom the admiration for his forthright character that the "man who knows," whether he has learned to know in Poona, Penang, Pretoria, or some other Imperial city, in his simplicity expects.

The nature of English economic life, the interweaving of English interests with those of most countries in the world, has helped to prevent the growth of complacent indifference to foreign ways. London has been, for a century, the centre of services, insurance, banking, shipping, for all the world, and a large toleration of foreign ways has developed as well as a great deal of first-hand knowledge of how things are done in all the continents. It is an old and justifiable complaint that the English businessman is slow to learn to adapt his product to the foreign market, that he is reluctant to admit that the customer is always right. But it is worth noting that it is just in those fields of commerce where fundamental salesmanship is most important, the field of services instead of goods, that English supremacy has lasted longest. Shipping and insurance have kept their competitive place better than cotton or woollen goods.

There is, in the great British cities, nothing odd or novel in doing business with China or Peru or any feeling that it is very different from doing business with Montreal or Melbourne or even another British city. People who allow their national passions to rise go bankrupt in the free-for-all world of international trade.[2]

It is probably an explanation of some of the folly that marked English foreign policy in the years between the two wars that the economic and political weight of the export industries and of the international services declined in comparison with the increasing strength of the industries catering to the home market. It is not an irrelevant accident that Mr. Chamberlain's home town, Birmingham, is the only one of the great British cities that is not a great port. A Lord Mayor of Liverpool or Manchester, a Lord Provost of Glasgow, would have hesitated before making plaintive remarks about remote countries of which so little was known. The inhabitants of these cities knew only too well that there were no regions of which Britain could afford to be ignorant, no problems which did not touch the nation of international shopkeepers.

The insularity of the Englishman is genuine and incurable, but it is compatible with a wide view of the world because it is tolerant. On great issues he finds it hard to believe that there is not a common religion of all sensible men; in minor matters of dress and deportment he thinks that the other peoples ought to be allowed to go their own way. For to be really right in these matters is a result of being English, not of going to the right tailor or the right school. It was Bismarck who warned the world against the Englishman who speaks French without an accent. The Englishman feels something of the same distrust at the sight of the more numerous class of foreigners who try and, in their own eyes, succeed in passing as adopted Englishmen. It is better for an American to stamp himself as indubitably American, say by shooting a fox, than to get to that point of ironical acceptance when he is referred to as "the unknown Etonian."

If the English view that the whole world is trying, unsuccess-

2 "There is little risk in the shipowner's case of a narrowed, sectarian outlook. His daily correspondence tells him more about the economic and political condition of the world than the whole daily press put together and, when that condition deteriorates, he is among the first to suffer."—R. H. Thornton: *British Shipping*, p. 46.

fully, to be English is kindly meant, it is, in fact, both insulting and misleading. It is in vain that Americans, Frenchmen, Germans insist on some particular point of difference. Below it all, it is firmly asserted, there is a common ground of political, ethical, economic principles. You have only to dig down a little to find this common ground. This illusion is one of the most expensive a nation can entertain. For it prevents objective study of the things on which nations do agree. It prevents a just assessment of the things that the United States and England have in common with each other, but not with other countries; it also prevents a just assessment of the things in which England and the United States have in common with other countries, but not with each other.

One thing both England and America have in common is a sincere belief that "righteousness" does in fact exalt a nation. What both fail to notice is that many nations do not believe this, or give a meaning to the word "righteousness" which the "Anglo-Saxon" finds it hard to realize is meant seriously. Thus it is complacently asserted that the Germans are "politically immature," which is only true if you accept as self-evident the doctrine that political maturity is equivalent to political democracy, which is just what a great many honest, able, learned, and candid Germans have been denying for a century past. Not all Germans deny this alleged axiom; not all Germans have any views on the subject. But it is an impediment to the most sympathetic understanding of the German problem to talk as if we were still in 1860, before the triumphs of Bismarck and the failures of the Liberals had shaken German faith in liberal, democratic methods.[3]

[3] It is worth remembering that many liberals really thought the triumph of Bismarck's Prussia over Austria and France was a triumph of liberalism, because Prussia was Protestant, modern, highly educated. Such illusions, combined with lingering German patriotism, made it quite natural for Henry Villard to call his new boom-town Bismarck. But such an error was far less excusable in 1914 and is still less excusable today. Yet we find an eminent German-Jewish exile like Herr Emil Ludwig defending Bismarck's work. A German patriot can easily defend him, but what the world is mainly suffering from at the moment is German patriotism.

It is not only Americans but Englishmen who see nothing odd in the lumping together by Mr. Henry Wallace of "the American Revolution of 1775, the French Revolution of 1792, the Latin-American revolutions of the Bolivarian era, the German Revolution of 1848, and the Russian Revolution of 1918. Each spoke for the common man in terms of blood on the battlefield." [4] For the real German Revolution was not that feebly attempted by the Frankfurt Parliament and the handful of South German militants or Berlin rebels, but that achieved by Bismarck, and if there had been any liberal as intelligent as Goethe present at Sadowa, he, like Goethe at Valmy, might have dated from that decisive battle the beginning of a new world, the world with which the American and English peoples (and the heirs of the defeated German revolutionaries of 1848) are at war.

For it is most important to realize that progress can work backwards; that there is more than one solution possible to many political problems, in this case the problem of the union and political future of Germany. After all, Lincoln knew this. He knew that he and the North were fighting a doubtful battle in which victory was not assured, that it was a question "whether this nation or any nation so conceived and so dedicated can long endure." It still is a question. A world in which Lincoln had failed and Bismarck had succeeded would be very different from the present world. So, too, would be a world in which Lincoln had succeeded and Bismarck had failed. For Bismarck's triumph, which provided the military, political, and economic framework for Hitler's extension and completion of the revolution begun by that Junker-*cum*-Jacobin of genius, is a fact about Germany that we must begin by weighing and assessing before we can talk intelligently about the future of Germany. To explain how it was that Germany got Bismarck when England got Gladstone and America Lincoln is, perhaps, a good way of curing Englishmen and Americans of too easy moral superiority. But it does not alter the importance of the fact. *Tout*

[4] Speech of May 8, 1942.

comprendre c'est tout pardonner is a moralist's maxim which is out
of place here and which prevents obedience to the more relevant
counsel of *tout comprendre c'est tout comprendre* and no more—
a beginning, not an end.[5]

It was a sign of the profound shock that the last war gave to

[5] The difference between Lord Vansittart and his critics is rather hard
to set out in words, for both schools seem to say the same thing. Thus
Professor Laski says (*New Statesman*, October 31, 1942): "I think it is
important to distinguish between national *character* regarded as a constant, and national *behaviour* which is the expression of impulses conditioned by historical circumstances." I cannot see why Lord Vansittart
should not accept this clear statement. But what is national character anyway? I can see no distinctive meaning in the term. The use of phrases like
"*German* character," "*German* people" is shorthand for a group of human
beings living in an identifiable historical community. Their national character is, in fact, what results from their historical experience. It is necessary to study that result and it is unnecessary to invent a (to me) meaningless entity called "German character" in the abstract. German character
is German national behaviour, "the expression of impulses conditioned by
historical circumstances."

The problem is to assess objectively the end-product, which is *contemporary* German national character or behaviour. The invocation of
Tacitus is, I think, unnecessary. I don't think he is as good a witness to
the background of Hegel and Bismarck, or to the English system of parliamentary government, as used to be thought a generation ago. The
Germania of Tacitus is rather like the intelligent English traveller's report
on the U.S.A. or the U.S.S.R. based on somewhat tendentious reading
and a short visit. Tacitus did not even make the ritual short visit. But we
can be sure that the Germans of Tacitus and the Germans of the age of
invasions were barbarians like the Gauls of the age of Vercingetorix, the
Britons of the age of Cassivelaunus, or even the Irish of the age of Queen
Maeve. The question is how far the Germans have got from that state. As
far as the English or the French? Further? Less far? And it is modern
Germany, not the Germany of Tacitus, Arminius (Hermann, as the Germans call that only too successful fighter for the right to remain savage),
Alboin, Luther, or the Grand Duchess of Gerolstein that we are concerned
with. Germany from Frederick the Great will do. Germany from Bismarck
will do. Their "national behaviour" expressing "impulses conditioned by
historical circumstances" is sufficiently different from English, American,
French, Russian national behaviour to make it wise to begin to study the
German problem with no *a priori* belief that the Prussians, any more than
the Russians, have been resisting a temptation to belong to another nation,
which turns out to be England as seen by Left-wing intellectuals.

the moral sensibilities of the Western democracies that in the years in which Germany was preparing for war, the English people were at least as much concerned with having an absolutely clear conscience as with being prepared for the coming ordeal in the material sense. This was true, also, of the American people and in both countries there was beneath this moral preoccupation and a necessary support of it a naïve national pride, a conviction that victory was certain and that only if there were some moral flaw in the British (or American) case could the forces of evil triumph. No one in fact thinks this way in private life or expects virtue to triumph over better-equipped evil or cunning, but one aspect of this time was the application to states of a high moral standard that was not demanded of individuals. To refuse to do business or to associate in politics or in social life with individuals whose characters or political attitudes did not meet the severest tests of chemically pure moralists was to be intolerant, uncooperative, smug. But nations were to be held to strict accountability for their past and present. Their journey to the penitent seat was to be made at once, in due humility—or else. Or else they would not get the support of various high-minded critics who preferred to sink rather than be saved by such ambiguous characters as the British Empire, the Third Republic, the Soviet Union. Not since the young woman in the French romance refused to let herself be saved from drowning by a sailor who was unfortunately naked have higher standards of political morality been asserted than it was fashionable to parade in the period between 1933 and 1939.

In face of Hitler's obvious plans and increasingly formidable power, it was idle to discuss the wickedness of the occupation of the Ruhr or the follies of the Treaty of Versailles. These explanations of the causes of the Nazi plague were, in fact, the basis for an evasion of responsibility for dealing with the fact that there was a plague. Even if the Germans were an innocent people, the victims of a disease injected by the French or at least exposed to contacts by the victors of 1919, the important fact was that the Germans had the plague. Typhoid Mary was an innocent carrier, but she was a carrier all the same. Tammany Hall's sabotage of the public health problem may have been the real cause of her sad condition, but she had to be dealt with all the same, even if that meant collaboration with leading New York officials and politicians who had had traffic with the accursed thing. But the English equivalents of the political moralists who would not work with Al Smith or with Senator Wagner because they were active members of the great New York machine instead of being ineffective sermonizers on the side-lines allowed position after position to be abandoned to Hitler while they were pondering their exact moral duty to the German-speaking inhabitants of the Sudeten lands or the rights or wrongs of the plebiscite in Upper Silesia. That so many people in England had the unconscious courage, the innocently optimistic outlook that was such a godsend to the Führer is a tribute to that old, admirable and, in its place, useful English tradition that refuses to separate morals from politics or to identify the state with the good in the high Germanic fashion. But it was a liability in a world in which power was not any longer on the side of the moralists.[6]

An eighteenth-century English divine is supposed to have explained his time-serving with the phrase: "I am too poor to keep a conscience." Britain was, in fact, too poor to keep the extravagantly tender conscience demanded of her by many of the makers of

[6] Even the war, the experience of German power, the fate of an innocent, non-imperialist, highly democratic country like Norway have not entirely cured the English intelligentsia of their passion for moral righteousness in a field of action where to search for moral perfection is in fact to surrender the power of making the only moral choice possible, between a bad solution and a worse. There is more excuse for Americans like Mrs. John Gunther, living in Connecticut, when they lay it down as a political axiom that "This war must be fought with planes, guns and ships, but first of all it must be fought with clean hands" (*New Republic*, August 10, 1942). The hands to be cleansed at all costs and at once are the English hands that, we learn, brought aggression into the world and all our woe by the conquest of India. Exactly the same readiness to lay down exacting conditions from a position of high moral superiority and physical remoteness characterizes the American critics of the Soviet Union.

British and American public opinion. But they did not know this and neither did the English people. Only a political Coal Oil Johnny could have satisfied the demands on the resources of the British Empire. With no very visible signs of support in arms or man-power from any other great power, the home and American critic wanted a firm stand to be made here, there, and everywhere, often in the barely concealed belief that Germany or Japan or the Soviet Union was bluffing. Even after the war had begun and the destruction of Poland and the German pact with the Soviets had revealed the terribly formidable power of the Nazi army and the skill of Nazi diplomacy, many honest and not pathologically combative people wanted Britain and France to take on Russia, too. The motives of some of the crusaders for Finland were less pure, but their errors, which were mistakes in political calculation, were less revealing of mental confusion and innocent national pride than the sentimentality of the honest believers in the duty and the ability of England to defend the weak everywhere, all the time.

It is the fact that the English people have learned this lesson, at last, that constitutes one of the chief barriers between the English and the American peoples. For it is wrong but not manifestly absurd to picture the United States as being in a position to refuse to deal with unreformed publicans and sinners while the battered, tired, toughened England that has had three years of dreadfully effective education in her own limitations has learned at last that completely free moral choice is a luxury that no state can now afford.

So far the evolution of English and American opinion on the outside world has been along the same lines. But the England of 1939 is not the England of 1942. Many optimistic views of progress have been killed. The English no longer believe that it is easy to put a case that any rational, open-minded German must see and be willing to act on. He has seen, in the German treatment of Poland, not only a shape of things to come but a revival from his own past of ideals and practices that he comfortably thought had died at least a century ago. He may reflect, if he is historically-minded, that the English in sixteenth-century Ireland behaved very much like the Germans in twentieth-century Poland and that some of the murderers and plunderers of Tudor Ireland were men of high cultivation and indeed of original genius. It is healthy for the Englishman to be reminded of this; but it is unhealthy of him to forget that he is not a Tudor Englishman, but a much more civilized being. That evolution can move unevenly, that many Germans, Christian, cultivated or at least educated, still think of the Poles as Walter Raleigh thought of the Irish, was a truth not widely enough known in 1939. It is more widely known today. Yet even today it is not felt as much as it is known.

The feelings of defeated, almost annihilated nationalities are very hard to understand from the outside, and it was natural that English intellectuals who, so far as they were patriots, for the most part were unconscious patriots, should in 1919 and after it have been contemptuous or ignorant of the force of national feeling. So they kept their eyes on "real" things like trade barriers and trade unions and class organization and ignored, or underestimated, the great and passionate force of nationalism. In their private lives they were abandoning the inadequate utilitarian psychology that had so markedly influenced nineteenth-century thought, but, perhaps from want of a lead from abroad in a new scientific jargon, they expected in public affairs far more rationality, far more prudence, far more vulgar self-interest than the mass of men could supply. The fault was not solely English or American. French and Dutch and Norwegians and other fortunate people made the same mistake. They could not understand, as Czechs and Poles and Serbs could understand, one of the least English poems in the English language:

Shall mine eyes behold thy glory, oh my country?
Shall mine eyes behold thy glory?
Or shall the darkness close around them ere the sun-blaze
Break at last upon thy story?
When the nations ope for thee their queenly circle,

As sweet new sister hail thee,
Shall these lips be sealed in callous death and silence,
That have known but to bewail thee?
Shall the ear be deaf that only loved thy praises,
When all men their tribute bring thee?
Shall the mouth be clay that sang thee in thy squalor,
When all poets' mouths shall sing thee?
Ah! the harpings and the salvos and the shoutings
Of thy exiled sons returning,
I shall hear, tho' dead and mouldered, and the grave-damps
Should not chill my bosom's burning.
Ah! the tramp of feet victorious! I should hear them
'Mid the shamrocks and the mosses,
And my heart should toss within the shroud and quiver
As a captive dreamer tosses.
I should turn and rend the cere-cloths round me—
Great sinews I should borrow
Crying "Oh my brothers, I have also loved her
In her loneliness and sorrow!
Let me join with you the jubilant procession,
Let me chant with you her story:
Then, contented, I shall go back to the shamrocks,
Now mine eyes have seen her glory."

This type of emotion, however unreasonable, is one of the most powerful political forces in the world. Its power is now felt by Frenchmen and Dutchmen and Norwegians as it could not be felt by them in 1939. It is, of course, felt by Germans, too. To stamp out such expressions of patriotic feeling among the Poles has been, for generations, the policy of all rulers of Germany. But neither the feeling nor the reaction against it of another nationality, convinced of the superiority of its way of life, is easily understood by English and American intellectuals. The English intellectuals can feel this poem, since Fanny Parnell's verses about Ireland awake in them, not sympathetic understanding, but that somewhat inadequate but morally admirable English substitute, a bad conscience. But had the poem been a Polish poem by an antagonist of Bismarck, it would not have seemed nearly as relevant to the German-Polish problem as (not quite raw) statistics of railroad clearings in Upper Silesia or the tonnage figures of Danzig and Königsberg. But such a poem would, in fact, have more relevance.[7]

In the years between the wars this truth was hidden from many intelligent and well-meaning Englishmen. For they were too intelligent to like some naïve, unhistorical, unfashionable views expressed by backward leaders of backward peoples, and being well-meaning themselves, they did not suspect that other intelligent, up-to-date spokesmen of modern interests might, in fact, be well-meaning in a very different sense. Many an English liberal has been the victim of a German equivalent of an Ulsterman, and men who would be unduly hostile to the case of Lord Craigavon

[7] The habit of writing-down or writing-off the small nationalities which were not created by the Treaty of Versailles, but revealed and liberated by the collapse of the Second Reich and the empires of the Romanovs and Habsburgs is shown by the language of one of the most acute of British economists. "The costs of transporting goods from one area to another are often artificially increased by the protective policies of governments; it was for this reason that many of the small states with which Europe was littered after the Peace of Versailles were made poor by the smallness of their populations; they paid with poverty for what proved to be a very transitory independence" (J. R. Hicks: *The Social Framework*, p. 52). The choice in a scientific treatise of a word like "littered" is significant, the more significant if it was unconscious. So is the statement that it was the small size of the new states that caused their poverty. But it was, on Professor Hicks's own showing, their choice of a wasteful tariff policy, a policy which was not more foolish than that of, say, Canada, where the results of a thin population and a high tariff policy could also be illustrated. And whether such small states as Latvia would have been at a higher economic level if they had been absorbed by the Bolshevik system, or if the traditionally inferior "natives" had been absorbed by the Germans, is a question to be discussed, not treated as settled. But if an English economist of the rank, the culture, and the historical learning of Professor Hicks automatically writes this way, what can we expect of mere publicists?

have, when it was a controversy between Pole and German, been uncritically receptive of claims that had less claim to attention from a democrat, a liberal, a humane citizen of the world than have the claims of Protestant Ulster.

That nationalism and its parent, patriotism, should have this power of survival, this power to demand and receive service of a more heroic, more selfless, and more effective kind than any other cause receives, naturally annoys the intellectual who has long since shown their irrelevance and announced their decease. The game of "cheat the prophet," which Chesterton describes, was never played more vigorously by history than in the years when we were all being adjured to rise above the narrow bonds of the nation state, the obsolescent fetters of old-fashioned patriotism, and serve a cause wider than our parochial ancestors knew, all in common purpose with kindred spirits who, in other ages, would have been called by the ludicrous name of foreigner. It would be going too far to say that something of the kind has not occurred. There have been instances of just this superiority to the old patriotic limitations of the "my country right or wrong" type; there have been cases of men preferring their cause to what older times would have called their plain patriotic duty. A very well-known example is Quisling, who, by the standards of the past, is a traitor, but who by the standards of the present is perhaps on the wrong side of an international barricade, but is certainly more progressive than the Norwegians who are fighting to free their country, not specifically from Nazi, but from German rule.[8]

Fortunately for us, progress has not progressed very far, patriotism of the old kind is not dead, and, in country after country invaded by the Nazis, men have not stopped to weigh the issues in a modern spirit, but have resisted the invaders. And not only democratic countries, with democratic governments threatened by the ideological consequences of German triumph, but dictatorially-ruled peoples have resisted, supporting their own undemo-

[8] I owe this example to my brother Colm.

cratic government against the foreign version, applying the Byronic principle:

> *A tyrant, but our masters then*
> *Were still at least our countrymen.*[9]

At what may have been a turning-point in modern history, the whole free world is indebted to the fact that in October 1940 this old-fashioned view was not "to the Greeks foolishness." [10]

A country in which the social structure is badly strained, in which for any reason old-fashioned patriotism is weakened, does not replace it with a new crusading zeal for a non-national cause, as the case of France shows. And when invasion and conquest show a people that their country does matter to them, patriotism revives as well as social zeal. Many of the Frenchmen murdered by Germans in the last two years were described by the murderers as Communists and were not. But many were Communists, and these, like the others, died with *"Vive la France!"* on their lips. The abdication of the French upper classes, their failure to justify their role as defenders of French patriotism, is one of the most important events in modern French history. It restores the duty and the chance of remaking France to the people who again can say *"Vive la nation!"* while their betters are shouting *"Vive le maréchal!"* as

[9] The text is not guaranteed; I cannot find the quotation in the *Oxford Dictionary* and I cannot lay hands on a Byron.

[10] At such moments as I have forgotten that there is no obligation on anyone, least of all on an Englishman, to be consistent, I have wondered at the fact that so many friends and acquaintances of mine are hostile to the very idea of nationality, have no belief in its present or future importance, think that the historical devotion of a people to its own past is dying superstition, and are yet Zionists who understand, or think they understand, why Jews want to go to Palestine and not to Madagascar or San Domingo. I am also puzzled to find that people who attach no importance to the practical services imperialism can do in raising the economic level of a backward country freely produce such arguments when it is a question of Jewish immigration into Palestine. I am in favour of Jewish immigration into Palestine, but I think there is more to be said for forcing people up to a higher economic and technical level than liberals, in general, admit.

their spiritual ancestors shouted *"Vive le roi!"* at Valmy or Fleurus.

Patriotism is not enough, but no substitute for it has been found. And the Englishman, thoroughly disillusioned in many ways, scornful of the easy flag-waving patriotism that had power as late as 1914, is yet obscurely convinced of this. He does not think that the religion that has held together the Poles, the Dutch, the Greeks, the Serbs, the other resisting peoples, has lost either its power or its usefulness, or has yet been replaced by any faith that the mass of men are ready to die for. And faiths that men are not ready to die for have hard sledding in these days. The plain American probably grasps this truth better than the American intellectual does.[11]

An English scientist of the last century gave as his definition of tragedy "a theory killed by a fact." It is a tragedy so dreadful that most of us evade it by denying the awkward fact and clinging

[11] "Under his plan there would be no European states in the old sense; there would simply be Europe—a Europe in which the various peoples could freely develop their own cultures, but in which they would work together for the welfare of all. Thanks to the work of destruction already performed by Hitler, Mr. Carr's program has become possible to achieve in terms of power politics. If adopted now by the United Nations, it would not only put them on the road toward winning the peace, but also—by its appeal to the oppressed peoples of Europe, including the Germans—it would do more to win the war than ten armored divisions landed on the coast of France." So Mr. Malcolm Cowley sums up the argument of Professor E. H. Carr (*New Republic*, September 21, 1942). It would be most unjust to hold Professor Carr responsible for Mr. Cowley's paraphrase. But the implication that the peoples of Europe are awaiting liberation from their own national existence seems to me to be pure fantasy. And new and powerful reasons why the merging of nations of very unequal strength, in a common pool, is emotionally terrifying, not attractive, are given on the same page of the same paper in Mr. Stephen Vincent Benét's review of what the Germans have done to make neighbourly relations between them and the Poles one of the most difficult problems in human history. If we are talking in terms of power politics, well and good, for then Mr. Cowley might be forced to contemplate that he will need to use his ten armored divisions to force this unity on Europe. And the European will be inclined to reply *"que messieurs les Américains commencent"* by rationalizing (by the methods of power politics) the absurd political structure of America north of Venezuela and Colombia.

desperately to our dear theory. And the decline of nationalism, the replacement of narrow parochial patriotism by the wider loyalties, has been predicted so often, so warmly, and so long that it has not been noticed that it has not occurred. That the power of nationalism has increased, is increasing, and ought to be diminished is a statement I subscribe to, but the chances of its being diminished are slight if you think that it is losing ground. When G. K. Chesterton wrote *The Napoleon of Notting Hill* he was more of a prophet than he knew, for his hero bestrides a great part of the world, but he is less attractive in real life than in fiction. The experience of the last few years has shown that the mass of men fight far better for their own country than they fight for any general cause, that the transformation of the general old-fashioned view that it is the proper thing to die for one's country into the new view that one's country is not worth dying for but that some cause is, is far harder than used to be thought. The Russians, who reward Soviet soldiers with the orders of Alexander Nevsky or Suvorov, which have no power of evoking enthusiasm except in Russians, show that they know this. The view that men will only fight warmly for a new social order is not proved. No one is, in fact, at the moment fighting for a new social order except possibly the Germans.[12]

The effect of the war on the Englishman is too early to estimate. But it has brought home to him that he is part of Europe (if only because Europe is where the bombs come from). He has acquired a new estimate of nations of which he knew nothing (like Poland) and of which he knew little and that mixed (like Russia). He keeps his fingers crossed about the future, but he does not expect or want to go back to 1939 as in 1918 he expected to go back to an improved version of 1914. After all, there are hundreds of thousands of men serving in this war who served in the last. And the sons

[12] We are often told that the generally poor show put up by the Italians shows that their hearts are not in this war, that they do not think they are defending their country. What does the superb show put up by the Germans, not only against us but against the Russians, show?

of the soldiers of 1914–18 have imbibed from their fathers some of the bitter wisdom of the deceived. A man who is betrayed twice has only himself to blame. And in their silent, unrhetorical, undramatic way the English people seem to be registering a vote of no confidence in their recent rulers, if they have not yet got to the point of finding new leaders to trust or even to follow.

It is obvious that these truths are not true, with equal force, of the American people though if the war lasts long enough and transforms American life as deeply as it has transformed English life, the two peoples may (there is no must about it) move in the same direction. But before that time comes, if it ever comes, there is a necessary period of close association and close co-operation that has to be gone through with the maximum of mutual serviceability and the minimum of friction. And there will be friction, not only because there always is friction between allies, but because there are special chances for friction between two allies who speak basically the same language and have, in fact, so much in common.

Over all discussions of Anglo-American relations there tends to hang a pall of well-meaning but disastrous tact. It is feared that neither country can stand either the truth about the other, or the truth about the attitude of Englishmen to Americans or vice versa. And there hangs not only a pall of tact, but there linger wisps of what once were truths but which are truths no longer. Thus it was true a generation ago that Americans were more interested in England, in English ways, and in English scenes than Englishmen were in Americans or their ways or their country. But not only has the Englishman lost a great deal of his smugness and traditional condescension, he has acquired a far more lively interest in America as such. He is still not interested in American history. He is, except in a muddled, romantic, and scrappy way, not interested in his own history. But he is interested, very interested indeed, in contemporary America. That interest ought to be counted to him for righteousness, but it is not, for it is a general and lively interest in America as a different, more lively, disorderly, and generally less "browned-off" country. It evokes no warm response in an average Englishman to tell him that Boston is like an English town. He has seen quite enough English towns and would rather hear about New York or Chicago, which are not like English towns.

Still less does the Englishman want to be told that America has come of age, settled down, put away the things of a child. For he finds England quite settled-down enough, and if America is as staid and stodgy as England, he has no use for imitations. And to tell him that the days of the West are over is to destroy a deeply cherished illusion, for if few Englishmen have heard of Andrew Jackson, thousands have heard of Buffalo Bill. The great legend of the Wild West is as much part of the inheritance of the English boy as of the American and he sees in every American visitor today, not the countryman of Emerson and Poe, but of the frontiersman.

To the secure, established, slowly moving England of the nineteenth century, the American legend of the prairie was a most welcome way of escape. Few boys, indeed, had not, illicitly or licitly, read the magic phrase: "Ping went my trusty rifle and another redskin bit the dust" or, changing roles, had not put feathers in their hair and played that they were Sioux or Mohicans. And if those days were passing, if America was becoming more like England, settled, safe, progressive, was that a gain? If they had known it, thousands of good citizens would have murmured the nostalgic lines:

Across the plains where once there roamed the Indian and the
   scout
The Swede with alcoholic breath sets rows of cabbage out.[13]

---

[13] The same sentiment with a different local cause inspired the famous lines of Swinburne:
. . . But these thou shalt not take,
The laurel, the palms and the pæan, the breasts of the nymphs in the brake.
Swinburne did not really expect to undo the work of Christianity and to make of Putney another Paphos. English and Americans who dreamed dreams of the vanishing West did not expect to undo the work of Mr.

In his heart of hearts the Englishman knows that those great days are over, but why should he be expected to rejoice? And as the gloomy truth has sunk in that the buffalo no longer fill the prairies round Chicago, gloom has been lightened by the thought that Hollywood has arisen to take its place, to enable America to play the role for which all Europe, including England, has cast her, as the fairyland where anything is likely to happen and in a timeless, amoral world, like that of a Restoration comedy. For to the average Englishman, the unsophisticated man in the street, America is like the movies, and if she is not, why, more's the pity.

In the late seventeenth century one of the most distinguished and original Scots was Andrew Fletcher of Saltoun. He is now remembered (so far as he is remembered at all) in part for his premature despair over the prospects of teaching the average Scot to take thought for the morrow, have an eye to the main chance, and, in general, respond to normal economic stimulus. His despair is to be commended to the large class that knows what national characteristics are, have been, and always must be. His remedy was slavery, a remedy that, under faint disguises, appeals to persons of the same pessimistic turn of mind in Kenya, Georgia, Prussia, etc. His other claim to attention is more lasting. For he knew "a wise man" who "believed that if a man were permitted to make all the ballads, he need not care who should make the laws of a nation." [14] If by ballads we mean, today, the whole apparatus of popular distraction, songs and stories, plays and pageants, the wise man is still right. And in this context the most important modern version of the ballad is the film.

This simple truth, when stated, evokes resistance in two different quarters: from those who think that the film industry is still in its infancy and should be treated as an infant—and a backward infant—and from those who think that the movies are an adult art

---

Oswald Garrison Villard's father and restore the Dakotas to the Sioux. Each unattainable dream was a protest against the world of Queen Victoria, Bismarck, and progress.

[14] Text from *The Oxford Dictionary of Quotations*.

and that Eisenstein and Euripides are brothers under the skin. The first school, the contemners of the movies, are especially vocal and numerous in any discussion of Anglo-American understanding. How often those of us who have been forced or who have chosen to discuss this topic have had to listen to lamentations about the fact that so many English people interpret the American scene in terms of the movies! It is the picture made by the movies that we are to erase from the minds of the English; another picture is to be substituted for it, one more high-toned, more respectful, more cultured. Sometimes a concession is made to the spirit of the times. *Good* movies are all right.[15] And good movies usually turn out to be historical movies that mislead the ignorant and impose cruel and unusual punishment on the learned. But in the main the drive is against any movies at all. They are not truthful and they prevent more valuable clues to the secret of America being followed up. It is possible (though I doubt it) that what the English public needs is to be induced to read more grim tales of New England spinsters laying down their thumbed copies of some Sanskrit classic as they lapse into day-dreams about the lover who left them, twenty years before, to seek fresher woods and newer pastures in the California gold mines or in the insurance business in Hartford, Connecticut. But if this is what they need, they are hopeless. The English are frivolous and ill-disciplined in their literary tastes. Their appetite for culture is limited, and when they read, they read for fun. Their notion of fun is very elastic, but no sense of duty to the common Anglo-Saxon heritage is going to drive them to drink at the fountains unsealed by Mr. Van Wyck Brooks. What is good enough for Hollywood is good enough for

[15] More than once I have been told in America, by kind and well-meaning women, that they had made great efforts to get a really "worth-while" movie brought to a local theatre. But when it had been brought, the populace, with a practically unanimous "include me out," ignored it and went to see the current Hollyhood hit. And how right the public was! The woman's-club notion of a "worth-while" movie, like Hollywood's own, is deplorable. But Hollywood, at least, "warbles its native wood notes wild" ten times for the one that it decides to go in for art.

them and they would agree (did they know of it) with Mr. Elmer Davis's dictum that the greatest gift of Indiana to American culture was Miss Carole Lombard. And since her death the only possible successor to this title in English eyes is Mr. Cole Porter. It is in vain to talk of Dreiser and Tarkington and James Whitcomb Riley. For Dreiser is entered in a race in which Dostoievsky is making the pace, Mr. Tarkington is running against Dickens and Flaubert; and all that can be done for the Briton in the way of simple sentiment has been done, once for all, by Robert Burns and his local allies. But Miss Lombard and Mr. Porter are winners in a race in which nearly all the runners are Americans. They are chief ballad-makers in a nation of ballad-makers. The average Englishman who starts with movies may go on to other and possibly higher things, but in nine cases out of ten the Englishman who thinks the movies are beneath him thinks the same of all American phenomena except Mr. T. S. Eliot.

If the movies represent nothing in America other than themselves, the game of Anglo-American understanding is up. Nothing can erase the picture made by the pictures.

That the picture of America painted by Hollywood is not either absolutely just or in proportion may be admitted at once. It is absurd to expect of a great industry a scrupulous scholarship and academic conscience that one can demand and often get from universities and foundations which appeal, as far as they appeal at all, to a small body of professional students of politics and sociology. No artist, good or bad, does in fact show proportion or justice in this academic sense, and so it may be hinted that, valuable as they are, these qualities are not the only qualities that count. The movies have other qualities; above all, they have the quality of inspiring interest. They, more, much more than any other single force, have put the contemporary United States on the map. To the childish interest in cowboys and Indians they have added what is in years, at least, a more adult interest in America as a going concern. This is their most important achievement, and it is not an artistic achievement, but a political and social achievement. On the movies as an art form I have no views. Neither have the overwhelming majority of picture-goers who (like me) pay for their seats. They want to be interested. And they *are* interested in the subjects treated by the movies, and the main basic subject is America. No doubt films are about love, but it is love in America; they are about money, but it is dollars, not pounds, that gild the nuptial cage. They are about crime, but it very decidedly is American crime. The millions of simple movie-goers are willy-nilly (and much more willy than nilly) constantly exposed to the sight of America and the sounds of America. And despite the protests of the purists (the type of occasional film-goer who calls the movies the Cinema, or even the Kinema) and of the British film industry, the English man, woman, and child love it. For the average movie-goer the films are American films, and, with less certainty, America is the films.

What picture of America does he (or more commonly she) get from the films? A picture of what America looks like that is more complete and more accurate than any picture of another country that any people has ever had. For whatever faults Hollywood may have, it is in its presentation of the visual side of America that it is most conscientious and successful. This is not a mere matter of artistic probity but an obvious necessity, since the main Hollywood market is the United States itself. The American movie public may have a very vague idea of what Europe looks like, may put up with edelweiss on Yorkshire moors or note with indifference that the Battle of Actium is, in the movies, fought on land. But bold treatment of the background that is good enough for films like *Wuthering Heights* is definitely not good enough for films like *It Happened One Night* or *The Palm Beach Story*. In *Cleopatra* Miss Claudette Colbert was given a barge the size of the *Queen Mary,* but the bus in *It Happened One Night* had to be a real and plausible bus. In *Bluebeard's Eighth Wife* Miss Colbert was able to recline on the sands of Nice even though there are no sands at Nice. But there could be no question of providing the rock-bound coast of Maine instead of the more placid landscape of Florida in

The Palm Beach Story. The house of which Miss Rosalind Russell had to be proud in *Craig's Wife* had to be a real American house; so had the jail in which she had to perform in *His Girl Friday.* No confusion of the Tower of London with the Bastille there. This was Cook County or, at any rate, Buncombe County jail, and so deserving of more accurate presentation than the living tombs of *Aïda* or the *Tale of Two Cities.* When it is necessary for the purposes of a *Between Us Girls* that Mr. Robert Cummings should inspect and admire a house inhabited by Miss Kay Francis, it has to be a real, modern American house, not a fine higher synthesis of all possible houses that might do were the locale Paris or London and not a New York suburb.

Nor is the care of Hollywood confined to backgrounds. It is manifest in the casting, especially in the casting of minor roles. Pool-room spongers, taxi-drivers, policemen, senators, gangsters have to look like their prototypes, even if that involves their not being ladies or gentlemen or not giving the impression of being cadets of noble houses unbending in charades—an impression too often made by British films. An *aficionado* of American life when confronted with a totally bad film can avert boredom or madness by studying the minor characters. His time will not be totally lost.

Of course, the picture of America painted by the pictures is not just (that divine attribute). It does, to some extent, foster English complacency. He is inclined to imitate the old lady who said of a performance of *Antony and Cleopatra,* "how unlike the home life of our own dear Queen!" But no one, not even an Englishman, goes week after week at his own expense to foster his sense of superiority and rightness. In any case, this sense in an Englishman requires no new nourishment after birth.

The America he sees in the films is an energetic, precedent-breaking, very amusing, fabulous country where anything goes and anything is possible. He does not want England to be like that, but he is glad America is like that and sorry for Hitler that he is on the opposite side to the land of miracles. Many things, the genuine and unconscious democracy of the films, unconsciously and slowly, alter his own standards. American houses, American ways of life, awake doubts about the necessary connection between "character" and "discomfort." That things can be done in an un-English way and nothing terrible ensue is news, disturbing news, but there is the proof in black and white and occasionally in techni-colour.

On the other side must be set an easy source of misunderstanding for which England is herself to blame or her representatives are. In no country has so much talent been devoted to misrepresenting the essential character of a nation as in England. The films, the novels, the plays do a fine job of presenting an England that is no more representative of the real England than the rural and sporting life of Warrenton, Virgina, is of the realities of the Alabama iron mines or Mississippi cotton fields. The sins of the movies are new, the sins of the theatre are old. But the failure of fiction to give anything like a reasonably proportioned picture of English life is new. Most people in England live in large industrial towns; but they are not written about. Millions live in the great urban aggregate that is called London without seeing Piccadilly Circus or St. Paul's once a month. Mr. Priestley has done a good deal to restore the balance, but no one has done what Arnold Bennett did: give a view of English life outside London and the country that was accepted as a natural literary phenomenon. We have gloomy stories of the depressed areas; we have innumerable detective stories. But Love on the Dole and Murder in the Home Counties do not cover all, or nearly all, of English life. The English people show that they know this, by reading American fiction with avidity, just as the American people show their good judgment in preferring their own more lively, human, and truthful fiction to the English standard brands. And the great sin of English fiction, English movies, English plays, English public relations in general is the refusal to admit that the Englishman is a townsman.

When Henry Adams came to London eighty years ago, he was struck, as all Americans then were, by the unique sight of the

"Black Country." Only in England had the industrial revolution as yet produced the most characteristic and important phenomenon of the modern world, the concentration of the major energies of a people on industry and their removal from the countryside where, from the beginning of history, the majority of mankind had lived. Even a century ago most of the English people had already left the land, and each generation saw a greater concentration in the towns. Sixty years ago only 12 per cent of the English people were engaged in agriculture, and today only 6 per cent are. All the powerful nations of the world have followed England's example and are powerful in proportion as they have followed it, but no great country, not even Germany, not even the United States, has yet reached the almost complete state of industrialization and urbanization that marks the pioneer nation of machine civilization.

As a consequence, there is no country in the world in which feeling for the soil as a *factor of production* is as rare as in England, or where knowledge of farming as a way of making a living is so much a specialist knowledge, in which the most romantic and unrealistic views of country life can be advanced with less danger of brutal contradiction from people who know what agriculture, as an economic and social system, involves. This truth should hardly need stating. To believe that a people who have for generations lived in towns, of whom only a small proportion has any direct connection with the land, has, in some mystical way, evaded the consequences of this state of affairs is to believe in miracles. To believe that England is full of workers anxious to return to the land which their great-grandfathers left is to show oneself even more capable of simple faith than the American Zionists or Irish romantics who believe that the two most urbanized groups in American society are really longing for the rural simplicities of Palestine or Connaught. But this illusion is widely spread in England, because two different things are confused: the love of flowers, gardens, open space, and the holiday delights of rural life, with the less picturesque, less common, less literary passion for the utilization of the land that marks the true farmer or the true peasant. No one who has lived among peasants, who has seen at close quarters the love of the soil as a way of economic life, with its own profits and its own burdens, is in much danger of confusing that not always attractive or rational attachment with the æsthetic view of the country as a natural way of life, composed of flowers, fresh air, scenery, and some work which is, directly or indirectly, subsidized by salaries, investments, other forms of employment. A nation of flower-growers like the English is a nation of shopkeepers, not a nation of farmers.[16]

It is probably true that a larger proportion of the English population which has comparative economic freedom uses that freedom to spend a part of its time in the country than the same class does in America. There it can quote Ruskin, or William Morris, or think of the spiritual and physical values engendered by a little digging, or quote Cowper:

> Not rural sights alone, but rural sounds,
> Exhilarate the spirit and restore
> The tone of languid nature.

So the fiction of English rural life as being normal and customary is fostered. It is pretended that most Englishmen either live in the country or would live there if they could, and the part that rural pastimes and rural ways of life play in the English make-up is cheerfully exaggerated in face of all probability.[17]

[16] The *Committee on Land Utilisation in Rural Areas* (the "Scott Report"), published by the Stationery Office, August 1942, talks of "the love of the country and country life" as "an innate national characteristic and in a large number of cases the 'pull' of the towns is economic" (p. 16). It is rare to find British official documents dealing in "innate national characteristics," but, that point apart, the "pull" has been operating for over a century and has produced a population whose alleged innate preference for the country has not exercised any very visible effect for generations.

[17] Thus Mr. Bernard Darwin can assert that "perhaps we may say that fox-hunting is, with cricket, the most typically British of all our ways of exercising and diverting ourselves; and they have this in common, that both are very democratic pursuits in that very different classes of society can meet on common ground" (*British Life and Thought*, p. 304). The

THE ENGLISH AND THE OUTSIDE WORLD

So a picture is painted which has as little to do with the realities of farming as a way of life as Marie Antoinette's haymaking in the grounds of the Petit Trianon. As long as it remains a hobby and an innocent illusion of the literary gentleman it does not matter. He is at liberty, as he sees the village handyman going down the lane from cleaning the London surgeon's car to set out the vicar's bulbs, to murmur a Virgilian tag:

Fortunatos et ille, deos qui novit agrestes,

and to turn to writing his daily stint of abuse or jokes at the expense of the modern machine-ruled world for the million-circulation newspaper that pays for his little bit of *urbs in rure*. It does no great harm, and least of all to the rustic, whose mind is ten times more likely to be filled with the images of Hollywood than with any rural folklore. It is picturesque, but it is not farming as it is understood in countries where real farmers abound—and the United States is such a country. The typical Englishman does manage to make his great cities more rural in appearance than those of Germany or the United States, but that is quite enough for him. The real country bores him; he has been too long cut off from the soil.[18] And far more typical of the English attitude to the

vast majority of the English people live in cities with no more chance of taking part in fox-hunting, even as spectators, than they have of playing roulette at Monte Carlo. "Our ways" in this, as in so many other cases, reduces the English people to two small groups: those who live in the country because they have to and those who live in the country because they want to. That both classes are small minorities is statistically provable; that they will remain small classes is an intuition of my own which I cannot prove, but which is as scientific as the Scott Committee's intuitions.

[18] This view is borne out by the views of the headmaster of the school for children evacuated from East Ham to Hindhead. "He was inclined to pooh-pooh the general conviction that East End evacuees have been so knocked of a heap by sylvan delights that after the war they won't want to go back home. 'They like the country but they'll want to go back all right,' he said. 'These children are cockneys, bred in the bone. They like the streets, the shops, the lights.' "—Mollie Panter-Downes in the *New Yorker*, September 26, 1942.

[2 7 7]

country than John Clare, or Thomas Hardy, or Edmund Blunden, is the old nursery rhyme that tells how:

> *Upon Paul's steeple stands a tree*
> *As full of apples as can be.*
> *The little boys of London town,*
> *They run with hooks to pull them down.*
> *And then they run from hedge to hedge,*
> *Until they come to London Bridge.*

The little boys had then had enough of the country and went home again.

This attitude is not to be confused with a real farmer's view of the country as something to be exploited, any more than a classical English rural landscape is to be confused with one by Grant Wood. The real farmer's attitude is far better expressed in the spirit of an American popular song of eighteen years ago than in idyllic verse that stresses the beauties rather than the resources of the land.

> *She's a corn-fed Indiana girl, but she's mamma to me.*

So say all real dirt-farmers—in England a small class.

Of course there are real farmers and real farms in England. In the eastern counties of England (and Scotland) are the best farmers in the world, but these are not the areas where the gracious and profoundly artificial English landscape is seen at its best.

"God make the country, and man made the town," is untrue of the greater part of England. Man made both, but from the point of view of the beauty-fancier, he made a better job of the country. Most English towns are drab, and some parts of all English towns are drab. And it is not enough to say that in most parts of most English towns the majority of the inhabitants are poor, which, of course, is true, or that the climate makes it hard to be picturesque and easy to be down-at-heel at the same time. There is a lot of un-necessary drabness that is a reflection on the taste, the energy, and the public spirit of the people.[19] And when all allowances are made for the fact that England is very crowded, that most of the big towns had their period of exuberant growth in the middle of the nineteenth century, when public buildings were generally badly designed and horribly furnished in most countries, the fact remains that the acceptance of unnecessary urban dirt, dullness, and boredom is in part a result of the refusal to settle down to the problem of organizing the life of an overwhelmingly urban country. And that refusal is, in turn, partly due to the unwillingness of the representative Englishman of the ruling classes to admit that most Englishmen do and will live in towns, not in country cottages or even in model rural villages.

But although the rural English landscape is one of the most masterly creations of man, it is also, in places, one of the most admirably utilized sources of agricultural wealth. The American is inclined to ignore this, because he does not see the outward and visible signs of good farming as he knows them, the great wheatfields, the great barns. But the wet, mild climate of Britain is not designed by nature for cereals, and that same wet climate makes unnecessary the great capital investment of the American farmer in shelter for his cattle against the great handicap of the bitter American winter. The huge Iowa barn, like the huge and cumbersome American railroad engine, is an indication of the handicaps imposed by a continental climate and long, profitless hauls. The small, wet island is here competitively better off. The English can afford small farm buildings and small but extremely efficient railway engines.[20]

[19] Sir Richard Livingstone contrasts the "dreary surroundings in which so many W.E.A. [Workers Education Association] classes meet, the bare room taken for an evening in a school or institute or cooperative hall in the crowded streets of a big city, with the pleasant buildings of a Danish High School, its gardens, pictures, music and corporate life. . . . Education is atmosphere as well as instruction."—Sir R. W. Livingstone: *The Future in Education*, pp. 50-1.

[20] I can well remember as a child being driven past a not very beautiful stretch of East Lothian landscape and my father pointing it out to me: "That's Harry Hope's farm, the best farm in the world." My father more

The reasonable American scepticism at the romantic type of "farming" called to his attention by the Virgils of our day not only blinds him to the really excellent high capitalist farming that is done in Britain, but, more important, blinds him to the basic fact about English power in peace and war. It is because England "neglected her farming"—that is, did not make the support of an artificially enlarged agricultural population a charge on her economy—that she was able to resist Hitler. Whatever may have been the case a generation ago, victory in war today goes to countries, not with a high proportion of bold peasants, but with a high proportion of machine-tenders.[21] It is true that a country like England which follows this policy runs the risk of being starved. But the alternative is to incur the certainty of being conquered. Only a highly industrialized, unpicturesque, urbanized country, with its national tradition thoroughly unagricultural, could in the desperate crisis of 1940 have held out and been ready, in the next year, to help to arm Russia, to despatch and maintain a great army in Egypt, and to wage war on sea and air on the other great industrial nation of Europe, which had made machines do the work of Pomeranian grenadiers.

If this is remembered (and the English make it difficult to remember it), the miracle of English resistance and of English power is made comprehensible. England and Europe were saved by the men who lived in dull city streets and worked at dull mechanical jobs.

Another source of confusion is the national or the middle- and upper-class habit of avoiding shop. Most people are more interesting when they talk shop than when they talk non-shop, since they have something to say which is their own, however silly, when

---

than once told me of the lazy Californian farming he had seen at the end of the eighties, mere mining of the virgin soil.

[21] For the disastrous results of the opposite policy in France, see Robert Vacher: *"La Politique agricole française"* in *La France Libre* (November 1942).

they discuss how they make or do not make their living. The foreigner may well get the impression that he is living in a nation of dullards or of hawkers of second- or third-hand opinions on ill-understood subjects. This is an error. If he can seduce his English colleague or acquaintance into talking about what occupies his days and his thoughts, he not only will learn a lot but will be saved from the dangerous illusion that comes so easily to Irishmen, Scotchmen, Americans, and Jews that the English are lazy and stupid. Many Englishmen are both; but many are neither, and the second discovery is sometimes made too late. Nor should the verbal frivolity of English speech be taken too seriously. It is a bad habit and one common in all ranks of society.[22]

This convention means that only the thickest-skinned and thickest-headed Englishmen can talk easily on serious subjects with comparative strangers. A distressing result of this taboo is that while in any country but England overheard conversations in public vehicles or restaurants often add to the public stock of innocent amusement and sometimes are well worth listening to, an Englishman who raises his voice almost always does so to utter some intolerable banality. In no country is less lost by obeying the rule of good manners that forbids one to listen to other people's conversation than in England.

To ask for specific information, to ask for a definite judgment, is, in England, bad manners, and so except among friends conversation is misleadingly dull. Far better is the American habit of providing a topic by exchanging information or views from which

[22] "The Englishman who belongs to the upper classes, or wishes to belong, suffers from the uneasy feeling that in order to show he is a gentleman he must always be slightly amusing. To the American or Frenchman who believes that humour has its hour and place, the result is invariably baffling when not wearisome" (Struthers Burt: *The Other Side*, p. 177). This is true and well said as far as it goes, but it does not go far enough. The legend of Cockney humour has made it a point of honour with certain classes of London workers to find a joke of some kind for all occasions.

progress can be made or a complete inability to find any common topics be established.[23]

The difficulties of intercourse that arise from these different national views of how the art of conversation should be conducted, are serious. The direct approach, the candid willingness to talk that is one of the greatest charms of American life (and one of the most useful attitudes of the American official), has so much to commend it that only ingrained habit makes a certain type of intelligent Englishman allergic to it. But that type exists.[24] And it is not so much a case of not understanding what the American is driving at as being prevented by the manner from giving due weight to the matter. On the other hand, the English habit of understatement, of allusion, of apparent moderation in statement combined with inflexible maintenance of the original point of view, is not only an irritating mannerism but a real cause of misunderstanding. The American not only does not like the way the Englishman is putting his case; he does not always realize what the case is. The class structure of England again takes its toll by making the habit of free discussion outside a narrow circle almost impossible. There is often no malice intended, no snub planned, simply a crippling realization that an expensive education has made the speaker incapable of conveying his thoughts to a small group who know them already. And this shyness, this *gaucherie,* are reflected in action. The young woman in *The Rains Came* who wondered if the English subalterns, with their determined "ragging," were quite normal maybe had something there, for the passion for noisy games of the type that appeal to not very pre-

[23] There was a good deal to be said for the American hostess who, having a totally unknown British friend of her son's landed on her on Christmas Day, began by asking him what he thought of the Incarnation. At the time, the appropriateness of the topic did not appeal to me, as I was a very shy young man who could only mumble that I thought it very important.

[24] It should be said that the willingness of some able Americans to squeeze the last drop of meaning out of the obvious and to prove the uncontested at excessive length has been known to tire even Scotchmen.

cocious children gives, again, a false view of the Englishman, who may turn from pillow-fights to Proust or to the geology or archæology of the Sinai Peninsula. But of course the boy who never grows up is not an exclusively English type.

For reasons that are discussed elsewhere, the type of Englishman who never grows old or up is more likely to be shielded from the realities of the world by memory of his school days than of his college days. There can be little doubt that America gains from the fact that its equivalent type is a perpetual sophomore, not a perpetual sixth-former. On the other hand, college is less unlike life than school is, and the sophomore may not really accept the fact that college standards are fictitious and that no one really cares who beat Yale, the last time Harvard did beat Yale, and that having been an All-American quarterback is a detail of minor importance in the political qualifications of a congressman. The Englishman who realizes that he will never be so great a figure as he was when he kicked the winning goal for Llanaba or scored sixty not-out for the glory of Mr. Chips, is less of a nuisance than the American who thinks he is still a great figure because he was mentioned as the only possible rival to Red Grange. Schoolboy adoration of athletes is healthy and normal. There is a good deal to be said for the English system that makes the high-water mark of this adoration come at the age of seventeen or so. University athletes are, of course, great people, but not nearly so great as schoolboy athletes. It is not inconceivable that a man should prefer getting the greatest of Oxford academic distinctions, the Ireland, rather than a blue.[25] And there is at least one known case of a Cambridge rowing-man preferring to go to the United States to study, to saving Cambridge from one of her rare defeats in the boat-race.

There is one last difference: the really athletic Englishman is

[25] It is of course to be noted that academic distinction in England pays far better in money than athletic distinction. I have known an American win more money in Oxford by brilliance in his studies than he could have got as a brilliant football-player in the most unreformed American college.

probably still playing some team game, or if he has given up playing football or cricket, he has also probably stopped talking about them.[26]

The most important difference of all between the Englishman and the rest of the world is his attitude to his own country. Whatever it may have been in the past, it is no longer flaunted or often put into words. When it is put into words, the words may be banal, unworthy of the countrymen of Shakespeare and Churchill. But the union in the average Englishman's mind of himself and his country is one of the great forces of the modern world. He is not the most patriotic man in the world (there are many peoples as patriotic as the English). But he is the least touchy patriot in the world. And this good humour or unshakable complacency is shown in small things and great, in the diversions of boys and in the most august political formulas.

The role of the English (and Scots) in inventing new patterns of life that could stand exportation was not confined to organized games. We are inclined to forget, in contemplating with horror the youth movements of Germany or Italy, the schools for barbarism that Hitler and Mussolini regard with such pride and which the Pétain regime has honoured with the compliment of its feeble imitation, that England was a pioneer in this field too. But the difference between the Boy Scouts and the Fascist boys' organizations is not merely obvious; it is significant.

First of all, the Boy Scouts were not merely international, encouraging friendly emulation among the boys of all nations; they were, in their symbolism and ritual, marked by that English indifference to national vanity which is one of the most healthy and engaging national qualities. There was no search for some English precedent, dating back to Robin Hood or earlier.[27] With a cheerful

[26] I formed this possibly jaundiced view of the exaggerated importance attached to the glories of college football when I had to suffer the full rigours of the Harvard-Princeton feud of 1926.

[27] A youth movement calling itself the "Kibbo Kift" did, in the inter-war years, pride itself on a kind of national ritual. But it was a small and unimportant body compared with the Scouts.

eclecticism, the founder drew on the great legend of the Wild West and on the *Jungle Book* of Kipling. And the great beanfeasts of the movement took their name from the tribal festivities of the Australian aborigines. In the word "jamboree" how much national good humour, how little national vanity, is revealed! And the founder of this organization, which canalized in non-military channels the gang spirit of boys, was himself a soldier. His military reputation was based on the unorthodox defence of Mafeking in the least glorious of British wars. And the relief of Mafeking had been the occasion of the most discreditable outburst of vulgar patriotism in British history. But Baden-Powell was not responsible for "Mafficking," and the inventor of the Scouts was a benefactor of mankind. But how many countries could produce soldiers with his inventiveness and his unorthodox ideals? No drill, no toy guns, no military emblems, no preaching of national arrogance! General Baden-Powell was less of a professional soldier in his tastes than Corporal Mussolini or Corporal Hitler. He was a countryman of the author of *Alice in Wonderland,* not of Baldur von Schirach.[28]

Today, I am told, the appeal of the Boy Scouts is weakening. The R.A.F. has captured the imagination of English boys, and the innocent imitation of life on the prairie or the veldt is replaced by preparation for war in the air. But this contagion of the world's slow stain is not the fault of England.

There is some resemblance between England and old China in the cultivation of the national religion of good form. The precepts and practices of the sages of English decorum are revered as were (and possibly are) the precepts of Confucius. To know when to wear a white tie or brown boots; to know the social priority of the Eton and Harrow cricket match, of the University rugger match

[28] Lord Baden-Powell belonged to a distinguished academic family. Professor Baden-Powell was Professor of Geology at Oxford and an extremely opinionated and individualistic theologian. He was one of the contributors to the heretical volume *Essays and Reviews.* Another but more orthodox contributor who yet refused to disown his colleagues was Dr. Temple, then Headmaster of Rugby, later Archbishop of Canterbury and father of the present Archbishop.

(and whether or when to call it "Varsity match"); the relative weight of Ascot and Goodwood; the ritual of the hunting field and of the grouse moors or deer forests—these are essential elements of the *savoir faire* of the English gentleman. Still more important is the knowledge of the constant changes in what is smart; there are fundamental laws which do not change, but there are minor modifications going on all the time. To be always correct is not a happy state to be attained, once for all, either as a gift of birth or as a reward of labour.

But as in old China, the cultivation of the rites is a national system; it is not confined to a small upper class, to a kind of "café society." Great national festivals which are solemn and popular like the great military parade, the "trooping of the colours" on the King's birthday, are not peculiarly English.

What was peculiarly English was the choice of music to celebrate the great military festival of the Guards. The regiment chosen for the honour marched with ballet-like perfection to the music of the best of all guyings of the pride, pomp, and circumstance of glorious war, *"Non più andrai"* from *Le Nozze di Figaro.* It is doubtful if this irony would be to the taste of an American audience even in New York, where one of the authors of the joke at the expense of the "gloria militar" was long a professor. As for Nürnberg or Berlin!

When that most important act of a sovereign legislature, the grant of money to the executive, is completed in the English Parliament, it is by the utterance of this formula: *"Le Roi remercie à ses bons sujets, accepte leurs benevolences et ainsi le veult."* When an ordinary bill becomes a statute, the same final assertion of sovereign will is made in the formula: *"Le Roi le veult."*

So the will of the English people to alter its laws or to pay for its wars is expressed in an obsolete language and implies a totally obsolete political organization, one in which effective power lay in the hands of the heir of the Norman adventurer who, in 1066, imposed the French tongue on the conquered English people and seized for himself and his fellow land-pirates the riches of the

Kingdom. Other nations have been conquered and plundered; other nations have had to take over institutions and phrases from their conquerors. But is there any nation but the English that has only one historical date firmly fixed in its own memory? And that not as a Serb may remember the date of Kossovo or a Pole the date of the last Partition, with bitterness and a resolve to wipe out the stain, but with complacency and even snobbish satisfaction that, at last, England was ruled by nice people? In vain historians dig up the Saxon or Celtic past. In vain poets or pamphleteers try to induce the public to go behind the fateful date. Before 1066 there was King Arthur and King Alfred and his cakes. There was also King Ethelred the Unready, so useful for humorous parallels with the incompetents who are ruling and ruining the country at any given moment of crisis, but English history, *real* history, begins with the Norman Conquest. After that date England remained unconquered and uninvaded and, with sound historical instinct, the English man in the street has decided that English history begins when the people of England, high and low, got a chance to go their own way without any further interference from outside. It matters not at all that this view involves the omitting of some important parts of subsequent history; that it involves the ignoring of the almost successful attempt of an aristocratic party in the early thirteenth century to put a French prince on the throne by the aid of a foreign army, or the successful attempt to put a Dutch prince on the throne by the same means in the late seventeenth century. It involves forgetting other episodes, too. But the English are the world's masters of the most useful historical talent, the talent for forgetting anything that interferes with the gratifying picture of their national past which assures them that however dark the present, however unknown the future, nations that get into wars to the death with England don't win them. In vain, rhetoric and argument are wasted on them by the enemy, by the candid friend, by the native critic spoiled by knowing too much. The Englishman sticks to his dogmatic, false, and immensely valuable view of his own history: before 1066 nothing of importance; after 1066 a series of "good things," some of them blessings in disguise indeed, but blessings all the same. So it was, so it shall be.

When we consider how much of the misery and evil of the modern world is due to the postponement of present good until some past wrong has been avenged, English bad memory is one of the happiest national gifts. "Have you ever considered how much happiness as a nation we owe to our habit of forgetting everything that occurred last week and assuming that everything before that was a win for our side? You know the account the Glastonbury man gave of his Abbey, that Oliver Cromwell put he up and William Norman pulled he down." [29] Happy the country that has such history! And how few such countries there are! Of course, English history has had its bitter quarrels, its internal feuds, its external hates. In their dealings with recalcitrant peoples like the Irish, the English, or at least their rulers, have sometimes exemplified the force of Dryden's verse:

> Forgiveness to the injured does belong
> But they ne'er pardon who have done the wrong.

And few things can be more maddening than the cheerful English forgiveness of the trespasses committed against others, than the firm refusal of some English thinkers, even at this moment, to give way to what we are left to assume is their passionate anger against the iniquities committed against the Poles by the Germans. An Irishman put his finger on an English weakness when he told an English friend: "You have sympathy for our ideas but none for our feelings." It is a weakness, but in this sorry world, a weakness that one could wish wider spread. As, in fact, it is not widely spread at all, the English assumption that all nations, like the English nation, have bad memories and an unshakable self-esteem is a dangerous illusion, a Utopian dream. It is a natural illusion in the natives of a country which, in the short sacred way of their capital city, has, at one end of Whitehall, a statue to Charles I and at the other a statue to Cromwell, who cut off Charles's head. How

[29] G. M. Young: *Daylight and Champaign*, p. 80.

can such people understand the feuds and hates which are a product of past history in Europe and America and which are now being bred by the Germans with all the energy and skill of a mad pathologist? [30]

The average Englishman's patriotism does not take the form of vanity; it takes the form of pride. His gratification at being English is not based on an accumulation of gratifying facts about England, but on being English. Other countries may have better telephones, trains, movies, schools, hospitals, planes, but they are not England. This attitude reaches its most perfect form in the Londoner. He may know that he lives in the largest city in the world, but that is not what makes him proud of being a Londoner. He may know that London has been a large city since Roman times, but that is not what makes Londoners proud of being Londoners. "London pride" is more than the name of a flower, it is the perfect description of an attitude which at a turning-point in world history determined how it should turn. It is easily misunderstood by the visiting foreigner. The Londoner may be mildly gratified at being complimented on the excellence of his subway system. But he would not be more than mildly irritated if he had to admit that it was no better than New York's. He tolerates the chaos of the South London waterfront and the snail-like progress of the new high-speed roads on the outskirts. He likes, but takes for granted, the comparative abundance of parks and squares, but in those parts of London which are least well off in this respect local pride is as deep and complacent as it is in Richmond or Battersea. No man is freer from the booster spirit. When the *Daily Express* (owned by the Canadian Lord Beaverbrook) asserted that Trafalgar Square was finer than the Place de la Concorde, the Cockney was merely bored. If

[30] Dr. Edward Thompson wrote an admirable tract on this theme when he pointed out to his countrymen in *The Other Side of the Medal* the permanent scar left on Indian memories by the savage repression that followed the Mutiny. The average Englishman, having forgotten his rage at the massacre of Cawnpore, expects the Indian to forget his anger at the vengeance for Cawnpore, or, rather, he would expect this if he had got to the preliminary stage of remembering anything about either.

he had ever seen the Place de la Concorde, he knew that it was untrue, but whether he knew this or not, he didn't care. Trafalgar Square, like the Strand and the City, the Borough and Hammersmith Broadway, were all parts of London, each unique as London is unique. The Cockney exile who enlisted in Canada in the last war and gave his birthplace as "London" was asked: "London, Ontario, or London, England?" "London, all the bloody world." So say all Cockneys.

In this Londoners are like New Yorkers and Parisians, but the London attitude is merely an extension and intensification of the English attitude. Other English cities may try to show off in the presence of London, but none of them want to show off in the presence of outsiders. So it is in vain to try to impress the Englishman with statistics. He is not dazzled by the brilliant growth in population, bank-clearances, real-estate values of an American city, since he neither knows nor cares about the corresponding figures for his own city. A Scot may be tempted to score off the unsuspecting American by producing his own statistics, of shipbuilding tonnage on the Clyde, or the miraculous growth of Dagenham, or the number of new houses built since 1920. The Englishman affects a resigned pessimism on these points. He does not generally realize that wealth and welfare by almost any standard of comparison were rising steadily if not dramatically in England between the two wars. That many British war planes are better, type for type, than American surprises him almost as much as it does the American accustomed to believe that he has a monopoly of mechanical efficiency. When the boot is on the other foot, he is more pained than angered, not at all surprised and inclined to murmur: "Well, it's the same old story."

And he is inclined to smile at the American passion for progressive statistics, because he does not realize that this discounting of the future, this refusal to "sell America short," of which the ready list of figures to prove that the federal census was wrong and pessimistic, is a sample, is a necessary attitude in a country where faith was literally required to cross mountains and deserts, to face flood and drought in the belief that, in a year or two, the foresight of the pioneers would be shared by others. It was necessary to win others to the faith in this boom-town rather than that, for in the not very long run the contest was decided by the informal plebiscite of those who settled—and stayed settled. All these questions were decided so long ago in Britain that no one cares today. Rutherglen may think it was mere bad luck that made Glasgow the metropolis, Bewdley recall the days when it was bigger than Birmingham, but these are idle dreams.[31]

In a dozen other ways the two peoples, now so closely thrown together, have different standards, different aims. The American has no passion for order, and it was a wise friend of mine who, when asked why he did not think England was a democracy, replied: "Because you can't hit a cop." [32] And American readiness to break the rules if that is the way to get things done is a quality that Englishmen admire, but which they cannot acquire for themselves. On the other hand, obeying the rules is often, in England, the only way of getting things done. And toleration for that point of view comes hard with many Americans.

It is possible, indeed easy, to take too seriously the problem of ill-tempered and bad-mannered criticism between allies. English phlegm, English self-esteem, and, a more recent national trait than the other two, English international good manners save the aver-

[31] If I were asked to state a fundamental national difference between the two countries in a sentence, I should say: "England is a country where real estate is not news."

[32] The English attitude I once saw manifested during a strike in a great Middle Western city. A strike picket had just caught a couple of policemen stealing some of the property they were supposed to guard. The pickets were divided in mind what to do. All but one rejoiced in a sensible way at having got something on their natural enemies and proposed to do a deal with the guilty pilferers. But the minority of one was an Englishman, settled in America for some years, but still full of English horror of irregularity. He wanted to complain to the Mayor, to write to the Governor, to get a question asked in the City Council. The Americans, better used to the realities of the class war in America, were quite content to keep the guardians of any potential scabs frightened.

age Englishman from undue irritation, even at irresponsible and almost malignant criticism. Had the English people been different, they might have done themselves, and Europe, and France irreparable harm by expressing anger and scorn at the withdrawal of the French government from the war, in defiance of a very recent undertaking not to do so and in breach of the common loyalties of Allies. But the English people did not cry "perfidious France." In a puzzled, not very intelligent, but admirable way they realized that they were not blameless and that the tragedy of France was so great that mere recrimination was unworthy of a nation that had been, as enemy and as friend, bound to France as to no other nation. The decision of the men of Bordeaux and Vichy not to continue the fight in the French Empire has cost thousands of English lives since it has closed the Mediterranean route. The only fighting done by regular French troops since the armistice has been against British and Free French troops. Yet few outbursts of popular enthusiasm have been more touching and more revealing, not only of generosity but of political sagacity, than the welcome given to the Free French celebration of the 14th of July in London in 1942. And if part of that enthusiasm was due to the heroic defence of Bir Hakim by the Free French a few weeks before, the genuine pleasure and pride felt by the Englishman in the street at the news of Bir Hakim was again a proof of generosity and political sagacity.[33]

Even the enemies of England have been treated in this war with decent respect. The truth about the German Army has been, indeed, almost too dreadful for the English people to believe. And although there has been a certain amount of frivolous comment on Italian military prowess, it has been really moderate when the

[33] Of course England has its share (proportionately a low share) of complacent, uncritical, and boorish patriots who freely condemn other peoples for all kinds of faults. But of reasonably well-informed and intelligent persons with whom I have discussed the French disaster, only one, and he not strictly speaking English, took the line of high moral indignation at French conduct. I may add that I have no reason to expect that had the critic been a Frenchman, he would have been an antagonist of Vichy.

provocation of contrast between Italian words and deeds has been taken into consideration. And although there was a good deal of laughter during the first great Wavell campaign, there was even more satisfaction at the humiliation of the Italian *miles gloriosus* by the Greeks.[34]

It is with this national temper in mind that the freedom of comment of certain American newspapers and certain American political leaders should be considered. It may be an irritating fact, but it is nevertheless a fact that the Englishman in the street is only slightly allergic to foreign criticism. He may be a little surprised that people who are, if not engaged in the same cause, at any rate are in the same boat should be so free from inhibitions of either comradeship or good manners. But he does not worry greatly. He might resent the criticism of his war record that stresses less the slowness and incompetence of his leaders (a topic of national jest in which Cockney humour sometimes flowers magnificently[35]) than his own courage and tenacity. This criticism (did he know of its existence) would certainly surprise him and might irritate him.[36]

That the English people is saddened by the dreadful price of war is true. They have every reason to be. Although their losses in the last war were much lower than those of the French or Germans, they were, nevertheless, very high.[37] So the Englishman is

[34] Again, the worst example of mere contempt for the Italian people which has come my way has been the work of a journalist writing, indeed, for the English press, but whose name and style suggest a fairly recent central-European origin.

[35] As in the popular London bar joke that followed a too optimistic view of the military situation in Libya: "Rommel's on the run, but he hasn't caught us yet."

[36] No people would be more surprised by it than the Irish in Ireland. Too many of them have fought with and against the English (or, in a good many cases, have done both) to be taken in by this non-traveller's tale.

[37] The losses in dead of the British Isles (not the British Empire) were, when allowance is made for the difference of population, between fifteen and eighteen times those of the United States.

not really angered by what seems to him so absurd a charge. He may, when criticism comes from Stalingrad, feel distress or anger that he is not bearing more of the burden, of the price (in blood) of victory. He will, indeed, spontaneously feel this way unless he is provoked by the too noisy advocacy of persons who did not see any merit in the blood of Dunkirk or the sufferings of London or Coventry. But he will not take seriously criticism of this kind coming from quarters where no comparable willingness to shed blood or make sacrifices had, up to December 7, 1941, been manifest. He may have full sympathy with the point of view of the American nationalist who sees in the present conflict no common interest but survival, but he is a little astonished to find this common platform turned into a pulpit from which one-way sermons are preached. But in very few cases does the problem affect him at all.[38]

Nevertheless, the Englishman in his new role as a tolerant observer of the national weaknesses of others, and in his old role of the citizen of the world least affected by the opinion of the world, can be startled and even angered. Certain things can be said with a smile that cannot be said with a sneer; and there must be

[38] A good example of the acceptance of the need for new and dreadful sacrifices has been given in the past weeks. The news of the offensive in Egypt (rightly welcomed in the United States) was given in a form that was intended not to lead to early or extravagant hopes. More than that, it represented the attack as being a straight-forward assault on an elaborately entrenched line. The early communiqués awakened in many minds memories of the Somme, of Ypres, of Gaza, of Passchendaele, of the desperate and dubious attacks of the last war, since written down under the influence of fashionable politico-military doctrine as blood-baths organized by Blimps. The first news, indeed, awakened memories in millions that only a few Americans now alive, those who can remember the summer of 1864, the Wilderness and Cold Harbor, can understand, the memory of bloody, apparently fruitless battles endured by a war-exhausted people. But the offensive was welcomed all the same. Even if it failed, it was due to the Russians that it should be tried. And the English people (and their leaders) have been rewarded for their courage, for their imitation of the two most famous former citizens of Colonel McCormick's Illinois, Abraham Lincoln and General Grant, by their joint resolution "to fight it out on this line if it takes all summer."

[294]

reciprocity of the right of criticism. The national habit of understatement that is often mistaken (even by Englishmen) for
modesty, leads to misunderstanding. The Englishman does not
expect the American to agree too heartily with his verbally contemptuous references to his rulers, to the Army, Navy, R.A.F. or
whatever institution is, at the moment, the scapegoat for fatigue,
or irritation, or the victim of the habit of "grousing." Or, if agreement is accepted, it is on the understanding that the American is
equally ready with verbal denigration, not merely of comparatively
unimportant institutions like Congress, but of sacred national belief like the efficiency of the war-production methods of the American automobile industry. It was a doubt, perhaps an unreasonable
doubt, of the complete equality of exchanges in this matter that
misled some Englishmen into palliating the disastrous effects on
the total war effort of Pearl Harbor. They forget, as some Americans forgot too, that *Kraft durch Schadenfreude* is a very poor
motto for a nation or for an ally.

But there is possibly one exception to the rule that the Englishman is indifferent to blame and not very grateful for praise. Once
in the recent past the English people had to make a dreadful decision, the decision to make war. They insisted that their rulers
should make war and they have not forgotten that this was their
decision.[39] When they insisted that England should keep her word
to Poland, no matter what Russia or France did, they were inviting
unknown terrors on their heads. Those terrors came, a year later,
in a more dreadful form than even the English people had anticipated. The world saw their courage with astonishment and admiration ("A garland briefer than a girl's"). But that the English

[39] This truth, put rather clumsily by Lord Croft, was the occasion for a
high-school wise-crack by *Time*: "So did France, Costa Rica, Cuba, the
Dominican Republic, Guatemala, Nicaragua, Honduras, Haiti, El Salva-
dor, Italy and Japan." *Time* is widely read in educated circles in England,
and in newspaper offices like the office of the *Evening Standard*. Had the
man in the street seen this piece of wit, he might have been sophomoric
enough to retort in kind.

people would stand up to what they had invited was proof only of courage. It was their earlier decision to invite destruction rather than submit to the endless extension of tyranny over Europe and the world that showed them to be a great political democracy, worthy of their past. September 1939, even more than September 1940, was their proudest hour.

Index

46, 50, 55, 146
Ruskin, John, 276
Russell, Bertrand, 62
Russell, G. W. E., 83
Russell, Lord John, 129
Russell, Rosalind, 273
Russell family, 59, 76
Rutherford, Lord, 183
Rutherford, Mark, 85
Rutherglen, 291
Ruyter, Michel de, 249

St. Aldwyn, Lord, 140
St. Helena, 178
St. Leger races, 143
St. Lucia, 160
St. Paul's School, Concord, N. H., 22
St. Paul's School, London, 29, 30, 43
Salazar, Dr., 199
Salisbury, Lord, 68
Salisbury Plain, 243
San Francisco, 182
Sanderson, Robert, 72
Sandford, E. G., 28
Sankey, I. J., 84, 85
Santa Cruz, Admiral, 249
Santayana, George, 96-7
Sarrail, General, 155
Sartines, Gabriel de, 151
Schools: public, 20-32, 33, 34, 39-40, 42-56; private, 20-1, 32, 35, 39, 103; board, 32-5; council, 32, 33-41; Catholic, 38
Schuster, George, 224, 225
Scotland, 70, 80, 85, 89, 105, 112, 115, 120, 121, 126, 207, 228-9, 278; Church of, 64, 65, 99-100
Scott, Sir Walter, 97
Scott Report, 276, 277
Seaham Harbour, 116
Seward, W. H., 131
Shaftesbury, Lord, 68, 76

Shakespeare, 284
Shaw, George Bernard, 7, 128, 194, 199
She Married Her Boss, 148
Shelley, P. B., 43
Sheridan, General Philip, 215
Sherman, William Tecumseh, 216
Shrewsbury, Earl of, 97
Shirach, Baldur von, 285
Siegfried, André, 78
Sikes, Professor, 60
Sikhs, 207, 209, 210, 213
Simon, Sir John, 11, 74, 91
Singapore, 229, 247
Slave trade, 5, 157, 167
Smith, Adam, 227, 229
Smith, Alfred E., 258
Smith, F. E., 10, 79
Smith, J. Russell, 180
Smollett, Tobias, 4
Smoot-Hawley tariff, 162, 170
Smuts, General, 163
Smyth, Canon, 60
Smythe, Charles, 26
Somerset, 89
South Africa, 160, 163, 173, 202, 237
South African War, 7-9, 11, 71, 233, 285
Spectator, 81
Spee, Admiral von, 249
Spencer, F. H., 34, 35, 37, 44, 103
Spurgeon, Charles H., 89, 91
Stalin, Joseph, 128, 224
Stephen, Leslie, 29
Stephenson, George, 6
Sterne, Laurence, 251, 252
Stevenson rubber scheme, 176
Stiffkey, Rector of, 79
Stolypin, P. A., 224
Strachan, Archdeacon, 100
Strauss, David, 190
Sudan, 237
Suffren, Pierre André, Bailli de, 247, 249

INDEX

A NOTE ON THE TYPE

The text of this book is set on the Linotype in Fairfield, the first type-face from the hand of the distinguished American artist and engraver Rudolph Ruzicka. In its structure Fairfield displays the sober and sane qualities of a master craftsman whose talent has long been dedicated to clarity. It is this trait that accounts for the trim grace and virility, the spirited design and sensitive balance of this original type face.

Rudolph Ruzicka—who was born in Bohemia in 1883 and came to America in 1894—set up his own shop devoted to wood-engraving and printing in New York in 1913, after a varied career as a wood-engraver, in photoengraving and bank-note printing plants, as art-director and free-lance artist. He now lives and works at his home and studio in Dobbs Ferry, New York. He has designed and illustrated many books and has created a considerable list of individual prints—wood-engravings, line-engravings on copper, aquatints. W. A. Dwiggins wrote recently: "Until you see the things themselves you have no sense of the artist behind them. His outstanding quality, as artist and person, is *sanity*. Complete esthetic equipment, all managed by good sound judgment about ways and means, aims and purposes, utilities and 'functions'— and all this level-headed balance-mechanism added to the lively mental state that makes an artist an artist. Fortunate equipment in a disordered world. . . ."

COMPOSED, PRINTED, AND BOUND BY
H. WOLFF, NEW YORK